NAIS

Journal of the NATIVE AMERICAN *and* INDIGENOUS STUDIES ASSOCIATION

VOLUME 11.1

Spring 2024

NAIS (ISSN 2332-1261) is published two times a year in spring and fall (Northern Hemisphere) by the University of Minnesota Press, 111 Third Avenue South, Suite 290, Minneapolis, MN 55401-2520. http://www.upress.umn.edu

Copyright 2024 by the Regents of the University of Minnesota.

All rights reserved. With the exception of fair use, no part of this publication may be reproduced, stored in a retrieval system, or transmitted, in any form or by any means, electronic, mechanical, photocopying, recording, or otherwise, without a license or authorization from the Copyright Clearance Center (CCC), or the prior written permission of the University of Minnesota Press.

Postmaster: Send address changes to NAIS, University of Minnesota Press, 111 Third Avenue South, Suite 290, Minneapolis, MN 55401-2520.

Information about manuscript submissions can be found at naisa.org, or inquiries can be sent to journal@naisa.org.

Books for review should be addressed to NAIS Journal, Centre for Indigenous Research and Community-Led Engagement, The University of Victoria, 3800 Finnerty Road, Saunders Annex 130C, Victoria, BC, V8P 5C2, Canada.

Address subscription orders, changes of address, and business correspondence (including requests for permission and advertising orders) to NAIS, University of Minnesota Press, 111 Third Avenue South, Suite 290, Minneapolis, MN 55401-2520.

SUBSCRIPTIONS
- **Individual subscriptions to NAIS** are a benefit of membership in the Native American and Indigenous Studies Association. NAISA's tiered membership ranges from $25 to $100 annually. To become a member, visit http://naisa.org/.
- For current **institutional subscriptions** and **back issue** prices, please visit: http://www.upress.umn.edu.
- **Digital subscriptions to NAIS for institutions** are now available online through Project MUSE at https://muse.jhu.edu.

GINA STARBLANKET COEDITOR
(Cree/Saulteaux, Star Blanket
Cree Nation)
University of Victoria

HEIDI KIIWETINEPINESIIK STARK COEDITOR
(Anishinaabekwe/Turtle Mountain
Band of Chippewa descent)
University of Victoria

SABRINA LAMANNA MANAGING EDITOR
(Mi'kmaw from Ktaqmkuk and
Italian/Irish descent)
University of Victoria

EDITORS EMERITUS

KELLY McDONOUGH
(White Earth Ojibwe/Irish descent)
University of Texas at Austin 2019–23

K. TSIANINA LOMAWAIMA
(Mvskoke/Creek descent)
2019–23

JEAN M. O'BRIEN
(White Earth Ojibwe)
University of Minnesota 2013–19

ROBERT WARRIOR
(Osage)
University of Kansas 2013–19

EDITORIAL BOARD

JENNIFER ADESE
(Otipemisiwak/Métis)
University of Toronto, Mississauga

CHADWICK ALLEN
(Chickasaw ancestry)
University of Washington

ALEJANDRA DUBCOVSKY
University of California, Riverside

MISHUANA GOEMAN
(Tonawanda Band of Seneca)
University at Buffalo

ALYOSHA GOLDSTEIN
University of New Mexico

JOYCE GREEN
(Ktunaxa Nation & Yaqit ʔa·knuqɬiʔit/
Tobacco Plains Indian Band)
Professor Emerita, University of Regina

HI'ILEI JULIA HOBART
(Kanaka Maoli)
Yale University

ELIZABETH SUMIDA HUAMAN
(Wanka/Quechua)
University of Minnesota

ARINI LOADER
(Ngāti Raukawa te au ki te tonga)
Te Herenga Waka
Victoria University of Wellington

MAY-BRITT ÖHMAN
(Lule/Forest Sámi, Tornedalian heritage)
Uppsala University and Luleå
University of Technology

RAYMOND I. ORR
(Citizen Potawatomi)
Dartmouth College

JAMAICA HEOLIMELEIKALANI OSORIO
(Kanaka Maoli)
University of Hawai'i at Mānoa

KEITH RICHOTTE
(Turtle Mountain Band
of Chippewa Indians)
University of North Carolina–
Chapel Hill

MARK RIFKIN
University of North Carolina,
Greensboro

DEONDRE SMILES
(Leech Lake Band of Ojibwe)
University of Victoria

CRISTINA STANCIU
Virginia Commonwealth University

DAVID TAVÁREZ
Vassar College

JOHN TROUTMAN
National Museum of American
History, Smithsonian

EVE TUCK
(Aleut Community of St. Paul Island)
University of Toronto

CAROLINE WIGGINTON
University of Mississippi

JANI WILSON
(Ngāti Awa, Ngā Puhi, Mātaatua)
Te Kūnenga o Pūrehuroa
Massey University of Wellington

MICHAEL JOHN WITGEN
(Red Cliff Band of Lake
Superior Ojibwe)
Columbia University

Journal of the NATIVE AMERICAN *and* INDIGENOUS STUDIES ASSOCIATION

CONTENTS
VOLUME 11 ● ISSUE 1
Spring 2024

  1 GINA STARBLANKET *and* HEIDI KIIWETINEPINESIIK STARK
Editors' Remarks

Articles

  3 DAVID DRY
"Ready to Be Terminated": Guy Jennison and Ottawa Traditions of Autonomy through Elimination

35 SUSAN JACOB
The Moving Mountain: Performance for Mauna a Wākea during the Protect Maunakea Movement

71 DANA E. POWELL
Life Beyond Ruin: Diné Presence in the Anthropocene

Reviews

114 HŌKŪLANI AIKAU
Cooling the Tropics: Ice, Indigeneity, and Hawaiian Refreshment by Hiʻilei Julia Kawehipuaakahaopulani Hobart

116 **BRYDON KRAMER**
Settler Memory: The Disavowal of Indigeneity and the Politics of Race in the United States by Kevin Bruyneel

118 **ROSE STREMLAU**
Allotment Stories: Indigenous Land Relations Under Settler Siege edited by Daniel Heath Justice and Jean M. O'Brien

120 **TRACI L. MORRIS**
Tribal Administration Handbook: A Guide for Native Nations in the United States edited by Rebecca M. Webster and Joseph Bauerkemper

122 **VALERIE LAMBERT**
Paternalism to Partnership: The Administration of Indian Affairs, 1786–2021 by David H. DeJong

124 **SAMUEL COOK**
Native Agency: Indians in the Bureau of Indian Affairs by Valerie Lambert

126 **COLL THRUSH**
American Indians and the American Dream: Policies, Place, and Property in Minnesota by Kasey Keeler

128 **MICHAEL D. WISE**
People of the Ecotone: Environment and Indigenous Power at the Center of Early America by Robert Michael Morrissey

130 **JULIANA BARR**
The Great Power of Small Nations: Indigenous Diplomacy in the Gulf South by Elizabeth N. Ellis

132 **TIFFANY KING**
Being Indigenous in Jim Crow Virginia: Powhatan People and the Color Line by Laura J. Feller

135 **MICHAEL P. TAYLOR**
Assimilation, Resistance, and Survival: A History of the Stewart Indian School, 1890–2020 by Samantha M. Williams

137 **LYNN STEPHEN**
Scales of Resistance: Indigenous Women's Transborder Activism by Maylei Blackwell

140 **GILLIAN CALDER**
Reconciliation and Indigenous Justice: A Search for Ways Forward
by David Milward

142 **KRYSTAL S. TSOSIE**
Inventing the Thrifty Gene: The Science of Settler Colonialism
by Travis Hay

144 **JAMES COX**
The Makings and Unmakings of Americans: Indians and Immigrants in American Literature and Culture, 1879–1924 by Cristina Stanciu

146 **KAI PYLE**
Making Love with the Land by Joshua Whitehead

148 **CHRISTOPHER PEXA**
The Dakota Way of Life by Ella Deloria (Raymond J. DeMallie and Thierry Veyrié, eds.)

151 **CELIA HAIG-BROWN**
The Boy from Buzwah: A Life in Indian Education by Cecil King

153 **DAVID DELGADO SHORTER**
Dancing Indigenous Worlds: Choreographies of Relation by Jacqueline Shea Murphy

155 **CARTER MELAND**
Dance of the Returned by Devon A. Mihesuah

157 **FREDERICK WHITE**
Raven's Echo by Robert Davis Hoffman

159 **JOSÉ ANTONIO LUCERO**
Cinematic Comanches: The Lone Ranger *in the Media Borderlands* by Dustin Tahmahkera

162 **AMY GORE**
"Vaudeville Indians" on Global Circuits, 1880s to 1930s by Christine Bold

164 **MARK MINCH-DE LEON**
Visualizing Genocide: Indigenous Interventions in Art, Archives, and Museums edited by Yve Chavez and Nancy Marie Mithlo

EDITORS' REMARKS

GINA STARBLANKET *and* HEIDI KIIWETINEPINESIIK STARK

AS THE THIRD PAIR OF COEDITORS for the *Journal of Native American and Indigenous Studies* (*NAIS*), we are thrilled to take over responsibility for the journal from K. Tsianina Lomawaima and Kelly McDonough, who finished their four-year editorial term at the conclusion of the NAISA annual conference in Toronto, on May 12, 2023. We began our term after working together throughout the spring to ensure a smooth transition in the work of the journal.

In bringing the *NAIS* journal to a new institutional home at the University of Victoria (UVic), we hope to carry it forward as an intellectually and ethically rigorous forum for critical Indigenous scholarship at local and global scales, building on UVic's long-standing commitment to Indigenous research and extensive relationships with communities across North America and the Pacific. We raise our hands to Qwul'sih'yah'maht Robina Thomas (vice-president Indigenous at the UVic) whose commitment of financial support made it possible for us to take up this work.

As a team, we bring shared interests in Indigenous, decolonial, antiracist, and feminist thought, and an established history of working together on a range of intellectual and pedagogical activities. Our collaborative work includes community-based research initiatives, coauthoring and copublication, and cofacilitation of academic and community-based partnerships and engagements. In all these contexts, our working relationship has been guided by a shared professional and political commitment to the advancement of Indigenous scholarship that is critical, rigorous, ethical, and grounded in the aspirations and needs of Indigenous people and communities.

We see the *NAIS* journal as a forum for generative and transformative interventions, conversations, and knowledge exchanges about Indigenous people around the globe. Under our leadership, we aim to create space for original and inspired inquiries and analyses in traditional, creative, and emergent forms.

As we assume coeditorship of *NAIS*, we understand our role and responsibility as recognizing the critical historical juncture that we are at and that our field must attend to. In addition to long-standing social, political, and economic inequities, we stand in the wake of a global pandemic and are facing unprecedented crises in not only how we relate to one another as humans but how we relate to creation. We acknowledge that scholarship, too, will be transformed by these contexts as our members work to interrogate the conditions of our times and envision new terms of change. We know that Indigenous theorizing and research continue to arise in the context of long-standing and evolving structures of colonialism, policies deployed in the service of colonialism, and racist and sexist ideologies that have legitimated and continue to legitimate ongoing colonial projects around the world. We are therefore committed to foregrounding Indigenous theoretical and empirical works that decenter colonialism while centering Indigenous knowledge, pedagogy, and methods. This entails a commitment to Indigenous, Black, migrant, antiracist, abolitionist, feminist, and 2SLGBTQIA+ struggles for justice and transformation.

Our intention is to situate the journal as a place where scholars will engage analyses of Indigenous movements toward decolonization and social, economic, and political transformation but also projects of Indigenous recovery, revitalization, and resurgence. Our approach reflects the ongoing need for analyses that explore and critically engage with the diversity of Indigenous communities and movements, and/or that deconstruct the colonial and capitalist contexts in which they exist. These include inquiries into specific forms of legal and political revitalization being undertaken by Indigenous communities across geographic regions and cultural groups, land-based practices, critical methodological and pedagogical interventions, Indigenous political theories and practices, Indigenous critiques and contestations, and Indigenous activism, coalition building.

Finally, our practice recognizes the crucial importance of encouraging and mobilizing knowledge across generations. To this end, we take seriously the contributions of scholars across ages, locations, and educational backgrounds. Embracing the significant work of Indigenous scholars in creative and artistic disciplines, the journal will continue to speak to and feature the work of those situated in conventional disciplines while also highlighting the importance of scholarly contributions from new and innovative sites of knowledge production.

ARTICLES

DAVID DRY

"Ready to Be Terminated": Guy Jennison and Ottawa Traditions of Autonomy through Elimination

Abstract

The 1950s and 1960s policy of tribal termination is justly regarded as a genocidal federal effort to extinguish tribal sovereignty and identity. Some tribal leaders, however, like Guy Jennison, chief of the Ottawa Tribe of Oklahoma from 1930 to 1962, supported termination. Jennison's advocacy for termination developed out of an Ottawa political tradition that sought greater autonomy through embracing federal policies aimed at tribal elimination. In this political tradition, the Ottawa endeavored to escape federal control through eliminatory policies while subverting the eliminatory intentions of policymakers by ensconcing their community in other dimensions of the dominant society. For Jennison, endorsing termination was a strategy to escape federal paternalism and gain greater control over tribal affairs. In anticipation of termination, Jennison led the Ottawas to reestablish tribal government through a state-chartered nonprofit corporation; by perpetuating tribal identity and prerogatives through this vehicle, the Ottawa undermined the eliminatory intentions of termination policy. Placing Jennison's advocacy for termination within a longer tradition of Ottawa activism reveals the Native intellectual genealogies that informed his perspective and demonstrates how policies intending tribal elimination represented a complex site of Ottawa struggle against federal authority.

IN AUGUST 1955, Guy Jennison, chief of the Ottawa Tribe of Oklahoma, testified before a House of Representatives Indian Affairs subcommittee hearing held at the federal courthouse in Muskogee, Oklahoma. "Every time we have a change in the United States administration," he said, "they change our Indian policies. It has been sort of a shell game with us, now you are under the blanket, now you ain't, until it has got to where we have not got any blanket whatsoever and we are perfectly ready to be terminated as soon as possible and relieve the United States Government of any obligation whatsoever."[1] The five-person Ottawa Business Committee endorsed termination a few months later, and Congress passed legislation to that effect in August 1956. The federal government formally ended oversight, services, and recognition of the Oklahoma Ottawa in August 1959.

Forged in the hardened nationalism of the early Cold War, termination policy sought to strip Native nations of their sovereignty and political distinctiveness.[2] By openly abrogating federal trust responsibilities and recognition of tribal sovereignty, termination represents one of the most explicit twentieth-century examples of the settler-colonial impulse to eliminate tribal identity.[3] Amy Den Ouden and Jean O'Brien, among others, have aptly described termination as a genocidal federal policy.[4] In this context, a tribal leader openly supporting the enterprise appears perplexing. Why would any tribal leader support the elimination of trust status and federal acknowledgment of tribal sovereignty? This article argues Jennison's advocacy for termination developed out of an Ottawa political tradition that sought greater autonomy through embracing federal policies aimed at tribal elimination. Jennison endorsed termination to escape federal paternalism and gain greater control over tribal affairs. While he championed termination, most Ottawas were never consulted about the policy. After the passage of termination legislation, Jennison's largely unilateral decision led to a tribal backlash from those who vehemently disagreed with the efficacy of disavowing federal recognition. After termination, however, tribal members of all persuasions worked cooperatively to achieve Jennison's vision of tribal life outside of federal acknowledgment and control.

Termination policy was intended to close out federal obligations and financial responsibilities to Native nations and had devastating consequences for many tribal communities. House Concurrent Resolution 108, passed in 1953, inaugurated the policy, and Congress ultimately passed termination legislation that affected 109 tribes. Most were small tribes receiving few federal services, and a handful were large and resource-rich tribes. The termination of the Klamath and Menominee tribes collectively removed nearly 1.1 million acres from trust and affected over five thousand tribal members: representing the vast majority of the land removed from trust and a large proportion of the Indian people directly impacted by the policy.[5] To eliminate federal trust responsibilities, legislation mandated the sale or division of tribal trust lands and resources and the removal of all restrictions and trust protections on allotted lands. Final tribal rolls were created to facilitate disbursements of tribal lands or monies from land sales. No longer regarded as Indians by the federal government, members of terminated tribes could not participate in federal health, education, or support services intended for Indian people. Policymakers expected the removal of federal acknowledgment, services, and trust protections to extinguish tribal identities and affiliations. After termination, many tribal communities faced widespread land loss with the removal of trust protections, and termination triggered devastating social and economic consequences. As Nicholas Peroff noted, in perhaps the most well-known case study, Menominee people experienced "increased economic instability, higher unemployment, decreased public services, aggravated racial discrimination, lower morale and personal self-esteem, deeper political alienation, and renewed factionalism."[6]

While not minimizing termination as a destructive policy intending tribal elimination, this study also demonstrates termination policy as a site of Native activism, refusals, and assertions of autonomy from colonial administration. Chief Jennison pursued termination as a deliberate rejection of the constraints imposed by federal authority. In the case of the Klamath and Menominee, federal officials refused to authorize payments due to those tribes until they consented to termination.[7] By contrast, the Ottawa had no tribal assets to divide or sell and no monetary incentives to terminate. Instead, Jennison was motivated by how the government-to-government relationship, as represented by the Bureau of Indian Affairs (BIA) of that era, undermined his conception of the Ottawa as competent, self-reliant, and fully capable of managing their affairs. Jennison aimed to escape paternalistic federal control by exiting federal oversight through termination.

Jennison's vision of mobilizing Ottawa self-determination outside of federal supervision derived from long-standing traditions in Ottawa political activism. Beginning in the mid-nineteenth century, the Ottawa repeatedly engaged federal policies intending tribal elimination to gain greater autonomy from the Indian Office and escape the unbridled authority that federal officials exercised over Native people under the doctrines of federal plenary power and the guardian-ward relationship.[8] In the mid- and late nineteenth century, the Ottawa faced threats of removal, gross federal maladministration, and federal intrusion in tribal affairs. To insulate themselves from those impositions, the Ottawa pursued U.S. citizenship, the termination of federal recognition, and allotment. The Ottawa pursued those policies for autonomy, not the elimination of their political distinctiveness as desired by policymakers. Instead of abandoning their tribal identity and political affiliation, the Ottawa refashioned the opportunities afforded by U.S. citizenship. In defiance of dominant imaginaries, they carved a new foothold for their tribal community by adapting to sustain their community within and through American society. While recent scholarship has critiqued state-based recognition as a tool of settler domination, the Ottawa experience places this discussion within a longer chronology.[9]

Mirroring earlier Ottawa efforts, Jennison embraced termination but worked through other dimensions of American society to deflect the eliminatory intent of the policy. In anticipation of termination, Jennison led the Ottawa in reorganizing tribal government as a state-chartered non-profit corporation. The Ottawa perpetuated tribal identity and prerogatives through this new incorporated entity. Other Native nations, including the Eastern Band of Cherokee, historically used incorporation to reconstitute tribal government in the absence of federal recognition.[10] By remaking their political identity and ensconcing their community in other dimensions of settler society, the Ottawa forged their own path through the federal government's capricious attitude toward Indian affairs and subverted federal control and eliminatory intentions.

Kenneth R. Philp has outlined diverse Indian responses to termination that included some communities favoring aspects of the policy as a path toward self-rule, and Katrina Phillips has cogently established how attending to groups generally glossed over in discussions of termination expands our understanding of the complexities of the termination era.[11] Placing Jennison's advocacy within a longer political tradition of Ottawa activism builds on that scholarship to demonstrate the importance of Native intellectual genealogies. Viewing the termination policy era solely through the narrow ambitions of federal officials is inadequate to the task of forging Indigenous histories. Ottawa, not federal, viewpoints shaped the outcome of the policy. Jennison's perspective is centered here, but that perspective does not validate the bankrupt, ethnocentric, and indeed, genocidal policy of termination as envisioned by federal policymakers; nor do I seek to posit Jennison's rendering as a paradigm. Even if framed by a desire for autonomy, Jennison's support for termination allowed the federal government to shirk many of its responsibilities and helped endorse a policy that took a catastrophic toll on other tribal communities.

Traditions of Autonomy through Elimination

Efforts in the 1950s were not the first time the Ottawa manipulated federal programs intending tribal elimination—it was not even their first time evading federal control by exiting federal recognition. Eliminating tribal identity by disavowing recognition and removing land from trust represents a recurrent objective of Indian policies, and Ottawa approaches to these policies

FIGURE 1. Guy Jennison, 1956. Photo courtesy of the Oklahoma Historical Society, Oklahoma Publishing Company Photograph Collection, no. 2012.201.B0318B.0325.

exhibit strong continuities. Removed from their homelands in the Maumee River Valley of Ohio to Kansas in the 1830s, the Ottawa bands who would later come to be called the Ottawa Tribe of Oklahoma suffered devastating deprivation and loss of life following removal.[12] With the organization of the Kansas Territory in 1854, the Ottawa faced the gruesome specter of yet another genocidal removal.[13] In response, the Ottawa adopted a new strategy to protect their community and gain greater control over their destinies—they resolved to become citizens of the nation threatening their destruction.

The Ottawa in Kansas chose allotment and U.S. citizenship over removal in an 1862 treaty, but they engineered those policies to ensure their survival as a community. Guy Jennison's grandfather, James Wind, served as one of four Ottawa signatories to a June 1862 treaty that allotted the Ottawa reservation in Kansas and declared that the Ottawa "organization, and their relations with the United States as an Indian tribe shall be dissolved and terminated at the expiration of five years . . . and each and every one of them, shall be deemed and declared to be citizens of the United States."[14] In addition to avoiding removal, the Ottawa used the treaty to preserve community life, perpetuate tribal governance structures, and acquire the tools to navigate American society on their own terms. Tribal leaders negotiated that all Ottawas acquire U.S. citizenship, not merely an elite subset as in other naturalization treaties. The treaty also created two new Ottawa-led organizations: a board of trustees for a school the Ottawa endowed with twenty thousand acres and chartered to serve Ottawa students in perpetuity and an organization to manage the Ottawa Baptist Church and graveyard. Similar to other Native nations operating outside of federal recognition in the mid-nineteenth century, the Ottawa mobilized around education and religion to assert their distinctiveness and achieve group objectives.[15] Taking federal policies in unexpected directions, the Ottawa aimed to escape federal impositions through U.S. citizenship and allotment and to subvert the eliminatory intentions of those policies by ensconcing themselves in other dimensions of the dominant society. It would not be the last time the Ottawa adopted this strategy.

The Indian agent for the Ottawa defrauded tribal members of their allotments and funds in federal trust, and the Ottawa leaned on their newly acquired status as U.S. citizens to protect themselves from federal maladministration.[16] Robbed of their allotments and monies, the Ottawa negotiated a new treaty in 1867. By dint of federal error, the 1867 Treaty confirmed the U.S. citizenship of tribal members, merely delaying naturalization to 1869, but also permitted the Ottawa to purchase an approximately 14,860-acre reservation in Indian Territory.[17] After naturalization, the Ottawa attempted to use their U.S. citizenship to demand tribal funds held in trust on the basis their wardship had ended, claim the right to negotiate contracts without the approval of their Indian Agent, and hire lawyers to pursue cases in state courts independently of the Interior Department.[18] The contours of their rights as U.S. citizens remained woefully undefined, but the Ottawa harnessed their U.S. citizenship to challenge their subjection to Indian Office authority.[19] As one Indian agent complained of Ottawa resistance to federal regulation of reservation lands, "The Ottawas claim to be citizens . . . . they will never submit to live as Indians unless they can enjoy the rights of a citizen and be protected by the government at the same time. In fact, they want to do as they please, and are always ready for trouble when they cannot."[20] The U.S. citizenship of the Ottawas notwithstanding, federal officials continued to subject the Ottawa to the authority of the Office of Indian Affairs.

In the late nineteenth century, the Ottawa again sought to use allotment and U.S. citizenship as vehicles for autonomy from colonial administration. Policymakers championed allotment with the aim of expropriating Native lands and facilitating the dissolution of tribal polities, and they held out allotment as a path toward citizenship rights for Native people.[21] On the Ottawa reservation, Indian agents threatened Ottawa subsistence by expelling white renters and interfering in the management of lands by individual Ottawas and tribal government. The right to control land and participate in the market economy represented an essential component of U.S. citizenship.[22] By embracing allotment, the Ottawa aimed to mobilize those attributes of U.S. citizenship to gain freedom from colonial control over their activities. The Ottawa petitioned for allotment in 1882, five years prior to the Dawes Act, and the Ottawa reservation was formally allotted under the Dawes Act in 1892.[23] After allotment, the Ottawa continued to hold elections for a tribal Business Committee, pursue claims against the federal government for treaty violations, maintain a tribal cemetery, and sustain tribal identity and community within and beyond the allotted Ottawa reservation.

In the early twentieth century, the Ottawa consistently demanded autonomy from suffocating federal paternalism and wardship by asserting their rights as U.S. citizens. Although the Ottawa had been twice allotted and twice declared U.S. citizens, federal officials continued to restrict individual tribal members from leasing or selling allotments and tribal leaders from leasing or selling remaining unallotted tribal lands. Ottawa leaders protested these federal limitations on individual and tribal actions and objected to their premise in supposed Native incapacity as wards. As Ottawa leader John Earley argued in 1906, "When they made us citizens, they placed us on equal footing with the white people and they are allowed to manage their own affairs."[24] Born in 1886, Guy Jennison was the son of the tribal clerk in the decades after allotment and first won election to the tribal council in 1912. Throughout his youth, Jennison heard tribal leaders express the recurrent refrains the Ottawa were "capable of managing our own business" and "controlled as if we were not citizens of the United States."[25] He inherited a tribal political tradition that asserted "we should be treated as citizens . . . [and] we think that the [Interior] Department has no jurisdiction over our band of Indians."[26] In United States v. Sandoval (1913) and United States v. Nice (1916), the U.S. Supreme Court definitively outlined that U.S. citizenship did not place Indians outside of the scope of federal plenary power and wardship.[27] Those Supreme Court decisions reflected a long-standing reality for the Ottawa that U.S. citizenship did little to insulate Native people from Indian Office control. To escape that federal authority, Jennison would need to look for a recourse other than U.S. citizenship alone.

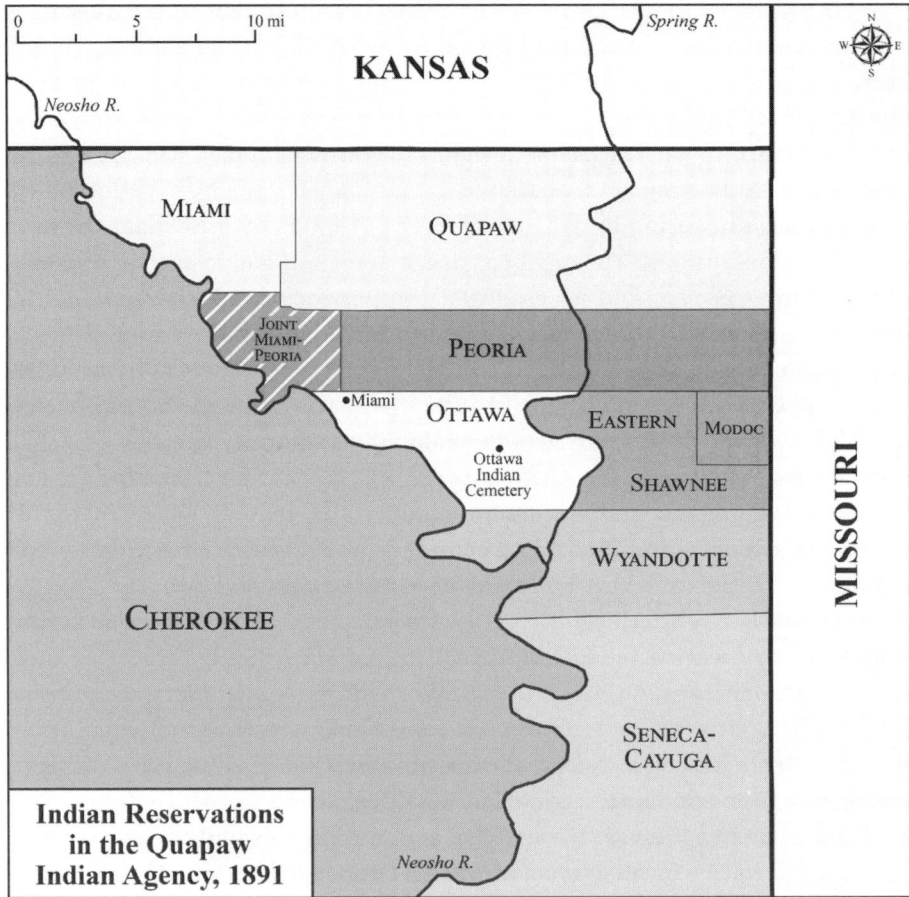

FIGURE 2. Indian reservations in the Quapaw Agency, 1891. The reservations of the tribes of the Quapaw Agency were allotted shortly after 1891. Map by Gabriel Moss. Data sources: Bureau of Indian Affairs, U.S. Domestic Sovereign Nations: Land Areas of Federally-Recognized Tribes, accessed September 30, 2021, https://bia-geospatial-internal.geoplatform.gov/indianlands/.

Guy Jennison: A Conservative Indian Progressive

Jennison's direct experience with federal paternalism influenced his desire to escape federal control and reinforced tribal political traditions that resisted colonial intervention in tribal affairs. Later in life, Jennison recalled how he was "forced to go to school by the BIA" with instructors he assessed as poorly trained for their work.[28] He particularly resented the indoctrination in Christianity that he noted "seemed so different from what my descendants [sic] had handed down."[29] Shuffled between multiple Indian schools, Jennison ultimately stormed out of Haskell Institute after an altercation with the superintendent. Making his way back to Indian Territory on foot, Jennison thereafter faced a permanent ban from attending any federal Indian schools.[30] Like most Ottawas of his generation, Jennison opted to send his own children to local public schools instead of paternalistic Indian schools following Oklahoma statehood.[31]

Jennison's early encounters with government regulations underscored the domineering authority the Indian Office exercised over Native people. After leaving Haskell in 1907, Jennison took up residence on his eighty-acre allotment. To him, the land "was not a gift from the government." It was his rightful "share of what we Ottawas salvaged from the million acres of land we lost in Ohio, Michigan and the Northwest Territory."[32] Nevertheless, in seeking to farm this land, he quickly ran up against federal restrictions. Although Jennison required capital to purchase a horse, federal guidelines viewing Indians as incapable of judicious management of their lands prevented him from legally selling or mortgaging the forty-acre homestead portion of his allotment still held in trust. As a result, he had to undertake a "complicated deal involving a mortgage on 40 acres" and "a $500 loan at 8 per cent interest."[33] To Jennison, full control of his land necessitated escaping trust status. In 1910, Jennison appeared before a federal "competency commission" that assessed his ability to manage his own affairs. After meeting their often arbitrary and racialized criteria, he secured the removal of restrictions on his land.[34] Contrary to popular expectations that Indians lacked the capacity to manage their lands, Jennison never sold his land and developed an over two-hundred-acre working dairy farm that served as his principal occupation. To Jennison, his own success provided undeniable evidence the Ottawa did not require federal "supervision."[35]

Although always clear to note the primacy of his Indian identity to his political ideology, Jennison's lifelong association with the Republican Party shaped his critiques of Indian policy.[36] In Jennison's telling, this political affiliation derived from his father's attachment to the Republican Party as a Union veteran and a hatred of Andrew Jackson's Indian policies.[37] Ascending to the position of chief in 1930, Jennison refashioned conservative critiques of expanding federal bureaucracy and New Deal programs to denounce federal Indian policy as archetypical of the threats to liberty posed by federal intrusion into the lives of U.S. citizens. Reviling how "Indian Affairs are big business," Jennison asserted "the fundamental cause of this abnormal growth, lies in the fact that the Bureau can and does exercise such complete control over the Indians and their property."[38]

Jennison's perspective on Indian policy also resonated with Progressive Era pan-tribal activism calling for the abolition of the Bureau of Indian Affairs. In the early twentieth century, leaders of the Society of American Indians (SAI) advocated for universal U.S. citizenship for Native people, an end to wardship, and racial equality; they argued the management and control of the Office of Indian Affairs was antithetical to these objectives.[39] Ottawas do not appear to have maintained direct connections with the SAI, but the strain of SAI thought that vilified federal control continued to resonate with many Indians in eastern Oklahoma in the late 1920s and 1930s.[40] In his unpublished autobiography, Jennison highlighted his conservative and Progressive leanings, noting, "Ottawa County is one of the leading Progressive counties of our state. We have two classes of people. The 'Pros and the Cons.' Progressives and the Conservatives. I sometimes wonder which side I am on."[41]

In his denunciations of federal Indian policy, Jennison found allies among the seven other Native nations headquartered in Ottawa County, Oklahoma, and under the jurisdiction of the Quapaw Indian Agency.[42] By 1930, members of these small tribes of the Quapaw Indian Agency were generally well integrated into the broader population, often received limited health or educational services from the Office of Indian Affairs, and resented federal paternalism.[43] In February 1933, Jennison helped found the Association of Indian Tribes (AIT), a largely northeast Oklahoma-based pan-tribal Indian advocacy organization.[44] The AIT council, of which Jennison was one of sixteen members, laid out their complaints for new Commissioner of Indian Affairs John Collier. Using unguarded language, AIT leadership inveighed against federal officials who "lead them on like dumb, driven cattle."[45] They demanded recognition of the individual rights of Indians "as other citizens" to conduct their affairs, rather than "await the pleasure of the Indian agent in order to confer or consult the Agency concerning matters."[46] Asserting their competency and self-reliance, AIT leaders spoke out against bureaucratic regulations and domineering federal control.

Far from addressing AIT concerns, Collier's reforms sparked additional complaints. As news of the proposed Wheeler-Howard Act began circulating in early 1934, the AIT would be the vehicle for opposition to the legislation in northeast Oklahoma. An AIT resolution referred to the bill as "an insult of the very basest kind toward not only the intelligence and integrity of all Indians, but also toward each and every Indian community of these United States."[47] Mirroring conservative critiques of other New Deal policies, AIT leaders described the bill as "strongly bordering on communism," and they maligned it as an attempt to place Indians "way, way back even beyond extreme primitive stages, almost to that stage of making monkeys of them."[48] On the campus of Northeast Oklahoma Junior College in Ottawa County, Oklahoma, on March 24, 1934, Commissioner Collier hosted one of his famous Indian congresses to consult with area tribes on his proposals, and over five hundred Indians attended the event. In heated exchanges, AIT members took the floor to denounce Collier's proposals and verbally quarrel with him. At the conclusion of the meeting, Jennison joined with four other area chiefs to author a resolution expressing their "emphatic DISFAVOR" of the proposed bill as an affront to "respectable, upright, and progressive" Oklahoma Indians.[49]

By the late 1930s, Jennison contemplated relinquishing federal acknowledgment and services as one means to escape federal control. With the AIT largely unsuccessful in shaping federal policy, Jennison and other like-minded Indians in northeast Oklahoma increasingly gravitated toward the American Indian Federation (AIF). A nationally focused pan-Indian organization, AIF members united around the shared goal of abolishing the Office of Indian Affairs.[50] In the late 1930s, the AIF pushed for the passage of the infamous "Settlement Bill" that called for a one-time individual payment and a release from wardship in return for disavowing any future federal Indian services for Natives who chose to take part. While often maligned as a precursor to termination policy, the bill held appeal for Jennison as it promised to hasten the abolition of the Indian Office and provided compensation for long-standing claims against the government. He cautiously supported the endeavor as "no more of a crackpot idea than what has been rammed down our throats in the past" and one way to overturn the reality that Indians "are not free citizens and are wards of Congress and so completely subjugated that they find their voice and interests drowned in the tumult."[51] The AIF bill died in Congress, but its objectives resonated with Jennison into the termination era. After winning election to three terms as county commissioner in the 1940s, Jennison emerged as a prominent local figure in the Republican Party and became a regular editorial contributor to the local newspaper in the 1950s. Through that outlet, he continued to outline his position on wardship as antithetical to Native equality and the capabilities of Native people to manage their own affairs without federal supervision.[52]

Choosing Termination

In the postwar era, the Ottawa endured a frustrating combination of ever more intractable BIA control and declining federal services that rendered disavowing federal recognition and oversight an increasingly attractive alternative. By the early 1950s, Jennison viewed Indian Affairs in bleak authoritarian terms. As Jennison noted in one editorial about the current state of Indian Affairs, "Most Indians are born Incompetent Wards. The bureau presides at our birth, supervises our lives, closes our eyes in death and wishes us well on our way to the Happy Hunting Ground!"[53] To Jennison, termination offered an escape. Shortly after the August 1953 ratification of House Concurrent Resolution 108 that inaugurated termination policy, Jennison argued the BIA "must be drastically reduced and in time totally abolished" and "the tribes who are ready for it will give full cooperation with the government in this respect."[54]

While federal recognition purported to provide a modicum of federal support for tribal sovereignty, federal control proved a more tangible reality for Jennison. By the 1950s the Ottawa had only $11.90 in tribal funds deposited with the U.S. Treasury, yet tribal members decades later still recalled how tribal leaders had to petition the BIA to use those funds to purchase a briefcase to hold the tribal secretary-treasurer's notes.[55] In a 1959 editorial, Jennison denigrated tribal authority under the BIA by calling tribal governments "puppet governments" and asserting "our activities are controlled with the BIA pulling the strings."[56] By incorporating Cold War language, Jennison invited comparisons between the conditions of tribal nations and states behind the Iron Curtain enduring Soviet authoritarianism, and he ridiculed the notion federal supervision engendered sovereignty.

Domineering federal oversight had long rested on premises of Native primitiveness and incompetence, and Jennison balked at these assertions.[57] Jennison had an established record as an adept businessman and local politician. A 1955 *Reader's Digest* article even placed Jennison in the ranks of such Native luminaries as ballet dancer Maria Tallchief (Osage) and athlete Jim Thorpe (Sac and Fox) by declaring him an exemplar of Indians who "made a good living from the soil."[58] Despite his widely recognized achievements, Jennison remained mired in the vacillating Indian policies of successive administrations in his leadership of the Ottawa, and he derided Indian policy as a "long series of experiments, super-imposed one upon the other."[59] While disavowing federal recognition might do little to erase societal perceptions of Indian capabilities, it could extinguish federal interference that rested on those presumptions.

While alleged Native incompetence justified paternalistic supervision, the BIA drew on evidence of Ottawa economic success and social integration to increasingly deny Ottawas services allocated for Indian people. As part of its targeted cost-saving and consolidation measures that foreshadowed termination policy, in the late 1940s the BIA shut down the Quapaw Indian Agency, which served the Ottawa and the seven other tribes headquartered in Ottawa County, Oklahoma. The BIA relegated the Quapaw Agency to a field office and transferred most services to the Muskogee Area Office, over ninety miles away.[60] Although he opposed these actions as subjecting the Ottawa to an even more distant and less responsive bureaucracy, Jennison was unable to prevent them.[61] In addition to reducing area services, in the early 1950s the Muskogee Area Office introduced new restrictions limiting hospital use for adult Indians to those of one half-degree Indian blood or more.[62] The Ottawa did not employ blood quantum as a metric of their Indian identity and maintained no blood-quantum requirement for tribal enrollment. Nevertheless, by government calculation, only 32 adults of the 630 Ottawas qualified for hospital services available to area Indians, and Jennison was unable to secure these services despite being the Ottawa chief.[63]

By the early 1950s, the BIA offered almost no services to Ottawas. In a 1952 report, federal officials related with pride that for the Ottawa the "Bureau rendered no service" in health, leases, welfare, training, and credit, among others, and concluded that "withdrawal [of services] is pretty well complete at the present time."[64] The Ottawa had little more than five hundred acres of allotted land in trust, almost all of it highly fractionated and in heirship, only a five-acre cemetery held in common, and no children in Indian schools.[65] As Jennison noted in advocating for termination, the Ottawa "haven't anything, in common, to terminate."[66] Neither considered fully competent nor sufficiently primitive, the Ottawa found themselves in a liminal space that offered neither services rendered on behalf of Indian people nor full control over their affairs. By the 1950s, the Ottawa had indeed, in Jennison's words, "not got any blanket whatsoever," as they received no substantive support from the federal government. With seemingly little to lose but their wardship, Jennison might realistically remark they were "perfectly ready to be terminated."[67]

While policymakers viewed termination as a tool to undermine tribal ties by subsuming Natives in American society, the changes termination intended to promote already characterized Ottawa tribal life. Ottawas had always strategically moved and interfaced with outsiders for subsistence, and in Kansas and later Indian Territory, Ottawas sustained their community amid deep-seated economic and social relations with white Americans and displacement outside of reservation boundaries.[68] After allotment in Indian Territory, Ottawas further adapted community life to manage the loss of most tribal lands, widespread intermarriage with outsiders, and the dislocation of tribal members across the United States. Thus, tribal mobility and interconnection with outsiders were nothing new for the Ottawa, and termination would not accelerate those processes. By the 1950s, only about a quarter of the tribal population still resided in Ottawa County, Oklahoma. To manage mobility, Ottawas had developed a community life where individuals regularly traveled long distances for events and networks of kin and communication linked tribal members together across the country.[69] Jennison recognized the Ottawa were "integrated into the general population,"[70] and for that very reason, he understood that termination posed little threat to existing tribal dynamics.

Jennison responded favorably to initial BIA overtures regarding termination and negotiated for legislation that addressed tribal priorities. Rejecting an omnibus bill wherein the BIA sought to rapidly extinguish all eight of the local tribes, Jennison insisted that negotiations take place on a tribe-by-tribe basis. Few tribal members attended the various meetings organized and hosted by the BIA regarding termination from 1954–1956, and meetings never included the necessary quorum needed for the General Council, the supreme Ottawa governing body, to conduct business. Jennison alone remained actively engaged throughout the process. At those meetings, he successfully pushed for the inclusion of several provisions not originally part of the model BIA legislation. These included a termination education program providing educational scholarships and the provision that all lands removed from trust should not be counted as taxable income.[71] As the Ottawa possessed no tribal assets to divide and sell, BIA officials proposed to forgo the creation of a tribal roll. Jennison insisted the composition of a tribal roll be included in the legislation, and seeking to dictate their own membership, the Business Committee compiled and submitted a complete accounting of all members recognized by the tribe.

In seeking termination for reasons other than elimination, Jennison was joined by the leaders of other Native nations headquartered in Ottawa County, Oklahoma. Lawrence Zane, chief of the Wyandotte Tribe of Oklahoma, adjacent to the Ottawas, joined Jennison in expressing his support for termination at the Indian Affairs subcommittee hearing held in Muskogee. Conveying how his intentions diverged from those of federal officials, Zane noted "the word 'termination' does not sound just right because we intend to exist as a tribe even after the supervision of the Government has and will be removed."[72] Similarly, the Business Committee of the Peoria Tribe, also adjacent to the Ottawas, approved termination legislation, but the Ottawa,

Peoria, and Wyandotte each maintained tribal governments after termination.[73] Although 109 tribes underwent termination, Congress passed only fourteen termination bills between 1954 and 1962, with many tribes in northern California and Oregon terminated in omnibus bills.[74] Thus, three of the fourteen termination acts were for the adjoining Ottawa, Peoria, and Wyandotte Tribes of Ottawa County, Oklahoma, and each act included unique provisions requested by tribal leaders to address tribal concerns.[75]

With the Ottawa shackled to an overbearing federal bureaucracy from which they derived little benefit, Jennison had few inhibitions about the Ottawa striking out on their own. Signed into law in August 1956, the Ottawa termination bill mandated a three-year preparatory period, with formal termination to occur in August 1959. After the passage of the bill, Jennison looked forward to when the Ottawa "will be able to go ahead and do business on our own."[76]

Contesting Termination

While Jennison championed termination, only the five-person Business Committee formally voted in favor of the proposition, and most tribal members did not know about the prospect of termination until after Congress had passed the legislation. By the 1950s, the elected tribal Business Committee managed the maintenance of the tribal cemetery, pursued claims, and interfaced with federal officials. As these administrative tasks seldom incited disagreements, the General Council of all members rarely met to debate issues, and in nearly thirty years as chief, Jennison had never faced an opponent in a tribal election. Jennison had long served as the spokesperson for Ottawa viewpoints without controversy, but after the passage of termination legislation, a group of tribal members objected to Jennison's unilateral decision to support the policy. This discontent erupted in a contentious 1958 tribal meeting where tribal members quarreled over whether the new status facilitated greater autonomy, as Jennison espoused, or needlessly renounced federal services.

Tribal member Norman Holmes, a BIA enrollment officer at the Anadarko Agency in Oklahoma, emerged as the most ardent Ottawa opponent of the policy. Born in Ottawa County in 1910, and twenty-five years Jennison's junior, Norman Holmes embarked on a career in Indian Affairs after graduating from Haskell Institute. In 1934, he secured a position as a stenographer at the Uintah & Ouray Agency, and by 1952, he had advanced up the ranks to chief clerk there.[77] While Jennison exhibited an almost clichéd hostility toward the BIA, Holmes expressed complex and sometimes conflicting views common among Natives working in Indian Affairs.[78]

Although he appreciated the beneficial services rendered by the BIA, Holmes had to implement policies he opposed. As the chief clerk of the Uintah and Ouray Agency, Holmes played an active leadership role in the termination of the Paiute Indian Tribe of Utah.[79] Likely convinced of the deleterious nature of termination by that episode, Holmes broke with his adherence to BIA directives by contesting Ottawa termination. Holmes joined the Anadarko Agency in Oklahoma as an enrollment officer in March 1956,[80] one month after the Ottawa Business Committee endorsed termination. Holmes, like many Ottawa, was unaware of that decision. In 1958, the BIA rejected the tribal roll composed by the Business Committee in favor of a BIA-produced roll, and controversy over the tribal roll sparked greater tribal awareness of impending Ottawa termination. As a result, Holmes and other Ottawa began to actively protest Ottawa termination.[81]

Risking his career, Holmes fought to overturn Ottawa termination. In April 1958, Holmes stormed into the Muskogee Area Office and demanded to see the Ottawa roll. As tribal affairs officer Marie L. Hayes related, Holmes "launched out in a critical manner on the Ottawa roll as prepared by this office, questioning our authority for preparing the roll and was most critical of a number of names which had been included on the roll, (largely those which had been recommended to be omitted at the time the Tribe prepared the roll)."[82] Within a few weeks, the BIA heard rumors that Holmes "very definitely was doing all that he could to bestir some activity on the part of members of the Ottawa Tribe to take a stand against not only the roll as prepared by the Area Director of the Muskogee Office, but to question the legality and authenticity of the action taken by the Business Committee on behalf of the Tribe with respect to termination."[83]

With his cousin Clarence King, Holmes circulated a petition calling for a special meeting to address termination and the issue of the tribal roll. Held May 3, 1958, the meeting brought together sixty tribal members, more than had gathered for a tribal government affair in over a decade. Representatives of the BIA also attended to defend their position and interests. Jennison defended his leadership and the actions of the Business Committee in supporting termination and argued "you have had an honest Business Committee. They have never stolen anything from you—they never had a chance to steal anything because you didn't have anything to steal."[84] Incensed by the unilateral action of the Business Committee, Holmes decried the lack of consultation with tribal members about a substantive shift in tribal status. In a dramatic gesture, Holmes requested, "Everybody stand up that didn't know anything about this termination."[85] When a majority rose, Holmes proclaimed, "There's your Indian people. This affects us from now on. That's the thing I am concerned with."[86] While recognizing many Ottawas did not receive or qualify for federal Indian services, Holmes felt Jennison ignored the interests of those who did, including Holmes's aunt, the only living allottee who still held her allotment in trust: "It seems to me that the Chief had determined in his mind what was good for us to do about termination and did not consider the wishes of people who still own land that is restricted, that it was his right to decide for the Tribe. Of course, it was no concern to him since he took his land out of trust years ago."[87] Rather than an opportunity for greater autonomy, Holmes maintained disavowing federal trust protections would compel his aunt to sell her land.

Tribal debates on termination came down to a vote. Surprised by the sudden criticism of his leadership, Jennison voluntarily resigned his post alongside the rest of the Business Committee to trigger an immediate tribal election. Nominations followed, with both Jennison and Clarence King, an opponent of termination and the cousin of Norman Holmes, put forward for chief. Although only three votes dictated the outcome, Jennison won reelection. It was the closest most Ottawas ever got to a vote on termination itself. Ultimately, the Ottawas reelected all the members of the Business Committee who had endorsed termination legislation and ran for reelection; however, in an act demonstrating their collective interests beyond the issue of termination, the Ottawas also elected Clarence King as second chief.

Holmes paid a price for his outspoken advocacy and federal officials forcefully silenced his opposition to Ottawa termination. A few weeks after the May 1958 tribal meeting, Commissioner of Indian Affairs Glenn Emmons wrote to William J. Pitner, area director of the Anadarko Agency, to condemn Holmes's actions. In Emmons's view, Holmes put the BIA "in the embarrassing position of having our own employees publicly disputing our actions."[88] Characterizing the activities of Holmes as a betrayal, Emmons questioned his "loyalty as an employee" and the ability of Holmes to fulfill his responsibilities and execute termination policy. Emmons gave Holmes a binary choice: "election as to whether he wishes to continue in his federal employment or to resign and devote his entire attention to tribal affairs."[89]

In the face of these coercive tactics, Holmes relented in his outspoken resistance to Ottawa termination. The May 1958 meeting had not elicited a comprehensive Ottawa condemnation of termination. In fact, it underscored ongoing tribal support for Jennison's leadership. With legislation already passed, his career jeopardized by continued activism, and a family to consider, Holmes discontinued further vocal opposition. In a letter to his supervisor, William J. Pitner, Holmes avowed his "loyalty to the Bureau" and stated his intention to stay out of Ottawa political affairs. Closing by declaring his commitments, Holmes noted, "My heart and soul is in my work with Indian people and my desire is to be of service to them as well as to support the policy of the Bureau and carry out the instructions and duties assigned to me."⁹⁰ Inserting a subtle critique in the face of overbearing pressure, Holmes distinguished between aiding Indian people and the work of the BIA. Perhaps nothing emblematized this disjuncture more than termination policy.

FIGURE 3. Clarence E. King, 1971, photographed by Victor Krantz. Photo courtesy of the National Anthropological Archives, Smithsonian Institution, NAA INV.10023000, neg. 71–2146.

Termination Without Elimination

While Holmes and Jennison disagreed on the efficacy of termination, neither faction equated termination with elimination. At the conclusion of the May 1958 meeting, Norman Holmes sought to quell the friction that had surfaced, and he shifted focus toward their shared future. Holmes congratulated "the council here on the way they have conducted the meeting" and stated he had "no hard feelings against anybody regarding this election."[91] Mutually outraged at the BIA commandeering the composition of the tribal roll, Jennison and Clarence King worked together to petition to excise those individuals who did not belong on the roll and plan the future for the Ottawa outside of federal supervision.

Divergent federal and tribal visions of termination came to a head at the May 1959 Ottawa General Council meeting, the last Ottawa meeting under BIA supervision. "In an effort to be of assistance," local BIA officials came to the meeting with a "proposed articles of incorporation for the Ottawa Indian Cemetery Association."[92] In short, the BIA wanted a convenient repository for the five-acre Ottawa cemetery—a place for the Ottawa, and seemingly their remaining tribal sovereignty, to go to die. Ottawas objected to this narrow mandate. As Ottawa tribal member Richard Montgomery cogently pointed out at the meeting, "if the Ottawas establish an organization just as a Cemetery Association . . . that is all they are going to be able to do."[93]

Headed by Jennison, the Ottawa Business Committee came to the meeting with their own plan to reorganize tribal government as a state-chartered nonprofit corporation. A leader in the AIT, the Ottawa County Farm Bureau, the Ottawa County Taxpayers League, and the Rural Electrification Administration, Jennison had a deep well of expertise leading nonprofit corporations.[94] The new Ottawa organization had three mandates: "to perpetuate the name and identity of the Ottawa Indians of Oklahoma; to maintain the Ottawa Indian Cemetery near Ottawa, Oklahoma for burial of persons having Ottawa Indian blood . . . [and] to act for and on behalf of the Ottawa Indian Tribe of Oklahoma insofar as Ottawa Indian tribal business is concerned."[95] Tribal leaders chartered the new organization to last in "perpetuity."[96] Far from acquiescing to elimination, the Ottawa perpetuated tribal identity and government, took control of remaining tribal lands, and continued to pursue tribal prerogatives—all key markers of nationhood.[97]

For tribal members, the new organization provided an opportunity to pursue their shared interests outside of BIA oversight. Tribal priorities included dictating their own membership. The newly proposed bylaws for the state-chartered organization featured a provision that called for future generations to be added to the tribal roll. Marie Wadley, tribal affairs officer for the Muskogee Area Office, objected to this provision at the 1959 meeting. Comparing Ottawa rolls to those of the Five Civilized Tribes, she noted the Ottawa roll "will be considered a final and closed roll" and "there is no authority to add to the rolls of the Ottawa Tribe which will be approved by the Secretary of the Interior under the Termination Act."[98] Tribal member Walter King countered Wadley's assertion by pointing out termination granted the Ottawa autonomy from federal control: "Since the Ottawas are going to be incorporated under the laws of the State of Oklahoma what is to keep them from adding names to their roll now that they are out from under the U.S. Government. . . . the Five Tribes rolls were not prepared under a termination program, such as the Ottawa Tribe, which is one of the first to terminate."[99] Walter King was correct. Unlike the Ottawa, BIA officials had never contemplated a tribal community enduring after termination. Wadley conceded the Ottawa could establish their own membership rules within the confines of their state charter—the BIA had no authority there.

The other immediate priority involved the management of the cemetery. The new state-chartered organization would gain control over this five-acre tract of land, and Ottawa leaders looked to gain secure title and expand the graveyard. According to existing property lines, the Ottawa Baptist Church adjacent to the cemetery, which had a mostly non-Ottawa membership, had encroached on cemetery land, and some gravesites had been located on church property. Prior to the 1959 meeting, Jennison initiated negotiations with church leaders. Church officials proposed to trade the land on which the church building encroached in return for a greater proportion of land to expand the cemetery site. Church leaders insisted, however, that the tract "be used solely for cemetery purposes" and that burial plots be made available to non-Ottawas living in the surrounding area.[100] Jennison objected to these stipulations. He observed, "I don't like their placing in there the provision that all people of the community should be buried there. I think it is up to the tribe . . . After we acquire the land, it is ours to do as we want to do."[101] Tribal members unanimously voted to reject the proposal of the Ottawa Baptist Church. After termination, the cemetery remained an Ottawa space, with burials restricted to tribal members or immediate relatives of whites already interred in the cemetery.

The new nonprofit organization reflected the priorities of tribal members in the 1950s. Jennison did not advocate to re-create in miniature the state-centered sovereignty of the United States. Instead, in emphasizing control over identity, control over the cemetery, and control over tribal affairs and activities free from BIA oversight, the organization reflected an Ottawa vision of tribal self-determination for that period. In their willingness to persevere as an Indian people after termination, the Ottawa consciously rejected federal and societal definitions of Indian identity that rested on federal acknowledgment, racialized blood quantum, economic status, and an antiquated image of cultural distinctiveness, each of which failed to account for the diversity of Ottawa tribal members or how the Ottawa identified themselves. At the helm of a new legal entity, built from an ancient edifice, Jennison led the Ottawa into the posttermination era. Jennison retired in 1962 and was succeeded as chief by Clarence King, but Jennison remained active in Ottawa affairs until his death in 1967.[102]

Conclusion

Senator Arthur Watkins, the leading congressional advocate for termination, portrayed the policy as an embodiment of the highest of American ideals. He championed it as "the road to complete citizenship rights" and declared "following in the footsteps of the Emancipation Proclamation of ninety-four years ago, I see the following words emblazoned in letters of fire above the heads of the Indians- THESE PEOPLE SHALL BE FREE!"[103] The Ottawa had heard similar propositions before. In June 1862, only a few months before Abraham Lincoln issued the Emancipation Proclamation, the Ottawa signed a treaty calling for tribal allotment, termination, and their acquisition of "all the rights, privileges, and immunities" of U.S. citizenship. In reality, both the 1862 Treaty and the policy of tribal termination that followed nearly a century later intended to facilitate tribal dispossession and elimination under the cloak of the expansion of democratic ideals and equal rights. Jennison and his grandfather James Wind embraced these policies not as a reflection of American values but to escape imposed, illiberal colonial administration. Ottawa ambitions of autonomy from colonial impositions intersected with the eliminatory aims of federal officials in these policies, but the Ottawa rebuffed the eliminatory intentions of policymakers. In both cases, the Ottawa worked to sustain their political community through dimensions of American society outside of colonial administration.

Equating Ottawa termination with elimination privileges state-centered recognition models over tribal actions.[104] Although outside the purview of this article, in the two decades following the passage of termination legislation, Ottawa leaders harnessed their autonomy from colonial administration and revitalized tribal cultural, political, and economic life in the 1960s and 1970s. As before, they continued to engage with federal policy on their own terms. Just as Jennison chose termination over paternalism, tribal leaders adjusted to the new rhetoric and realities of the federal policy of tribal self-determination in the 1970s. After heated internal debates, the Ottawa voted to pursue the restoration of federal recognition in 1972, but Ottawa leaders petitioned for federal recognition on the basis that they had never stopped functioning as a tribe.[105] The Ottawa Tribe of Oklahoma secured reinstatement in 1978.

By understanding Jennison's activism within the context of Ottawa political traditions, this article underscores the creative and subversive ways Native people have harnessed legal regimes designed to render them invisible to secure autonomy from colonial administration.[106] Ottawa termination experiences feature coercive dimensions found in other termination accounts, and they reflect a broader Cold War tendency to use undemocratic means to advance "freedom."[107] Both federal officials and Jennison disregarded consultation with most tribal members on termination, and the BIA used intimidation to quell dissent.[108] It might be tempting to cast Ottawa termination largely in terms of victimization and BIA manipulation, but such an account would obfuscate Jennison's sustained advocacy for termination and the long tradition of tribal activism that informed his perspective. Jennison's standpoint on termination as a path toward greater autonomy did not represent the only tribal perspective on the topic, but his activism shaped the outcome.

DAVID DRY is a citizen of the Ottawa Tribe of Oklahoma and completed his Ph.D. in history at the University of North Carolina at Chapel Hill.

References

Alfred, Taiaiake, and Jeff Corntassel. "Being Indigenous: Resurgences against Contemporary Colonialism." *Government and Opposition* 40 (2005): 597–614.

Andrews, H. A., to Ed Edmondson, April 23, 1956. Ed Edmondson Papers. Box 52. Folder 15. John Vaughan Library. Northeastern State University. Tahlequah, Oklahoma.

Andersen, Chris. *"'Métis': Race, Recognition, and the Struggle for Indigenous Peoplehood*. Vancouver: UBC Press, 2015.

Armstrong, O. K. "Give the Indians an Even Chance." *Reader's Digest* (November 1955): 101–5.

Arnold, Laurie. *Bartering with the Bones of Their Dead: The Colville Confederated Tribes and Termination*. Seattle: University of Washington Press, 2012.

Barker, Joanne. *Native Acts: Law, Recognition, and Cultural Authenticity*. Durham: Duke University Press, 2011.

Barlow, Lewis. Interview by Joseph Cash. June 5, 1976. Interview 1021. American Indian Research Project. Oral History Center. University of South Dakota. Vermillion, South Dakota.

Beard, Henry. *The Title of the Ottawa University, Kansas*. Washington, D.C.: Judd and Detweiler, 1873.

Beck, David. *Seeking Recognition: The Termination and Restoration of the Coos, Lower Umpqua, and Siuslaw Indians, 1855–1984.* Lincoln: University of Nebraska Press, 2009.

———. *The Struggle for Self-Determination: History of the Menominee Indians Since 1854.* Lincoln: University of Nebraska Press, 2005.

Blacklidge, C. N., to George Mitchell, April 24, 1871. M-856. Reel 36. Frames 495–498. Records of the Central Superintendency of Indian Affairs. Miscellaneous Letters Received. Record Group 64. National Archives and Records Administration. Washington, D.C.

Buckmaster, Edra. Interview by David Dry. August 12, 2019. In author's possession.

Cahill, Cathleen D. "Our Democracy and the American Indian: Citizenship, Sovereignty, and the Native Vote in the 1920s." *Journal of Women's History* 32, no. 1 (Spring 2020): 41–51.

Cash, Joseph H., and Gerald W. Wolff. *The Ottawa People.* Phoenix: Indian Tribal Series, 1976.

Chandler, H. E., to Elmer Thomas, "Resolution" [enclosure], November 18, 1933. Elmer Thomas Papers. Box LG 12. Folder 79. Carl Albert Congressional Research and Studies Center. University of Oklahoma. Norman, Oklahoma.

Cohen, Nancy. *The Reconstruction of American Liberalism, 1865–1914.* Chapel Hill: University of North Carolina Press, 2002.

Coulthard, Glen. *Red Skin, White Masks: Rejecting the Colonial Politics of Recognition.* Minneapolis: University of Minnesota Press, 2014.

Coward, John M. "Promoting the Progressive Indian." *American Journalism*, 14, no.1 (1997): 3–18.

Dawes, Henry L. "Petitions and Memorials," January 5, 1883. 47th Congress. 2nd session. *Congressional Record* 14, Part 1. Washington, D.C.: Government Printing Office, 1883.

Den Ouden, Amy E., and Jean M. O'Brien. "Introduction: Why 'Recognition' Matters." In *Recognition, Sovereignty Struggles, & Indigenous Rights in the United States: A Sourcebook,* edited by Amy E. Den Ouden and Jean M. O'Brien, 1–34. Chapel Hill: University of North Carolina Press, 2013.

Dennison, Jean. "The Logic of Recognition: Debating Osage Nation Citizenship in the Twenty-First Century." *American Indian Quarterly* 38, no. 1 (2014): 1–35.

Dyer, D. B., to the Commissioner of Indian Affairs, August 27, 1881. In *Annual Report of the Commissioner of Indian Affairs,* 96. Washington, D.C.: Government Printing Office, 1881.

Dyer, D. B., to the Commissioner of Indian Affairs, August 4, 1882. Quapaw Agency Records. Reel QA-5. Frame 236. Indian Archives Collection. Oklahoma Historical Society. Oklahoma City, Oklahoma.

Ellinghaus, Katherine. *Blood Will Tell: Native Americans and Assimilation Policy.* Lincoln: University of Nebraska Press, 2017.

Emmons, Glenn, to William J. Pitner, May 27, 1958. Records of the Anadarko Area Office. Personnel Files. Personnel Correspondence 1956–1958 File. Record Group 75. Federal Records Center. Fort Worth, Texas.

Finger, John R. *The Eastern Band of Cherokees, 1819–1900.* Knoxville: University of Tennessee Press, 1984.

Fixico, Donald Lee. *Termination and Relocation: Federal Indian Policy, 1945–1960.* Albuquerque: University of New Mexico Press, 1986.

Gracey, Marci Barnes. "Joseph Bruner and the American Indian Federation: An Alternative View of Indian Rights." In *Alternative Oklahoma: Contrarian Views of the Sooner State,* edited by Davis D. Joyce, 63–86. Norman: University of Oklahoma Press, 2007.

Hauptman, Laurence M. "The American Indian Federation and the Indian New Deal: A Reinterpretation." *Pacific Historical Review* 52, no. 4 (November 1983): 378–402.

Hayes, Marie L., to Paul Fickinger, April 22, 1958. Records of the Muskogee Area Office. Office Files of the Tribal Affairs Officer, 1947–65. Record Group 75. Federal Records Center. Fort Worth, Texas.

Hayworth, Rhonda. Interview by David Dry. August 15, 2019. In author's possession.

Hiraldo, Danielle V. "'If You Are Not at the Table, You Are on the Menu': Lumbee Government Strategies under State Recognition." *Native American and Indigenous Studies* 7, no. 1 (2020): 36–61.

Holmes, Norman, to William J. Pitner, June 4, 1958. Records of the Anadarko Area Office. Personnel Files. Personnel Correspondence 1956–1958 File. Record Group 75. Federal Records Center. Fort Worth, Texas.

Holt, Ronald L. *Beneath These Red Cliffs.* Logan, Utah: Utah State University, 2006.

Hoxie, Frederick E. *A Final Promise: The Campaign to Assimilate the Indians, 1880–1920.* Lincoln: University of Nebraska Press, 1984.

Indian Affairs: Laws and Treaties, Vol. 2, edited by Charles J. Kappler Washington, D.C.: Government Printing Office, 1903.

Jennison, Gene, with Lewis Barlow. Interview by Joseph Cash. June 3, 1976. Interview 1022. American Indian Research Project. Oral History Center. University of South Dakota. Vermillion, South Dakota.

Jennison, Guy. "Gift from White Man." *Miami Daily News-Record,* April 1, 1959.

———. "History Unfair to Original American." *Miami News-Record,* September 28, 1956.

———. "Let Indians Lug the Ball." *Miami Daily News-Record,* November 2, 1961.

———. "Ottawa Chief Airs Indian Problems." *Miami Daily News-Record,* January 22, 1954.

———. "Political Scalps Exposed." *Miami Daily News-Record,* April 24, 1960.

———. "Sparks from the Tribal Fire" [unpublished autobiography], circa 1956, Ottawa Tribe History Folder, Dobson Museum Archives, Miami, Oklahoma.

———. "Tribal Council Speech," July 10, 1965, Ottawa Tribe Folder, Dobson Museum, Miami, Oklahoma.

———. Typescript of Undated (c. 1953) Speech. Ed Edmonson Papers. Box 52. Folder 15. John Vaughan Library. Northeastern State University. Tahlequah, Oklahoma.

Jennison, Guy Jr. Interview by Joseph Cash. June 4, 1976. Interview 1018. American Indian Research Project. Oral History Center. University of South Dakota. Vermillion, South Dakota.

Jones, Hiram W., to the Commissioner of Indian Affairs, September 1, 1872. In *Annual Report of the Commissioner of Indian Affairs*, 243. Washington, D.C.: Government Printing Office, 1872.

Joplin Globe. "Boswell Named to Head Ottawa Bureau." June 5, 1921.

———. "Ottawa County Fair Ends Greatest Year." September 17, 1921.

King, Joseph B. "The Ottawa Indians in Kansas and Oklahoma." *Collections of the Kansas State Historical Society* 13 (1913–1914): 373–78.

King, Mary. Interview by David Dry. August 15, 2019. In author's possession.

King, Walter S. to Elsie Hand, January 3, 1958. Walter S. King Collection. Box 1. Folder 4. Oklahoma Historical Society. Oklahoma City, Oklahoma.

Klopotek, Brian. *Recognition Odysseys: Indigeneity, Race, and Federal Tribal Recognition Policy in Three Louisiana Indian Communities.* Durham: Duke University Press, 2011.

Lambert, Valerie. "The Big Black Box of Indian Country: The Bureau of Indian Affairs and the Federal-Indian Relationship." *The American Indian Quarterly* 40, no. 4 (2016): 333–63

Lomawaima, K. Tsianina. "The Mutuality of Citizenship and Sovereignty: The Society of American Indians and the Battle to Inherit America." *Studies in American Indian Literatures* 25, no. 2 (2013): 331–51

Lowery, Malinda Maynor. *The Lumbee Indians: An American Struggle.* Chapel Hill: University of North Carolina Press, 2018.

Maddox, Lucy. *Citizen Indians: Native American Intellectuals, Race, and Reform.* Ithaca: Cornell University Press, 2005.

"Meetings with Ottawa Tribe," November 23, 1954, December 13, 1954, Records of the Muskogee Area Office. Office Files of the Tribal Affairs Officer, 1947–65. Record Group 75. Federal Records Center. Fort Worth, Texas.

Metcalf, Warren. *Termination's Legacy: The Discarded Indians of Utah.* Lincoln: University of Nebraska Press, 2007.

Miami Daily News-Record. "300 County Indians Rap Bill Pushed by Collier." March 13, 1934.

———. "Agency Menaced." July 27, 1949.

———. "Andrews Again in Agency Job." January 7, 1948.

———. "Fireside Chat." July 7, 1940.

———. "Former Miami Boy Weds." April 9, 1935.

———. "Indians Meet for Election." January 9, 1934.

———. "Jennison Assails Act Seeking End to Indian Setup." April 18, 1948.

———. "Leaguers Urge More Reforms in Tax System." January 10, 1933.

———. "Locals." June 10, 1934.

———. "Quapaw Agency Records Leave County Aug 1." April 18, 1948.

———. "Seven Tribes Urge Return of Indian Agency to Miami." January 2, 1948.

Miller, Douglas K. *Indians on the Move: Native American Mobility and Urbanization in the Twentieth Century.* Chapel Hill: University of North Carolina Press, 2019.

Nieberding, Velma. "Wyandotte and Peoria Leaders View Progress." *Miami News-Record,* August 6, 1956.

———. "Wyandotte Tribe to Invite Bids Soon for Sale of K.C. Cemetery." *Miami News-Record,* February 22, 1959.

O'Brien, Jean M. "Tracing Settler Colonialism's Eliminatory Logic in Traces of History." *American Quarterly* 69, no. 2 (2017): 249–255.

Ostler, Jeffrey. *Surviving Genocide: Native Nations and the United States from the American Revolution to Bleeding Kansas.* New Haven: Yale University Press, 2019.

Ottawa Chief and Council to the Secretary of the Interior, March 22, 1877. Quapaw Agency Records. Reel QA-9. Frames 154–155. Indian Archives Collection. Oklahoma Historical Society. Oklahoma City, Oklahoma.

Ottawa Tribe of Oklahoma. Articles of Incorporation: Ottawa Indian Tribe of Oklahoma, June 1, 1959. Tribal Constitutions Folder, Ottawa Tribe of Oklahoma History Archives Library, Miami, Oklahoma.

———. Certificate of Incorporation. July 14, 1959. Tribal Constitutions Folder. Ottawa Tribe of Oklahoma History Archives Library, Miami, Oklahoma.

———. Ottawa General Council Meeting Minutes, May 3, 1958, Series 29, Ottawa General Council Folder, Historic Oklahoma Collection, Oklahoma Historical Society, Oklahoma City, Oklahoma.

———. Ottawa General Council Meeting Minutes. May 9, 1959. Tribal Minutes Folder. Ottawa Tribe of Oklahoma History Archives Library, Miami, Oklahoma.

"Ottawa Tribe of Oklahoma . . . Proposed Roll of Members." *Federal Register* 23, no. 57 (March 21, 1958), 1901–1906.

Peroff, Nicholas. *Menominee Drums: Tribal Termination and Restoration, 1954–1974.* Norman: University of Oklahoma Press, 2006.

Phillips, Katrina. "When Grandma Went to Washington: Ojibwe Activism and the Battle over the Apostle Islands National Lakeshore." *Native American and Indigenous Studies* 8, no. 2 (2021): 29–61.

Philp, Kenneth R. *Termination Revisited: American Indians on the Trail to Self-Determination, 1933–1953.* Lincoln: University of Nebraska Press, 1999.

"Progress Report of Reduction of Bureau Services by Termination," December 31, 1953. Records of the Muskogee Area Office. Office Files of the Tribal Affairs Officer, 1947–65. Record Group 75. Federal Records Center. Fort Worth, Texas.

Prucha, Francis Paul. *The Great Father: The United States Government and the American Indians.* Lincoln: University of Nebraska Press, 1984.

Puisto, Jaakko. *'This Is My Reservation, I Belong Here': The Salish Kootenai Indian Struggle against Termination.* Lincoln: University of Nebraska Press 2016.

"Report on Meeting with Members of the Quapaw Tribe," January 9, 1955. Records of the Muskogee Area Office. Office Files of the Tribal Affairs Officer, 1947–65. Record Group 75. Federal Records Center. Fort Worth, Texas.

Rifkin, Mark. "Indigenizing Agamben: Rethinking Sovereignty in Light of the 'Peculiar' Status of Native Peoples." *Cultural Critique* 73 (Fall 2009): 88–124.

Rountree, Helen C. *Pocahontas's People: The Powhatan Indians of Virginia through Four Centuries.* Norman: University of Oklahoma Press, 1996.

The Roosevelt Standard (Roosevelt, Utah). "Employees Leave Staff." March 15, 1956.

———. "Final Rolls Completed." February 23, 1956.
———. "Meeting at Fillmore on Indian Legislation." January 7, 1954
Rosier, Paul C. *Rebirth of the Blackfeet Nation, 1912–1954.* Lincoln: University of Nebraska Press, 2005.
———. *Serving Their Country: American Indian Politics and Patriotism in the Twentieth Century.* Cambridge, Mass: Harvard University Press, 2012.
Stanciu, Cristina. "Americanization on Native Terms: The Society of American Indians, Citizenship Debates, and Tropes of 'Racial Difference.'" *Native American and Indigenous Studies* 6, no. 1 (2019): 111–48.
Survey of Conditions of the Indians in the United States, Oklahoma Part 15. Washington, D.C.: Government Printing Office, 1931.
The Indian Reorganization Act: Congresses and Bills, edited by Vine Deloria Jr. Norman: University of Oklahoma Press, 2002.
Ulrich, Roberta. *American Indian Nations from Termination to Restoration, 1953–2006.* Lincoln: University of Nebraska Press, 2013.
Unrau, William E., and H. Craig Miner. *Tribal Dispossession and the Ottawa Indian University Fraud.* Norman: University of Oklahoma Press, 1985.
U.S. House. *Hearings on Muskogee and Anadarko Area Indian Tribes before the Committee on Interior and Insular Affairs.* 84th Cong., 1st sess., August 25–26, 1955. Washington, D.C.: Government Printing Office, 1956.
———. *Hearings Before the Committee on Interior and Insular Affairs.* 95th Cong., 1st sess. July 14, 1977. Washington D.C.: Government Printing Office, 1977.
U.S. Senate. *Report of the Select Committee to Investigate Matters Connected with Affairs in the Indian Territory with Hearings.* 59th Cong., 2nd sess., November 11, 1906–January 9, 1907. Washington, D.C.: Government Printing Office, 1907.
Warrior, Robert. "The SAI and the End(s) of Intellectual History." *Studies in American Indian Literatures* 25, no. 2 (2013): 219–35.
Watkins, Arthur V. "Termination of Federal Supervision: The Removal of Restrictions Over Indian Property and Person." *The ANNALS of the American Academy of Political and Social Science* 311, no. 1 (May 1957): 47–55.
The Western Spirit (Paola, Kansas). "The Ottawa University." December 13, 1872.
Whittlesey, Eliphalet, to Clinton B. Fisk. December 15, 1882. In *Annual Report of the Board of Indian Commissioners to the Secretary of the Interior for the Year 1882,* 31–32. Washington, D.C.: Government Printing Office, 1883.
Wilkins, David E., and Heidi Kiiwetinepinesiik Stark. *American Indian Politics and the American Political System.* Lanham: Rowman & Littlefield, 2018.
Wilkins, David E. and K. Tsianina Lomawaima. *Uneven Ground: American Indian Sovereignty and Federal Law.* Norman: University of Oklahoma Press, 2001.
Wilkinson, Charles F. *Blood Struggle: The Rise of Modern Indian Nations.* New York: Norton, 2006.
———. *The People Are Dancing Again: The History of the Siletz Tribe of Western Oregon.* Seattle: University of Washington Press, 2010.
Wilkinson, Charles F., and Eric R. Biggs. "The Evolution of the Termination Policy." *American Indian Law Review* 5, no. 1 (1977): 139–184.

Wilson, John, and Ottawa Tribal Council to Commissioner of Indian Affairs, April 17, 1869. M-234. Reel 657. Frames 486–487. Ottawa Agency. Letters Received by the Office of Indian Affairs 1824–1881. Record Group 75. National Archives and Records Administration. Washington, D.C.

"Withdrawal Programming: Ottawa Tribe," September 15, 1952. Records of the Muskogee Area Office. Office Files of the Tribal Affairs Officer, 1947–65. Record Group 75. Federal Records Center. Fort Worth, Texas.

Wolfe, Patrick. "Settler Colonialism and the Elimination of the Native." *Journal of Genocide Research* 8, no. 4 (December 2006): 387–409.

———. *Settler Colonialism and the Transformation of Anthropology: The Politics and Poetics of an Ethnographic Event.* New York: Cassell, 1999.

Notes

I would like to express my gratitude to the *Native American & Indigenous Studies* Writing and Mentoring Fellowship for creating a venue for me to improve and workshop an article draft, and I would like to thank my mentor during that fellowship, Jeani O'Brien, for her detailed comments and our constructive conversations. I would also like to thank NAIS editors Kelly McDonough and K. Tsianina Lomawaima and the three anonymous peer reviewers for their thoughtful insights and feedback. Finally, I want to express my appreciation to my dissertation chair Malinda Maynor Lowery for her steadfast support and guidance. This article is the result of the time and efforts of many people, and I am ever grateful.

1. U.S. House. *Hearings on Muskogee,* 34 (statement of Guy Jennison).

2. Fixico, *Termination and Relocation,* 183; Wilkins and Lomawaima, *Uneven Ground,* 132; Wilkinson and Biggs, "Evolution," 153–54.

3. Fixico, *Termination and Relocation,* 183–197; Wolfe, *Settler Colonialism,* 3; Wolfe, "Elimination of the Native," 400.

4. Den Ouden and O'Brien, "Introduction," 1.

5. Of the 109 terminated tribes, 99 were small northern California and Oregon tribes terminated jointly in omnibus bills. See, Ulrich, *American Indian Nations,* 71–72, 114–15; Wilkinson and Biggs, "Evolution," 151; Prucha, *Great Father,* 1048.

6. Peroff, *Menominee Drums,* 169.

7. Peroff, *Menominee Drums,* 55; Beck, *Struggle for Self-Determination,* 139; Beck, *Seeking Recognition,* 153. For another example of financial incentives to terminate, see Puisto, *Salish Kootenai Indian Struggle,* 51–52.

8. Wilkins and Stark define wardship as a "legally specious" means "to justify any number of federal activities" and the assertion of plenary power as a "virtually boundless governmental authority and jurisdiction over Indian tribes, their lands, and their resources." See Wilkins and Stark, *American Indian Politics,* 296–97, 58–69.

9. Recent scholarship has noted federal recognition circumscribes the sovereign claims of tribal nations by inducing tribes to acknowledge themselves as under federal authority, on federal terms, and by presenting the recognition

of tribal nationhood as justice. See, for example, Coulthard, *Red Skin, White Masks,* 17–33; Alfred and Corntassel, "Being Indigenous"; Barker, *Native Acts,* 1–26; Andersen, *Métis,* 20–21; Dennison, "The Logic of Recognition"; Rifkin, "Indigenizing Agamben," 96–99. Another line of recent scholarship has assessed how tribes have navigated the advantages and liabilities of federal recognition, see Klopotek, *Recognition Odysseys,* 1–9; Hiraldo, "'If You Are Not at the Table."

10. See, for example, Finger, *The Eastern Band,* 44–45, 170–75.

11. Philp, *Termination Revisited,* xi–xiv, 71, 85–88, 170–71; Phillips, "When Grandma Went to Washington," 39–40. For other works that substantively examine tribal support for termination, see Arnold, *Bartering with the Bones;* Rosier, *Rebirth of the Blackfeet Nation.*

12. King, "Ottawa Indians," 376.

13. On removal as genocidal, see Ostler, *Surviving Genocide,* 365–67.

14. *Indian Affairs: Laws and Treaties,* 830.

15. For similar strategies around tribal unity through educational and religious institutions, see Rountree, *Pocahontas's People,* 187–220; Lowery, *An American Struggle,* 94–124.

16. Unrau, and Miner, *Tribal Dispossession.*

17. *Indian Affairs: Laws and Treaties,* 960–69.

18. Wilson and Ottawa Tribal Council to Commissioner of Indian Affairs, April 17, 1869; *The Western Spirit,* "Ottawa University"; Unrau and Miner, *Tribal Dispossession,* 154–59; Blacklidge to Mitchell, April 24, 1871; Beard, *Title of the Ottawa University,* 4–26.

19. Federal officials described the U.S. citizenship of the Ottawas as an "anomalous condition" and how "their exact rights are not clearly defined." See Jones to the Commissioner of Indian Affairs, September 1, 1872, 243; Dyer to the Commissioner of Indian Affairs, August 27, 1881, 96.

20. Dyer to the Commissioner of Indian Affairs, August 4, 1882.

21. Prucha, *Great Father,* 716, 659–71.

22. After the Civil War, liberal reformers championed economic liberalism, or laissez-faire, that lionized the sanctity of property to rationalize limited government in market relations. Cohen, *Reconstruction of American Liberalism,* 84–109.

23. Ottawa Petition," in Whittlesey to Fisk, *Annual Report,* 31–32. As early as 1877, the Ottawa tribal council advocated for allotment. The 1882 Ottawa allotment petition, the first formal tribal petition for allotment, was endorsed by 96 of the 122 Ottawas. Ottawa Chief and Council to the Secretary of the Interior, March 22, 1877. Dawes, "Petitions and Memorials," January 5, 1883, 869.

24. U.S. Senate, *Report of the Select Committee,* 53–54 (testimony of John Earley, November 13, 1906).

25. U.S. Senate, *Report of the Select Committee,* 58 (testimony of Manford Pooler, November 13, 1906); U.S. Senate, *Report of the Select Committee,* 53 (testimony of John Earley, November 13, 1906).

26. U.S. Senate, *Report of the Select Committee,* 53 (testimony of John Earley, November 13, 1906).

27. For a summary of these cases, see, Wilkins and Stark, *American Indian Politics*, 65.
28. Jennison, "Gift."
29. Jennison, "Gift."
30. Jennison, "Sparks."
31. Jennison, interview.
32. Jennison, "Gift."
33. Jennison, "Gift."
34. Ellinghaus, *Blood Will Tell*, 45–69.
35. Armstrong, "Give the Indians," 105.
36. Jennison, "Ottawa Chief."
37. Jennison, "Political Scalps."
38. Jennison, "Ottawa Chief."
39. The perspective of Ottawa leaders reflects the efforts of the SAI to abolish Indian Office control and secure U.S. citizenship—sometimes demanding civil equality at the expense of tribal sovereignty. See, for example, Maddox, *Citizen Indians*, 166–175; Lomawaima, "The Mutuality of Citizenship and Sovereignty"; Cahill, "Our Democracy," 41–51; Warrior, "Intellectual History."; Stanciu, "Americanization."
40. Coward, "Progressive Indian."
41. Jennison, "Sparks."
42. Eastern Shawnee, Miami, Modoc, Peoria, Quapaw, Seneca-Cayuga, and Wyandotte.
43. *Survey of Conditions*, 6645–601.
44. *Miami Daily News-Record*, "Indians Meet."
45. Chandler to Thomas, November 18, 1933.
46. Chandler to Thomas, November 18, 1933.
47. *Miami Daily News-Record*, "300 County Indians."
48. *Miami Daily News-Record*, "300 County Indians."
49. *The Indian Reorganization Act*, vii–xvi, 328–67, quote on page 366.
50. Hauptman, "American Indian Federation," 378–402; Gracey, "Joseph Bruner."
51. Jennison, "Ottawa Chief."
52. *Miami Daily News-Record*, "Jennison Assails"; Jennison, "Gift"; Jennison, "History Unfair"; Jennison, "Let Indians Lug the Ball."
53. Jennison, "Ottawa Chief."
54. Jennison, Typescript of Undated (c. 1953) Speech.
55. Andrews to Edmondson, April 23, 1956; Hayworth, interview.
56. Jennison, "Gift."
57. Hoxie, *Final Promise*, 115–46.
58. Armstrong, "Give the Indians," 105.
59. Jennison, "Ottawa Chief."
60. *Miami Daily News-Record*, "Quapaw Agency Records Leave County Aug 1."
61. *Miami Daily News-Record*, "Seven Tribes Urge;" *Miami Daily News-Record*, "Andrews Again;" *Miami Daily News-Record*, "Agency Menaced."

62. "Progress Report of Reduction of Bureau Services by Termination," December 31, 1953.

63. "Ottawa Tribe," *Federal Register;* Jennison is listed as 3/8 degree of Indian blood.

64. "Withdrawal Programming: Ottawa Tribe," September 15, 1952.

65. "Withdrawal Programming: Ottawa Tribe," September 15, 1952.

66. "Report on Meeting with Members of the Quapaw Tribe," January 9, 1955.

67. U.S. House. *Hearings on Muskogee,* 34 (statement of Guy Jennison).

68. As much as half of the Ottawa resided outside of reservation confines prior to allotment in 1892. See, King to Hand, January 3, 1958.

69. Buckmaster, interview; King, interview.

70. U.S. House, *Hearings on Muskogee,* 33 (statement of Guy Jennison).

71. "Meetings with Ottawa Tribe," November 23, 1954, December 13, 1954.

72. U.S. House, *Hearings on Muskogee,* 40 (statement of Lawrence Zane).

73. U.S. House, *Hearings Before the Committee on Interior and Insular Affairs* (testimony of Robert Alexander, Business Manager for the Ottawa, Peoria, Wyandotte, and Modoc Tribes).

74. Ulrich, *American Indian Nations,* 247–48; Wilkinson and Biggs, "Evolution," 151.

75. Tribes in the Quapaw Agency whose leaders refused to endorse the policy escaped termination, while the Ottawa, Peoria, and Wyandotte tribes, whose Business Committees all consented, had termination bills enacted. The Wyandotte bill incentivized the federal government to address the longstanding issue of the Wyandotte Cemetery in Kansas City by stipulating it had to be resolved prior to formal termination. The Peoria bill similarly incentivized the federal government to settle their Indian Claims Commission cases. Nieberding, "Wyandotte and Peoria Leaders"; Nieberding, "Wyandotte Tribe."

76. Ottawa Tribe of Oklahoma, Ottawa General Council Meeting Minutes, May 9, 1959.

77. *Miami News-Record,* "Former Miami Boy"; *Miami News-Record,* "Locals"; *The Roosevelt Standard,* "Meeting at Fillmore," *The Roosevelt Standard,* "Employees Leave."

78. Lambert, "Big Black Box."

79. Holt, *Beneath These Red Cliffs,* 61–87; *The Roosevelt Standard,* "Final Rolls."

80. *The Roosevelt Standard,* "Employees Leave."

81. The roll compiled by the Business Committee excluded individuals they claimed had been illegally placed on the tribal roll during allotment in 1892. BIA officials argued the tribal constitution mandated that those individuals be included. As a result, the BIA rejected the roll composed by the Business Committee and took over composition of the tribal roll.

82. Hayes to Fickinger, April 22, 1958.

83. Hayes to Fickinger, April 22, 1958.

84. Ottawa Tribe of Oklahoma, Ottawa General Council Meeting Minutes, May 3, 1958.

85. Ottawa Tribe of Oklahoma, Ottawa General Council Meeting Minutes, May 3, 1958.
86. Ottawa Tribe of Oklahoma, Ottawa General Council Meeting Minutes, May 3, 1958.
87. Ottawa Tribe of Oklahoma, Ottawa General Council Meeting Minutes, May 3, 1958.
88. Emmons to Pitner, May 27, 1958.
89. Emmons to Pitner, May 27, 1958.
90. Holmes to Pitner, June 4, 1958.
91. Ottawa Tribe of Oklahoma, Ottawa General Council Meeting Minutes, May 3, 1958.
92. Ottawa Tribe of Oklahoma, Ottawa General Council Meeting Minutes, May 9, 1959.
93. Ottawa Tribe of Oklahoma, Ottawa General Council Meeting Minutes, May 9, 1959.
94. *Joplin Globe,* "Boswell Named to Head Ottawa Bureau"; "*Joplin Globe,* Ottawa County Fair Ends Greatest Year"; *Miami News-Record,* "Leaguers Urge More Reforms in Tax System"; *Miami News-Record,* "Fireside Chat."
95. Ottawa Tribe of Oklahoma, Articles of Incorporation: Ottawa Indian Tribe of Oklahoma, June 1, 1959.
96. Ottawa Tribe of Oklahoma, Certificate of Incorporation, July 14, 1959.
97. Wilkins and Stark, *American Indian Politics,* 297.
98. Ottawa Tribe of Oklahoma, Ottawa General Council Meeting Minutes, May 9, 1959.
99. Ottawa Tribe of Oklahoma, Ottawa General Council Meeting Minutes, May 9, 1959.
100. Ottawa Tribe of Oklahoma, Ottawa General Council Meeting Minutes, May 9, 1959.
101. Ottawa Tribe of Oklahoma, Ottawa General Council Meeting Minutes, May 9, 1959.
102. Jennison, "Tribal Council Speech," July 10, 1965.
103. Watkins, "Termination of Federal Supervision," 51, 55.
104. O'Brien, "Tracing," 251.
105. Cash and Wolff. *The Ottawa People,* 77–90; Barlow, interview; Jennison Jr., interview; Jennison, with Barlow, interview.
106. Ottawa engagement with termination contributes to scholarship that examines other eliminatory federal programs commandeered by Native participants to suit ends not envisioned by policymakers, including the relocation program that accompanied termination. Miller, *Indians on the Move,* 5–10.
107. Beck, *Seeking Recognition,* 162–164; Wilkinson, *Blood Struggle,* 77–81; Wilkinson, *People Are Dancing,* 279; Metcalf, *Termination's Legacy,* 16; Rosier, *Serving Their Country,* 181.
108. Jennison with Barlow, interview.

SUSAN JACOB

The Moving Mountain:
Performance for Mauna a Wākea during the Protect Maunakea Movement

Abstract

Between the period of July 2019 and March 2020, Kānaka Maoli (Native Hawaiian) kiaʻi (protectors or guardians) blocked the access road up to Mauna a Wākea, Hawaiʻi's tallest peak, to protest and prevent the construction of the Thirty Meter Telescope (TMT). This proposed development, spearheaded by a conglomerate of international scientific organizations, has become the catalyst for the latest movement for reestablishing Hawaiian sovereignty after a long history of appropriation, desecration, and broken promises. For Kānaka Maoli the construction poses a threat to their sacred land, burial sites, and the delicate ecology of the mountain. During these protests, kiaʻi demonstrated and reconfirmed their relationship to Mauna a Wākea through the mediums of music and dance in the newly created Mauna Protocol Ceremony performed at the protest site on Hawaiʻi Island, public performance venues, and online. Performing for the mountain at accessible locations allowed more people to view and interact with Mauna a Wākea without having to be on location. It is through the Hawaiian concepts of ʻike (know by doing), kū (stand firm), and hulihia (overturn) that I illustrate how kiaʻi effectively transform secular spaces into sacred ones through the act of performance.

FROM JULY 2019 TO MARCH 2020, a group of Kānaka Maoli (Native Hawaiians)[1] led a series of protests in opposition to the proposed construction of a Thirty Meter Telescope (TMT) on the summit of Mauna a Wākea, a dormant volcano and the tallest peak on Hawaiʻi Island, with resistance participants framing themselves not as protestors but as the kiaʻi (protectors or guardians) of the mountain. The choice of using the term kiaʻi frames the intentionality of the movement and the intimate relationship and kuleana (responsibility) Kānaka Maoli have to the land. Mauna a Wākea is named for the Hawaiian deity Wākea (the sky father), but the name is also often shortened to

Maunakea or Mauna Kea,[2] the latter meaning White Mountain (Case 2021, 25; Goodyear-Kaʻōpua 2020, 10; Herman 2015). This mauna (mountain) is a sacred place in Native Hawaiian culture, an honored and once restricted zone open only to certain members of the society. It is a place of creation for the Hawaiian people, a connector to the heavens, a burial ground for chiefs, and a site where Hawaiians practice sacred ceremonies to this day. Given the sacred qualities with which Hawaiians imbue this landmark space and its importance in Hawaiian life, it is little wonder that kiaʻi are making a stand and standing firmly—kū.

The proposed construction of this telescope, known colloquially as TMT, has sparked controversy and a series of very visible resistance events ever since the groundbreaking ceremony at the proposed site in October 2014 (Kelleher 2014). Although the start of construction was stalled by additional protests in April 2015 and a consequent series of legal battles (Casumbal-Salazar 2019, 205–6), the state eventually granted the necessary permits and announced that construction would begin on July 15, 2019. Two days prior to the intended construction date, however, kiaʻi gathered at the Mauna Kea Access Road and set up a campsite to block construction vehicles. This is a story of their fight to protect Mauna a Wākea, reaffirm Hawaiian values through the use of performative action, and unite a community by raising awareness of social and cultural wrongs.

This work examines how Maunakea protectors and their allies engage with Mauna a Wākea through song, dance, word, gesture, and digital media as a form of kū (standing firm). As organizers of the movement establish new traditions that emulate old styles, they link the past with the present. They also propel the movement forward and imbue it with the energy and performance of newly created rituals and recently composed songs that aim to foster direct connections between Mauna a Wākea and the community that supports the movement. Their goal is to protect the mauna in a contemporary Hawaiʻi while grounding their efforts in a respect and acknowledgment of Hawaiʻi's history and traditions. Through these actions they invoke the fundamental concepts of ʻike,[3] a Polynesian value that privileges "knowing by doing," kū (standing firm), and hulihia[4] (overturn). I argue that it is through the acts of singing and dancing that kiaʻi define the experience of the sacred while simultaneously celebrating and connecting Indigenized sites. Through the use of ancient and modern modes of performative expression and communication, they create a wide cooperative community of resistance and hulihia—of people united in action around concepts of sacred space, even when not geographically proximate. By relying on the values of ʻike, kū, and hulihia, the Protect Maunakea[5] movement has also done the impossible: it has helped a dormant volcano continue to grow.

FIGURE 1. Subaru, Keck, and NASA telescopes—summit of Mauna a Wākea. Photo by Robert Linsdell.

I recognize my positionality influences what I say and present in this work. I come to this research with outsider eyes, as a new arrival in the islands five years ago, and as someone both engaged in the study of ʻōlelo Hawaiʻi (Hawaiian language) and with prolonged training in hula: I have been a haumāna (student) of Hālau Hula ka Noʻeau under the tutelage of Kumu Hula Michael Pili Pang. Soon after my arrival I observed the anxiety surrounding the beginning of the telescope's construction, prompting conversations with professors, classmates, and members of the community. Coming from a secular Jewish background that hails the pursuit of science as unquestionably honorable, I was forced to reevaluate my understanding of the ethics of scientific conquest and how it can negatively impact people whose values differ from my own. I recognized how the field of ethnomusicology can contribute to the efforts of kiaʻi and help others engage with their own internal struggles balancing the desire for scientific advancement and the protection of Indigenous rights. It is my goal with this work to highlight the effectiveness of music as resistance for Indigenous Hawaiian causes and encourage people to gain empathy and understanding beyond their worldview.

I approach this research through qualitative practice as an observer participant in ceremonial and protest activity on Mauna a Wākea and the island of Oʻahu, attendance at concerts, and through interviews and conversations with kiaʻi, university coursework on Native Hawaiian politics and Hawaiian music, and cyber ethnography. Through these methods I endeavor to tease out the ways in which Mauna a Wākea's protectors engage with music and dance performance as a method of resistance and as a way metaphorically to "move" and "grow" a mountain as they transport the sacredness of Mauna a Wākea into otherwise secular spaces. Moving transpires on the levels of emotional engagement, geographical location, and calls to action through pilgrimage and the moving body. Growing takes place through education and the growth of knowledge as well as through expansion of the community in an ever-developing meshwork of connections (Ingold 2007).

This study explores dual themes of sacredness and resistance through the lens of Hawaiian epistemology and, specifically, the values of ʻike, kū, and hulihia to illuminate and inform how music functions in social and political activity in Hawaiʻi. I first discuss issues surrounding the sacred-secular spectrum. I then examine the ways in which Hawaiians turn to music as an operative force in resistance, both today and at key points in Hawaiian history. Exploring present-day modes of musical resistance in the Protect Maunakea movement as performative practice illuminates how music functions in decolonized spaces and relationalities. Finally, analyzing newly composed chant and hula performed on Mauna a Wākea and at satellite areas of protest—the University of Hawaiʻi at Mānoa campus, urban performance venues, and digital platforms—I show how sacred actions spill into secular spaces to form expanded communities of support. In the process, kiaʻi take secular space and render it sacred, either temporarily or permanently, through the performative action of shared musical experience. Using music with the stated purpose of educating people, kiaʻi move the mountain and bring the sacredness of Mauna a Wākea to places outside of Hawaiʻi Island, where previously untapped communities are able to support the cause of the movement as a regional, national, and international imaginary.

Comprehending the Sacred: ʻIke

In discussing the sacred, I acknowledge the critical discourse surrounding this term and the fact that Indigenous views of what is sacred do not always share the same distinctions as those encompassed in the Western binary of sacred-secular. Many Indigenous Peoples do not differentiate between these worlds or regard the sacred as bound within definable limits (Charlot 1985, 1; Deloria, Foehner, and Scinta 1999; Evans 2003; Holmes 2004; Kashay 2008; Keller 2014; Kim 2012; Liljeblad 2019; Rabinovich 2018; Sarmiento 2017; Silva 2004, 85–86; Twiss 2015). Rather, Indigenous spirituality often has a porous quality to it, allowing practices and ideas to flow smoothly from one realm to another to place the person in constant connection with the sacred.

Even within Western thought the term "sacred" is multidimensional, making a universal definition impossible (Evans 2003, 41). In many modern societies, government regulation pushes the sacred from the state and into the realm of "tradition," a problematic term in its own right (Bronner 1998). This association creates a (mis)understanding that the sacred is fixed and immovable. Hawaiian culture, however, known for its permeability and qualities of flexibility and openness to incorporating elements from other cultures into its own, disrupts the idea that the sacred must remain immutable in order to be authentic. The false standard of authenticity often imposed on Native Hawaiian and other Indigenous cultures by outsiders, in turn influences and shapes the discourse on Hawaiian values and ways of being, artificially forcing Hawaiians into uncomfortably bounded and limiting roles (Case 2021, 66; Stillman 2021). Just as most continental Americans do not live frozen in the past, Hawaiians do not confine themselves to ancient lifeways and are continuously developing contemporary elements of their culture (Brown 2016; Trask 1991, 164–65). Tension occurs when society labels some people as forward-thinking and innovative when embracing a new practice but views other people as inauthentic sellouts to modernity if they choose to innovate.

Acknowledging that Native Hawaiian culture avoids distinctions between porous and impermeable views of sacredness forces scholars to search for a way to recognize this difference while trying to understand and honor the values that form and maintain it. The black and white positioning of sacred versus secular ignores the nuances of various grays that exist within nondifferentiating cultures, a critique launched by younger scholars who embrace the need to integrate Indigenous viewpoints. "In many ways, the term sacred fails to capture what Kānaka [Maoli] experience when relating to their ancestral homeland" (Casumbal-Salazar 2019, 208). "As a pragmatic matter, those who come from Indigenous communities have to engage with the power of the dominant language terms . . . while those in the dominant communities rarely engage with the linguistically and culturally specific words and meaning of the Indigenous communities" (Keller 2014, 89). For example, the online Hawaiian language dictionary database, Wehewehe,[6] translates the term "sacred" as kapu. The dilemma of the insufficient reduction of a very complex thought to a mono-dimensional meaning and the inaccuracy inherent in its cross-cultural transposition becomes apparent when the definition is turned around, and the reader finds "sacred" as only one of many translations of kapu. As Casumbal-Salazar indicates, however, "sacred" is the closest word we have in the English language (2019, 208) to describe the condition of the spiritual, and it is with that caution—and its shortcomings as well as its potentials—that I use it here.

Differences in perception underline the challenges of translating cultural and linguistic meaning, especially in an encounter of conflicting worldviews. When talking to a group of settler-colonial children about Heart Mountain in Wyoming, Apsáalooke (Crow) elder Grant Bulltail stated: "I don't want to call it a sacred site because your idea of something sacred and my idea of something sacred are a little bit different" (Keller 2014, 88). Instead, drawing upon traditional Native American ways of transmitting knowledge and awareness of the world (Archibald and Xiiem 2018), he turned to the medium of story-telling[7] as he described to the children how his tribe experiences and connects with this revered mountain, even from a great distance where it cannot be seen (Keller 2014, 90).[8]

The sacred in an Eastern Polynesian worldview has an ongoing role in linking past, present, and future and is based primarily on a connection to place as a specific historicized and experienced or "lived" interaction with a geographical locale and the beings, artifacts, and forces of nature that it encompasses. "The island-world environment (land, sea, sky) is animate and comprises a web of interconnected and genealogically related elements (gods, land, sea, sky, humans, and all therein)" (Brown 2016, 155). In the Hawaiian worldview, environmental elements are akua (gods)[9] (Ku'ulei Kanahele pers. comm.) who have personified roles associated with their worldly function. For example, the volcano akua, Pele, is a creator of land, even as "her passionate nature and emotions drive her to both violence and love, which are demonstrated through the flow and eruptions of Kīlauea [an active volcano on Hawai'i Island]" (McDougall 2016, 28).

Native peoples from various cultures manifest their relationship to land, for example a particular tree or mountain, through reciprocal practices (Deloria, Foehner, and Scinter 1999, 232–38). One way that Polynesians foster connection with their environment is through the burial of the placenta or afterbirth, a practice that connects a newborn child with the land to create a physical and deeply felt affective genealogical link that renders the child an inseparable part of the land. In speaking of French Polynesia, Saura describes this as a cyclical and synergetic process wherein the pu fenua (placenta) in Tahiti is buried "at the base of a fruit tree so that the substance that nourished the foetus nourishes the tree" (2002, 127), and the tree in turn nourishes the individual. Placenta burial in Hawai'i takes on an aspect of genealogical safeguarding; "many of the families living on the slopes of Mauna a Wākea deposit the piko [umbilical cord] and 'iewe (afterbirth, placenta) of the family's newborn in hidden places on the summit to protect the child" (Casumbal-Salazar 2017, 5). In addition, mothers may choose to bury the piko and 'iewe at a particular location to imbue their child with certain qualities, such as longevity, hula expertise, or connection to birthplace (Barrère, Pukui, and Kelly 1980, 102–3). Moreover, for Kānaka Maoli, Mauna a Wākea is the piko (navel, center, point of connection) that links the Hawaiian people to the heavens (Peralto 2014, 236). In Hawaiian thought, Mauna a Wākea is not simply a geological formation but a familial connection that must be cared for, nurtured, and experienced on a physical and spiritual level (Cooper, Delormier, and Taualii 2019, 5). As explained by Native Hawaiian academic and activist Dr. Haunani-Kay Trask regarding the connection to land in precontact Hawai'i, "Our people looked on land as a mother, enjoyed a familial relationship with her and other living things, and practiced an economically wise, spiritually based ethic of caring for the land, called mālama ʻāina" (Trask 1991, 160).

This familial connection is evident in the phrase "We Are Mauna Kea," an expression used by kiaʻi in the Protect Maunakea movement to underscore and confirm that Kānaka Maoli and Mauna a Wākea are inextricably linked. Given this worldview, Hawaiians see the construction of the TMT as not merely about a building, the perception of uncontrolled scientific advancement, a fending off of rampant exploitation of limited island surfaces and natural resources, or the maintenance of power and control. Yes, it represents all those things. But on a much more profound level, TMT holds the potential to disrupt a place where Hawaiians connect—to their ʻāina (land), to their history, to their ancestors, and to their world. They do not accept the possibility of a rending displacement lightly.

TIO (TMT International Observatory) is a conglomerate of international scientific organizations that backs construction of the TMT. If built, the TMT would stand 56 meters tall (the equivalent of 18 stories), making it the largest of the 13 telescopes already housed on Mauna Kea (McLaren 2020). The TMT also would disturb untouched ground, thus setting the precedent for ever-expanding development on Mauna a Wākea. Some people favor a compromise wherein two existing unused telescopes would be decommissioned and the TMT built in their place, but there seems to be little interest from TIO in considering this measure. Faced with such conflicting views, the lack of progress in resolving these two positions is deeply troubling for opposers of the telescope who hold still unresolved spiritual, ecological, and ethical concerns about the construction.

One might wonder why scientists want to build on such a culturally significant place. The answer lies in the fact that Mauna a Wākea has the best "seeing" in the world, a term that references the conditions for astronomical observation. Mauna a Wākea is a shield volcano with an ocean backdrop and a view totally unobstructed by other land masses. Its sloping sides create smooth airflow, which decreases turbulence and results in far superior image quality. According to Keck Observatory astronomer Robert McLaren, "no place gets better images consistently than Mauna Kea" (McLaren 2020).

Optimal astronomical conditions matter little to Mauna a Wākea's protectors. Supporters of the telescope have accused kiaʻi of being antiscience, which ignores their true efforts in protecting what they consider sacred. "We're not against the science of astronomy," said Protect Maunkea activist Dr. M. Noe Noe Wong Wilson in an article published by Space.com. "We are against the [construction] of a building too big on our sacred mountain. And we really want to make that clear because that gets lost" (Urrutia 2020).

Western society conditions its population to believe that the pursuit of science is unfailingly just and necessary to the advancement of humanity, but this becomes complicated when Western desires invade Indigenous spaces and erode the meanings attached to them. Indigenous scientists have even joined the fight, such as Native Hawaiian astronomer Kealoha Pisciotta, who has worked on Mauna Kea for over a decade and has been a vocal opponent of TMT construction (Feder 2019).

There are, however, also Native Hawaiians who support the telescope, although their voices are noticeably quiet in the dialogue about the TMT. The website IMUA TMT (TMT first) publishes written and video testimonials by people who support the telescope, including Native Hawaiians. Leimomi o Kamehae Kuamoʻo Moʻokini Lum, the kahuna (priestess) of Moʻokini Heiau (Moʻokini Temple) in North Kohala on Hawaiʻi Island, states:

> I believe totally in getting the new telescope built on Mauna Kea. Our ancestors studied the heavens. Now a new generation of Hawaiians can have the opportunity to advance what they discovered. A telescope that can accomplish this maintains the sacredness of the mountain. With this and in other ways, we need to be open to the future to carry us forward to the many tomorrows yet to come. (IMUA TMT)

Kahuna Lum's words illuminate the complexity lying just behind the issues surrounding TMT. Like Western views on the sacred, there is no universal agreement among Native Hawaiians as to how sacredness should be experienced or expressed. Lum's words justify TMT by suggesting that the telescope would contribute to the advancement of Hawaiian Indigenous astronomical knowledge, which has been in practice for centuries and utilized to great effect for navigational purposes (Lewis 1974; Makemson 1938, 1939; Eckstein and Schwarz 2019).

A post on the discussion forum site Reddit, dated December 19, 2022, asked members of the r/space subreddit page for their thoughts on the construction of TMT and possible reconciliation of competing objectives (thedrakeequator 2022). As of January 2023, the post received over eighteen hundred comments, some from people who claim to be Native Hawaiian and in favor of TMT. Understandably, many comments in this forum post are in support of the project since the r/space subreddit page attracts users who are interested in astronomy, however, many people in the forum also express sympathy for the kiaʻi and discuss the possibility of alternative sites for the construction. Such controversies may cause a rift in society but provoke important conversations regarding reassessment and reconsiderations of how Indigenous and other worldviews navigate value systems and current practices—especially those so closely aligned to the sacred.

More Than Just a Song: Kū

While views of the sacred underpin much of the investment in and argument over TMT, the musical response to this dispute merits the attention of ethnomusicologists. Music as resistance occupies an established place in ethnomusicology literature (Damodaran 2016; Denisoff 1966, 1970; Edet 1976; Garratt 2019; Pratt 2013; Rodnitzky 2013; Street 2003; Way 2016), where scholars have generally approached the subject as music or musical activity connected to "any kind of oppositional thinking or subculture behavior" (Pratt 2013). Challenges, however, surround the determination of exactly what constitutes resistant musical practice. Despite agreement about the efficacy of protest music, "Theorists disagree . . . about the kind of activities that qualify as [music] protest activism" (Garratt 2019, 128). Music can be and *is* a powerful motivator and method of protest that has a long history within social movements, even if some protest songs often fail to enact any meaningful or wide-ranging social change on their own (Denisoff 1970, 822; Garratt 2019, 130–31). Rather, some scholars see music as shouldering crucial foundational work through its "support [of] the broader work of social change movements" (Garratt 2019, 130). The growing literature on Indigenous and Native Hawaiian music resistance (Fellezs 2019a; Lewis 1985, 1987; Love 2018; Sheffield 2011; Stillman 1989, 1999; Teves 2018) examines some of these determinants of efficacy while turning attention to musical efforts that challenge settler coloniality, protect Indigenous land, and build cultural solidarity. Such efforts find organized expression and purpose in Indigenous movements, such as the Protect Maunakea movement and the NoDAPL protests to stop construction of the Dakota Access Pipeline in the Standing Rock Sioux Nation (Love 2018).

Much research on music as resistance has focused on the functions of protest songs in social movements, such as sociologist Denisoff's establishment of six categories for analyzing social function in these songs (1966, 582). Of these, categories 2, 3, and 6 hold particular relevance for understanding how Hawaiians invoke and practice music within the Protect Maunakea movement:

2. The song reinforces the value structure of individuals who are active supporters of the social movement or ideology.
3. The song creates and promotes cohesion, solidarity, and high morale in an organization or movement supporting its worldview.
6. The song points to some problem or discontent in the society, usually in emotional terms. (582).

The use of Indigenous languages, including ʻōlelo Hawaiʻi (Hawaiian language), can complicate the message of resistance when much of it glides by the ear of audiences not versed in the language. In Hawai'i, the banning of the Hawaiian language in schools in 1896 (and its subsequent replacement by English in public spaces) resulted in its near extinction; despite concerted efforts to revive it, relatively few people today speak Hawaiian fluently[10] or understand the nuances of poetry and use of kaona (double meaning). In addition to the loss of linguistic understanding, Hawaiian music and dance fight a long colonial and tourist history of being taken as pure, lighthearted entertainment in a perception that renders protest songs as fun and easygoing due to their predominant use of major tonality, flowing melodies, strong lyricism, and the added graceful movements of a hula dancer. In the voices, actions, and understandings of the Indigenous population, however, these same practices do not diminish the message at all (Kaeppler 2010). Rather, the music of resistance resonates in deeply felt ways that reflect both the individual and the culture at large, accomplishing community-focused goals through the act of staying grounded in traditional views and practices.

Hawaiians have utilized music to protest American occupation since the era of annexation during the 1890s. The most famous protest song from the annexation era is "Kaulana Nā Pua" (Famous are the flowers), composed by Ellen Kekoaohiwaikalani Wright Prendergast in 1893 in response to the illegal overthrow of the Hawaiian Kingdom (Basham 2008, 163; Nordyke and Noyes 1993; Stillman 1989, 1999). Over the years, this song has appeared under multiple titles, such as "He Lei no ka Po'e Aloha 'Āina" (A symbol of affection for the people who love their land), "Mele Aloha 'Āina" (Patriot's Song), "Mele 'Ai Pōhaku" (Stone-eating song), and "He Inoa no nā Keiki o ka Bana Lāhui" (A name song for the children of the national band), to name a few (Nordyke and Noyes 1993, 27; Papakilo Database).

Each of these titles highlights important meanings found within the song. For example, the phrase Aloha 'Āina translates here in English to "patriot"; however, love of the land is a more literal and realistic translation (Silva 2004, 18). "Patriot" is gendered male and implies a relationship with a national imaginary, whereas Aloha 'Āina is gendered female and underscores a genealogical relationship between people and the land. "In the struggle against annexation . . . aloha 'āina [was developed] as a discourse of resistance, and simultaneously as a particularly Kanaka [Hawaiian] style of defensive nationalism" (18).

Two titles contain interesting references to the Royal Hawaiian Band and appear in the phrases 'ai pōhaku (stone-eating) and ka bana lāhui (the national band). Shortly after the overthrow of the Hawaiian Kingdom (1893) the "provisional government issued a mandate for goverment workers to sign a loyalty oath many [sic] persons resisted this order, including members of the Royal Hawaiian Band" (Nordyke and Noyes 1993, 27; Silva 2004, 134–35). Nordyke and Noyes provide an in-depth look at this song, but some points underscore the idea of immersive attachment to and identification with the land. The phrase ʻai pōhaku comes from the first two lines of the fourth verse: Ua lawa mākou i ka pōhaku/I ka ʻai kamahaʻo o ka ʻāina (We are satisfied with the stones/Astonishing food of the land) (1993, 29). Laced with kaona[11] (double meaning), these lyrics imply that rocks, or the land, will suffice (lawa) as food, providing sustenance that is more important than the American ideal of land ownership (1993, 33; Charlot 1985, 28).

"Kaulana Nā Pua" remains popular today as the unofficial anthem for Hawaiian sovereignty. Its profound meaning, although masked by a major tonality and pleasant, lyrical melody, is evident to those who can understand the Hawaiian language and the metaphorical allusions behind the song text. This shared understanding contributes to the conception and development of sovereignty among Kānaka Maoli, with the music serving as an amplification of those sovereign voices. The longevity of the cultural importance of this song, for over 130 years, serves as a measurement for how long Native Hawaiians have felt displaced in their homeland as well as a painful reminder of ongoing dissonance for the islands' Indigenous population.

In addition to the suppression of Hawaiian language and culture following the overthrow, Hawaiians also underwent a period of increasing marginalization and exoticization in their "new country," all of which contributed to reformatting the definition and perception of Hawaiian music and culture exported from Hawaiʻi on a global scale. Hawaiian musicians traveled global music circuits as the exoticized Other (Imada 2012), while predominantly white performers outside of Hawaiʻi appropriated and misrepresented Hawaiian music and dance for their own purposes as a form of "Polynesianface." The resultant well-known image of a sexualized and whitewashed female hula dancer, whose movements were mimicked via insensitive representations in movies and on television, came to occupy the international imaginary as a trivialized caricature of her and her art. Incredibly, this stubborn and specious trope still persists in the twenty-first century, including every sitcom with a Hawaiʻi vacation episode.

The exploitation of Hawaiʻi extends well beyond the misrepresentation of music, language, and iconic figures; it is part of the larger misuse and abuse of culture apparent today in even more pertinent threats to the environment and sovereignty. Protecting the environment from desecration, fending off cultural exploitation and distortion, and establishing sovereignty have been key motives for Kānaka Maoli activists in the latter half of the twentieth century and early twenty-first century.

The Hawaiian Renaissance[12] (from 1969[13] to roughly the mid- to late 1990s) marked a period of renewed interest in traditional Hawaiian cultural practices, the effects of which still echo today. Various resistive efforts during this era utilized popular protest songs reflecting what Denisoff calls "discontents" (Denisoff 1966, 582). During the Hawaiian Renaissance these discontents focused efforts to protect land from over-development and harmful military practices, promoted sovereignty, and highlighted issues surrounding the tourist industry and American occupation.

Many popular protest songs of this era utilized ʻōlelo Hawaiʻi, with layers of kaona—in the lyrical text and stylistic elements, and timbres such as steel guitar, ʻukulele, and falsetto singing that rooted these songs as distinctly Hawaiian, even while incorporating elements from "outside" local music traditions. Songs such as "E Kuʻu Morning Dew" (composed in 1973) by Larry Kimura and Eddie Kamae, "Waimānalo Blues" by Thor Wold and Liko Martin (also known as "Nanakuli Blues") (1975), and "Hawaiʻi 78" by Israel Kamakawiwoʻole (1993), to name a few, all contain themes of aloha ʻāina expressing concerns about the precarious state of Hawaiian lands. For example, "E Kuʻu Morning Dew" features lyrical text filled with kaona that on the surface appears to be a love song, however, reading between the lines reveals a love for the land, not a romantic interest. "Waimānalo Blues" and "Hawaiʻi 78" are more explicit in their expressions of resistance in their lyrical text mourning increased urban development.

Denisoff states that the vast majority of protest songs (1) have a publicly identifiable author, (2) are transmitted via audio-visual aids, and (3) rarely "survive beyond their historical genre or organizational milieu" (Denisoff 1968, 229). Both 1 and 2 are true of the previously mentioned Hawaiian songs of resistance, in addition to many others not mentioned. In contrast with statement 3, these songs escape the ephemerality that plagues both protest and popular music due to their broad resonance within the culture and continued struggles between Native desires and foreign interests. Preserved and disseminated on social media and audio streaming sites, these songs find continued life through professional-quality music videos, filmed live performances, and audio produced by the artists themselves and by media groups such as projectKULEANA and Mana Maoli.

Performance as resistance encompassed hula when, toward the end of the Hawaiian Renaissance in 1997, the Hawaiʻi state government attempted to pass Senate Bill 8, which would have greatly restricted gathering access to traditional plants used in hula by requiring practitioners to prove the authenticity of their genealogy, continuing blood quantum debates and the long history of the suppression of traditional practices (Kamahele 2008; Kapuaʻala 1998). Response to this proposed bill brought together kumu hula (hula masters) to form the ʻĪlioʻulaokalani (red dog of the heavens) Coalition, a group "committed to defending any encroachment upon Native Hawaiian culture in general and hula in particular" (Kamahele 2008, 88).

In a short three days, ʻĪlioʻulaokalani organized a twenty-four-hour protest demonstration to take place on February 25, 1997, at the State Capitol building. Every hour on the hour, hundreds of hula practitioners danced and chanted in the kahiko (ancient) style, accompanied by pahu (shark skin drums), which was considered the most sacred hula instrument. Over one hundred pahu sounded in the atrium of the Hawaiʻi State Capitol building, a deafening and "chicken skin"–inducing sound that observers reported hearing several blocks away from the site (Kamahele 2008, 90). Successfully blocking Senate Bill 8, the ʻĪlioʻulaokalani Coalition set a precedent for effective Kānaka Maoli art resistance.

Mele Aloha ʻĀina: Uniting Resistance and the Sacred

"How can we support you?
Write mele for us. Be our kūpuna the way that they wrote mele
for the Aloha ʻĀina of their time." (Osorio 2021)

The above quote by Kanaka Maoli activist, poet, and scholar Dr. Jamaica Osorio expressed the above in her online video presentation on April 2021 (Osorio 2021), recollecting a conversation from a twenty-four-hour vigil held in March 2015 at the University of Hawaiʻi at Mānoa. Organized in support of kiaʻi who ascended Mauna Kea during one of the earlier Protect Maunakea demonstrations, the 2021 online event—titled Mele Kiaʻi Mauna (Songs of the mountain guardians): Where Creativity and Community Commitment Collide—was a gathering of notable members of the kiaʻi as well as well-known musicians from different musical backgrounds. As in most Hawaiian presentations and ceremonial events, the program began with an oli—"E Hō Mai"—performed by Pua Case, kumu hula and one of the main leaders of the Protect Maunakea movement. "We are blessed today to be transported back to the mauna by Kumu Pua Case," said Dr. Osorio in acknowledging the phenomenological experience of Case's chant (Osorio 2021) and music's power to bring listeners, performers, and the mauna together to foster that sacred connection—even through a digital platform.

In various protests, demonstrations, vigils, and educational outreach events, music has remained an essential tool of resistance, amplifying the messages of protection and solidarity while serving as a vehicle to connect participants to Mauna a Wākea despite the physical distance. Looking to the manaʻo (thoughts, ideas, beliefs) of selected kiaʻi and, in particular, the mele hula (chant accompanied by movement) "ʻAi Kamumu Kēkē" from the Mauna Protocol Ceremony, I bring into focus the kiaʻi's efforts to protect Mauna a Wākea as expressed through performed embodiment. Kiaʻi have effectively shared and grown the use of this music by moving it into previously secular spaces, their transformative actions establishing satellite areas of sacredness and resistance. The satellite areas, metaphorically bound in Mauna a Wākea's orbit and balanced by the pull of the mauna's spiritual gravity, connect, amplify, and root musical activity.

The Mauna Protocol Ceremony
The Mauna Protocol Ceremony, one of the most significant ceremonial developments in the Protect Maunakea movement, is a performative tradition consisting of previously composed and newly created prayer in the form of mele (song), oli (chant), and hula (dance) in the kahiko (old; precontact) style. Closely tied to the mauna and Protect Maunakea resistance, in July 2019 the ceremony quickly became a recurrent performative rite of inclusion, sharing, and solidarity that is performed three times daily in tribute to Mauna a Wākea—every morning, midday, and early evening. The use of the kahiko idiom connects those present to a Hawaiian past, successfully perpetuating the old while keeping historical Hawaiian practices meaningful in a modern world. Musicians, dancers, and other cultural practitioners serve as the leaders of this movement, responding to the need to create "new" traditions to facilitate cultural expression, agency, and the experience of the sacred.

The Mauna Protocol Ceremony is performed and observed with kapu aloha. This is a recent term in the Hawaiian lexicon with old roots reaching far back in Hawaiian ideology. Kapu means simply "sacred, taboo, or prohibited"; the familiar term "aloha" means "love" but carries the deeper meaning of affection, compassion, and kindness. To define either word with a singular meaning discounts the intricacies and nuances of these terms. Combined they have become "a guiding principle of the protectors of Mauna Kea" (Teves 2018, 9) or what Kumu Pua Case considers "a manner in which one conducts themselves when they are in the sacred. You become the sacred" (Puʻuhonua o Puʻuhuluhulu 2019a). Kapu aloha means having compassion and respect for the land, the people, and the space around you even in moments of resistance and strife. It is through conducting one's self in the sacred with reverence and respect, connection, and action that the Protocol Ceremony invites sacred action into secular spaces to imbue them with heightened and transformative ideological change. Kapu aloha has been a guiding principle since the start of protest, expressing a way of conducting oneself and avoiding violent or aggressive actions.

On October 26, 2019, I traveled to Hawaiʻi Island to visit the Puʻuhonua o Puʻuhuluhulu encampment on Mauna a Wākea to observe the Mauna Protocol Ceremony firsthand. This is the puʻuhonua (camp) where kiaʻi first blocked the road leading up to the summit on July 13, 2019; they would eventually retreat only in March 2020 when then Hawaiʻi State Governor Ige declared a

FIGURE 2. View of Mauna a Wākea, shot from across Hilo Bay. Photo courtesy of Eric Tessmer.

stay-at-home order due to the COVID-19 pandemic. The puʻuhonua was set up at the T-intersection of the Mauna Kea Access Road and the Saddle Road that runs between Mauna a Wākea and Maunaloa where the black igneous rock from Pele's long-since-cooled eruptions marks this terrain. The temperature is cool at this high elevation of over 6,600 feet and, on that day, the clouds hung low, obscuring the view of Mauna a Wākea in a gray haze.

Upon arrival, I found a Kupuna Tent set up on the asphalt of the Access Road to house and seat the kūpuna (elders) while effectively blocking the road from vehicles. Participants stood off to the sides, and protocol leaders directed the ceremony from in front of the tent. Kumu Pua Case was directing the ceremony that day; as she gazed over the crowd, she announced proudly that she saw many newcomers and warmly encouraged onlookers to participate. Slowly, almost all kiaʻi and visitors joined in. People of all ages, backgrounds, and places, danced and chanted in unison to honor Mauna a Wākea and lend support to the kiaʻi in an expression of aloha—for the mountain, its guardians, the culture, and all present.

While some sections of the Mauna Protocol draw from older sources, many parts were created by kiaʻi leadership. These newly created mele and hula resemble those of the kahiko tradition but modified to accommodate the many participants in the protocol without previous experience in hula or singing in the Hawaiian language. The inclusive parts of the ceremony are simple, allowing participants to follow along in the back while those in leadership roles perform at the front.

The mele hula "'Ai Kamumu Kēkē" has emerged as one of the most inclusive and memorable parts of the protocol. It consists of a verse (figure 3) recited three times, accompanied by simple hula hand and arm movements. The motions in hula help to explain the poetry and give imagery to the words of the chant or song, serving as accompaniment to the all-important poetry of the chant (Zuttermeister 2020). The puʻuhonua featured educational classes, and during my visit, renowned Kumu Hula Kekuhi Kealiʻikanakaʻoleohaililani dropped in on a "how to" class dedicated to learning the song and movements for "'Ai Kamumu Kēkē." A descendant of Pele, member of the hula school Hālau o Kekuhi, and the wife of Hawaiʻi Community College professor Dr. Taupōuri Tangarō (who choreographed the hula and modified the text for this chant), she described the text as an onomatopoeic rendering expressing the sights and sounds of a volcanic eruption.

In conversation with Dr. Tangarō, he described the process of first choreographing "'Ai Kamumu Kēkē" back in 1997 when he started teaching at Hawaiʻi Community College. "I've always used hula in my classes, regardless if it was a hula class or not, because hula was the way the whole body and the multiple intelligences could play in the acquisition of knowledge" (Taupōuri Tangarō, pers. comm.). He recognized early in his career the struggles of BIPOC and female students in the Eurocentric American higher education system and utilized the performance of "'Ai Kamumu Kēkē" to decolonize his classroom (Akena 2012; Elbow 2017; Knopf 2015; Tuhiwai Smith 2021) and foster an environment for marginalized students to achieve academic success.[17]

HULIHIA KA MAUNA[14]

Hulihia ka mauna	Destruction and turmoil in the Pit
Wela i ke ahi a ka wahine	The fires of the Woman have done it
Wela nā ʻōhiʻa o Kūlili a i ka ua	Consuming the forests of Kūlili
A wela a nopu ke ahi o ka lua	Fires that boil from the depths of the Pit

ʻAI KAMUMU KĒKĒ

(na Taupōuri Tangarō)[15]

ʻAi kamumu kēkē	Consuming, crunching
Nakeke pāhoehoe, kē	A rattling lava flow
Wela i luna o Halemaʻumaʻu kē	It is hot above Halemaʻumaʻu (crater on Kīlauea)
Wela i luna o Halemaʻumaʻu kē[16]	It is hot above Halemaʻumaʻu

FIGURE 3. Song text from the Puʻuhuluhulu website ("Puʻuhonua o Puʻuhuluhulu" 2019b.) "'Ai Kamumu Kēkē" translated by the author.

The choreography for this mele is from the hula kiʻi (image, idol, or puppet hula) tradition, wherein dancers perform the embodiment of sacred kiʻi (anthropomorphic wooden or stone images) found in temples (heiau) (Luomala 1984). Most often this style of hula is performed using a puppet; however, the choreography of "ʻAi Kamumu Kēkē" utilizes the body of the dancer to represent the kiʻi. The choice to utilize this style was not arbitrary. In Hawaiian thought, the performance of hula serves as a means to acquire mana (spiritual power), allowing the dancer to access the realm of the sacred and become an akua.[18] In "ʻAi Kamumu Kēkē" the dancers themselves become the sacred kiʻi and therefore becoming godlike.

The performance of Dr. Tangarō's choreography of "ʻAi Kamumu Kēkē" is notable in that dancers remain in a stationary, bent-knee position, known as haʻa (lowered), for the duration of the dance. In standing hula, normally the feet and hips move in known lower body movement motifs; this stationary position breaks from that practice. The haʻa stance grounds the dancer, lowers the center of gravity, and strengthens the connection the dancer has to the ʻāina. Dancers prepare this stance by planting their feet firmly in position separated by a shoulder width, bending the knees slightly, and tensing their upper body as protocol leaders chant "Hulihia ka Mauna" (figure 3) which serves as a lead-in to "ʻAi Kamumu Kēkē" in the protocol ceremony, and signals designation as a Pele chant.[19]

The movements of this hula are also notable for the extreme tension in the arms and hands as mimetic gestures that depict the breaking of rock and the flow of lava. It is not uncommon for upper-body gestures in hula kahiko to be strong, but the arm and hand movements in "ʻAi Kamumu Kēkē" are particularly forceful as hands claw at and metaphorically destroy the sacred land in order to convey the power of volcanic eruption (figure 3). Vocal timbre and facial gestures are also tense, evoking an eruption through the energy and power of the voice and the tightened muscles of the face. This is performative kaona, wherein the voice, facial gestures, and atypical hand movements are metaphors for the fire burning within the kiaʻi, but these movements are not merely performative. Mauna Kea exists within the chant and in every performance of it. Through chant and movement, the performer embodies the volcanic action, viscerally feeling the scorching of the earth and the potential for continued injustice. Kiaʻi are not just simply miming an eruption. When they perform this mele hula, they become part of the ʻāina, erupting with spiritual energy.

While the movements of this hula are distinctly Hawaiian, the intense and energetic vocal recitation is inspired by Māori haka (Taupōuri Tangarō, pers. comm.), a chant style meaning "fire breath," which originates from Aotearoa New Zealand (Clements 2014, 21). Back in 1997, Dr. Tangarō chose to borrow haka's heightened vocalization in order to channel the anger his students felt about American colonization and militarization of the islands, the monarchy's decision to remain peaceful during annexation, and their families' adoption of Christianity (Taupōuri Tangarō, pers. comm.). Although "'Ai Kamumu Kēkē" is only performed three times during the Mauna Protocol Ceremony, he and his students have performed it as many as ten or more times to the point of exhaustion to expel that anger and energy. In our conversation, he compared this release to a form of spiritual sacrifice. In precontact Hawai'i, ki'i required a human sacrifice in order to gain sacred energy. The sacrifice transferred the spirit from the human form to the wooden or stone ki'i where it would live on. The release of energy during performances of "'Ai Kamumu Kēkē" is a form of self-sacrifice that instills the spirit of the performer in their ki'i form (Taupōuri Tangarō, pers. comm.).

Dr. Ku'ulei Kanahele, who trained in hula as part of Hālau o Kekuhi, explained that the choice of performing Pele chants, such as "'Ai Kamumu Kēkē," in the Mauna Protocol was to "set the foundation that [kia'i] were on a volcanic island . . . surrounded by beds of pāhoehoe (smooth, unbroken type of lava rock)" (Ku'ulei Kanahele, pers. comm). Without giving specific names, she divulged that some people "may have had the agenda [that] if Mauna Kea erupted again, maybe the telescopes would be gone" (Ku'ulei Kanahele, pers. comm.). Pele chants like "'Ai Kamumu Kēkē" end with a dedication "He inoa no Hi'iaka-i-ka-poli-o-Pele" (In the name of Hi'iaka-in-the-bosom-of-Pele), even if the chant has nothing to do with Pele's sister Hi'iaka. Kanahele remarked on the use of this closing dedication: "After the eruption you need that calm space. Environmentally you need that time for the land to heal. As a person, after performing these heavy dances you need that time to calm down and bring [you] back to yourself" (Ku'ulei Kanahele, pers. comm).

Performed in unison and in the duple meter typical of danced text in Polynesia, "'Ai Kamumu Kēkē" consists of a rhythmic recitation on notes of indefinite pitch, without the vocal techniques and embellishments that often mark Hawaiian chant. The rhythmic accent is placed on the first of every four beats, serving as a metronomic function that keeps a large group of performers in time. The simplification of performative elements benefits those without previous hula or chant training so all are able to come together and participate with ease in the protocol, thereby personally experiencing the embodiment of knowledge attainable through the 'ike of direct engagement with the mele and hula. This protocol ceremony also points to the importance of hulihia ("to overturn") in the performance of musical resistance where ease of participation facilitates the building of solidarity in communal action.

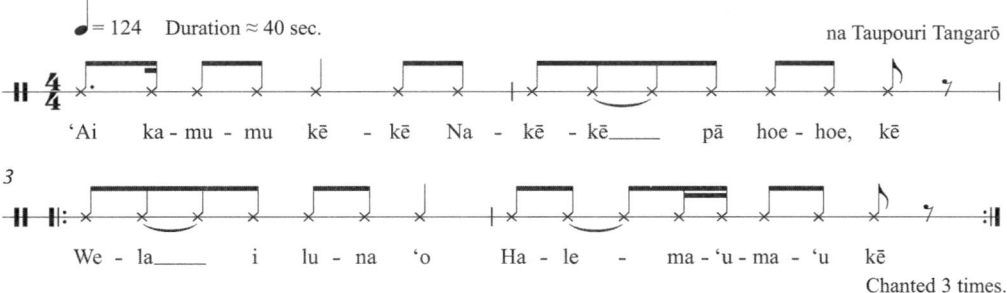

FIGURE 4. "'Ai Kamumu Kēkē" as transcribed from the instructional video available on puuhuluhulu.com ("Protocol—Puʻuhonua o Puʻuhuluhulu" 2019).

Performance as Community: Hulihia
Education is at the center of Protect Maunakea's community-building efforts and kiaʻi have expertly utilized various platforms to disseminate their knowledge and message to those who are open to learning. Social media and digital platforms have become essential venues for the performance and documentation of Protect Maunakea musical resistance. Early on in the protests of 2019, kiaʻi set up the website www.puuhuluhulu.com, where those interested could learn about the movement and lend their financial support. The website includes videos and chant texts from the protocol ceremony for educational purposes. Rather than following the hālau hula (hula school) model of repertoire as privileged information, the movement embraces an open-access model of widespread digital dissemination, making the repertoire accessible to people all over the world and bringing the fight to protect Mauna Kea directly into homes and electronic devices.

Organizers learned early on that they needed to expand beyond established local and national news outlets in order to disseminate their message. Their skillful utilization of social and digital media platforms effectively circumvented the barriers and filters of corporate news by allowing kiaʻi to connect directly with supporters. For example, Hāwane Rios, 2020 Nā Hōkū Hanohano winner for Contemporary Album of the Year and daughter of Kumu Pua Case, frequently shares pule (prayer) and her Mauna a Wākea experiences with fans on Facebook and Instagram.

The most impressive social media outreach conducted by kiaʻi during the 2019 protests occurred on August 11 at 11 a.m. HST—the Worldwide #Jam4Maunakea. This event featured a music jam recorded live from the Puʻuhonua o Puʻuhuluhulu encampment and streamed online from the Puʻuhuluhulu, Kanaeokana, and Mana Maoli Facebook pages. Organizers promised a medley of "Kū Haʻaheo" and "Hawaiʻi Loa" and, prior to the event, digitally distributed lyric sheets with song text, key and tempo markings, and chord progressions as well as an audio track with which to practice the melodies. Participants worldwide joined the Jam 4 Maunakea challenge by video recording their involvement and posting their performances online with the hashtag #jam4maunakea. Many of these performances became part of a compilation music video that featured participants from all over the globe: domestically across the Hawaiian Islands and the United States, and internationally from Japan, Brazil, the Netherlands, Aotearoa New Zealand, and Russia, to name a few (Mana Maoli 2020). Although the jam was scheduled for a thirty-minute timeframe, the streamed event lasted for up to two hours. After performing "Kū Haʻaheo" and "Hawaiʻi Loa" a few times, the crowd began performing other popular songs of resistance, such as "Kaulana Nā Pua" and "Hawaiʻi 78," morphing the event into a true kani ka pila (music jam, lit. "sound of the string instrument").

During the event, global participants shared their manaʻo in real time in the comments section on the Facebook feed, affirming their support for the mauna and the kiaʻi and sharing the geolocation from which they were watching. The large number of people at the site on Mauna a Wākea often caused the live stream to freeze and cut to black, prompting organizers to ask the crowd to limit their cellphone use. Many locally famous musicians, cultural practitioners, and activists were at the location on the mauna, including well-known people such as former congresswoman Tulsi Gabbard and actor Jason Momoa. News outlets reported that thousands of people flocked to the Puʻuhonua o Puʻuhuluhulu encampment for the event as well as other venues of cultural and political importance, such as ʻIolani Palace and the University of Hawaiʻi at Mānoa campus. The popularity of the event highlighted the global breadth of support for kiaʻi and a growing international trend to document social and political resistance through music on social media and digital platforms.

Moving the Mountain

The University of Hawaiʻi also has a relationship with the mountain, albeit one that is challenged by supporters of the Protect Maunakea movement. The university was tasked with managing the land on Mauna Kea and served to benefit financially if the TMT was built. Not surprisingly, the main ancillary or satellite area of protest outside of Hawaiʻi Island was on Wise Lawn, an open space fronting Bachman Hall, the main administration building at the university's Mānoa campus on Oʻahu. Figure 5 shows the ahu (ceremonial altar) constructed by kiaʻi in April 2015 in conjunction with the very first encampment on the mauna several years previously. Kiaʻi formed a chain stretching over half a mile, from the Kamakakūokalani Center for Hawaiian

Studies to Wise Lawn, and passed large rocks down the line to build the ahu (Garcia and Web Staff 2015). Replicating a historical tradition of transporting large rocks when voyaging to a new place and to establish points of connection, the kiaʻi built their ahu and, in that very act, reclaimed this secular colonial space as sacred to Hawaiians. In Fall 2019, student kiaʻi organized a semester-long occupation of the ground floor of Bachman Hall.

During the prolonged occupation, university students and people in the local community conducted the Mauna Protocol Ceremony three times daily at this campus site, mirroring the performative activity at the protest site on Mauna a Wākea and further amplifying and extending the sacredness of the ceremonial events to the UHM campus. An ever-changing group of university students and community members participated in the protocol ceremony at this satellite. Whereas the ceremony on Mauna a Wākea felt like a collective private moment with the mountain, the ceremony at the ahu on Wise Lawn, while still connecting to Mauna a Wākea, was clearly intended to be seen and heard by the larger community. Since the performances were in a public place amid an urban landscape, all those within earshot were aurally brought into the event. Reminded by protocol performers of the

FIGURE 5. Wooden structures around the ahu on Wise Lawn during the Fall 2019 semester announce names of kiaʻi arrested on Mauna Kea at the beginning of the protests. Photo courtesy of author, January 14, 2020.

message and actions underway to protect Mauna a Wākea, observers were themselves imbued with sacredness. Even now, the expectation is that kapu aloha is the norm that students and university personnel should practice when at this site. Although not an officially sanctioned university structure, the ahu remains steadfast—recalling the actual mountain itself.

As exemplified by the ahu and its surrounding physical and aural space, the performance of sacred traditions can invest secular places with temporary sacredness through collective musical experience. A notable example of such transformation, even if transitory, occurred on November 23, 2019, when Janet Jackson invited kiaʻi to perform mele and hula from the Mauna Protocol Ceremony and the Protect Maunakea movement during her concert at the Blaisdell Arena in Honolulu. In videos taken by audience members and published online, viewers witness the three key concepts of ʻike, kū, and hulihia in action—as enacted with adherence to kapu aloha by the kiaʻi on stage, audience members, and Janet Jackson herself. The audience responds with enthusiasm and passionate outbursts, crying "cheehoo" (a faʻaumu "shout of excitement" from Sāmoa adapted by Hawaiian culture) and participated along with the chanters onstage to amplify the energy of the experience. Janet Jackson, the ever-gracious performer, allows kiaʻi to be the stars on her stage and even attempts to join in at certain moments. In the context of this pop concert, onstage and offstage merge in sacred action that blurs the boundaries of secular and sacred. By enacting the geological occurrences described in "ʻAi Kamumu Kēkē," the performers bring Mauna a Wākea to this new stage, their bodies and voices becoming metaphors for the rock, lava, and the soundscape of eruption.

"ʻAi Kamumu Kēkē" has also been included in music events separate from the Mauna Protocol. For example, the Nā Wai Chamber Choir, a group created and directed by former University of Hawaiʻi at Mānoa professor and choral director Dr. Jace Kaholokula Saplan,[20] performed this mele on December 13, 2019, at Waiwai Collective, a small performance venue and workspace in Honolulu. This lecture concert, titled "Kūʻē [to resist]—a History of Sonic Resistance," featured locally well-known mele from various flashpoints of resistance in Hawaiian history. The repertoire chosen for this concert highlighted the resilience and continued relevance of these mele, which included works composed by Queen Liliʻuokalani, Liko Martin, and Israel Kamakawiwoʻole. Dr. Saplan explained the reason for including "ʻAi Kamumu Kēkē" in the program was to provide a more "universally relateable [perfomance] in the context of resistance . . . [as seen] through a Western lens" (Jace Saplan, pers. comm.). They echoed Dr. Kuʻulei Kanahele's statement about the need to create spiritual and emotional harmony between assertive and calm performative elements. In a reflection of the synergy between musical performance and environmental cycles, the assertiveness of "'Ai Kamumu Kēkē" was balanced by the uplifting melodies of other songs on the program.

Nā Wai also performed "Kaulana Nā Pua" at this concert, connecting modern songs of resistance to those of the past. A further examination of this song's musical composition as well as Nā Wai's arrangement reveals sonic influences of the Christian sacred that reflect Hawai'i's long complicated history with Christianity and the attempts of many cultural practitioners to reconcile the sometimes-conflicting value systems that surround Christianity in Native lives. Amy Stillman explains the incorporation of musical characteristics of hymnody as a process wherein Western concepts of "rhythm, scales, and harmonization . . . were combined with features from [I]ndigenous musical traditions" thus creating "contemporary idioms, many of which have extended beyond the sphere of Christian hymnody" (1993, 89).

My analysis is focused on Nā Wai's rendition of "Kaulana Nā Pua" and represents just one of the ways this song may be performed, although some of the characteristics I mention carry over from the original notated setting in 1895 attributed to J. S. Libornio.[21] A review of various audio and video recordings of this song reveals many divergences in melody, harmony, and timbre, a practice that aligns with Eastern Polynesian norms of spontaneous performance that make a song unique to the individual artist(s), occasion, or feelings of the moment. Figure 6 exhibits characteristics of nineteenth-century Protestant hymnody in "Kaulana Nā Pua" most clearly in rhythmic value and organization, pitch range, and use of Western harmonies. It is common for hymns to have a formulaic rhythmic pattern in the melody wherein a succession of notes of short duration resolve on a note of long duration at the end of the phrase as evidenced in the transcription of Nā Wai's performance. Additionally, the pitch range (minor 7th, E4 to D5 as indicated by the square-outlined notes) of the melody is fairly narrow, with a descending perfect 4th as the largest leap in the melody. This song also utilizes Western harmonies with a simple chord progression of I-IV-I-IV-I-V-I. Interestingly, lines one and two resolve using a plagal cadence (IV-I), which is frequently set to the "amen" text in hymnody. Although not pictured in figure 6, Nā Wai also performed their arrangement in homorhythmic texture and with blended voices, both of which are sonic markers of nineteenth-century Protestant hymnody. The application of well-known patterns in rhythm, melody, and harmony is not merely an aesthetic choice. These elements provide a predictable structure that fosters an ease of participation that is so important to both hymn and protest singing.

FIGURE 6. Transcription of the melody and chords from the first verse of "Kaulana Nā Pua" as performed by the Nā Wai Chamber Choir on December 13, 2019.

Although the lyrical text of "Kaulana Nā Pua" is secular, the communal aspect of hymn-tune singing unifies the singers and intensifies the feeling of a sacred shared experience. According to Holmes, the act of singing itself takes on the very qualities of sacredness (Holmes 2004, 170–71). This harkens to the Hawaiian concept of mana,[22] which can be gained through heightened vocalization. Therefore, the act of singing, especially singing with purpose, can serve as a way to harness sacredness regardless of genre. These mele find roots in particularly Hawaiian ways of musicking. Even though "'Ai Kamumu Kēkē" and "Kaulana Nā Pua" straddle differing realms of sonic sacredness, they both link back to the same source—Mauna a Wākea and the continued fight for Hawaiian sovereignty.

A final example I highlight of reclaimed space through sacred action occurred on October 5, 2019, when the Aloha 'Āina March in support of the Protect Maunakea movement filled the streets of Honolulu in an act of solidarity and community that took place simultaneously on each Hawaiian island. The O'ahu event started at the easternmost end of Ala Moana Beach Park, followed along Ala Moana Blvd. and Kalākaua Ave. through Waikīkī, and ended at Kapi'olani Park, a total of roughly 2.5 miles in the heat and humidity of Hawai'i's heavy October days that bring winds from Hawai'i Island in the south. The procession began with the long, sustained tones of

FIGURE 7. Photos of kiaʻi at the Aloha ʻĀina March in Honolulu, October 5, 2019. Photos courtesy of author.

multiple pū (conch shell trumpet), a sound that Islanders associate with signaling an event of significance. Various groups paused at the starting point to deliver chants and sing songs before continuing down the road. This important step required over twenty minutes for the main procession of thousands[23] to move past the starting point before organizers invited the general public to join the march.

The eclectic soundscape of music-making ranged from traditional chanting to communal singing to local hip-hop and reggae songs played from portable speakers—there was even a member of the kiaʻi who used drumsticks to play a frying pan hung from around his neck. Spontaneous chants in call-and-response form resounded as shouts of kū kiaʻi mauna (stand guard over the mountain), kūʻē (resist), aloha ʻāina (love of the land), and combinations of eo (victory) and ea (sovereignty) echoed along the route. A young boy passionately led the call and response chant "I Kū Mau Mau," a work song originally used to time the hauling of logs to be made into canoes but mobilized in Native Hawaiian protest activity in the twentieth and twenty-first centuries (Kahanu 2020, 21). Tourists looked on from the lānai (balconies) of their hotel rooms and the side of the road. Waikīkī is known to locals as being overrun by tourists, but during this afternoon it was the locals who took over, reaching beyond their physical presence on the street with the musical sounds of resistance as they restructured and redistributed sonic and geographical space.

Conclusions

Music continues to be important to the Protect Maunakea movement. The manifestations of musical resistance presented here are only a sampling of the many activities that aim to protect sacred land, to aid participants to engage directly with the sacred through performative action, and to educate the population about unresolved challenges to Mauna a Wākea that threaten the very essence of the mountain and the value it holds to the Hawaiian people. These performative and highly visible events demonstrate how music, already an integral part of life for Native Hawaiians, assumes a much deeper function than mere entertainment. They also provide a picture of how a people who are spiritually and genealogically tied to the land have found the structures and practices that allow them to move a mountain and touch the lives of far distant Hawaiian communities in a way that seeks inclusion and participation.

Through musicking, kiaʻi engage directly with and come to know and feel the mauna through their bodies and their actions (ʻike). They stand firmly (kū) to defend Hawaiian values and the mountain they hold dear. Through the innovative actions of hulihia, they expand sacred spaces beyond the geographical and successfully utilize social and digital media to disseminate their message and build ranks of supporters in a meshwork of solidarity.

This study points to critical ways in which Hawaiian voices and bodies are essential to an understanding of resistive strategies in the Pacific and signals the need for expanded research in this area. It brings focus to the why and how of Hawaiian activism and links music directly to resistance through Hawaiian ways of enacting ʻike, kū, and hulihia. For Islanders, music performance provides a unique and amplified call to activism that is participatory, corporeal, and rooted in the land itself.

Social media and digital platforms have played a significant role in Protect Maunakea awareness and the dissemination of documented musical resistance for the movement. Professional quality music videos of Mauna a Wākea songs of resistance accumulate far more views than Protect Maunakea videos that do not feature music. For example, as of June 20, 2023, the aforementioned #Jam4Maunakea compilation music video has 160,864 views on YouTube while the music video for "Kū Haʻaheo," featuring a choir of well-known artists from across the islands, has 2,789,734 views. By contrast, news or documentary-like videos have views in the hundreds or lower thousands. The COVID-19 pandemic moved the fight to protect Mauna a Wākea almost fully online and into the courtroom and legislative chamber, but the music has not stopped. Protect Maunakea organizers still communicate their message via social media, and kiaʻi perform through Zoom and Facebook, growing the network far beyond Pacific shores.

On July 7, 2022, then Governor Ige signed House Bill 2024, transferring the management authority of Mauna a Wākea lands from the University of Hawaiʻi to a newly established Mauna Kea Stewardship and Oversight Authority (31st Legislature, State of Hawaii 2022). On that same day, Satoshi Miyazaki, the interim director of the Subaru Telescope, one of thirteen telescopes already on the summit of Mauna a Wākea, released a statement regarding the transition of authority: "We recognize the many ways of knowing, sharing appreciation for and exploring the Universe, and are honored to be part of this important initiative to shape the future of Maunakea, Hawaiʻi, and astronomy" (2022). Keck Observatory director Hilton Lewis also released a statement that same day: "We believe this is a positive way forward, one that upholds our core principles, is inclusive of the native [sic] Hawaiian community in decision-making and is consistent with our commitment to a Community Astronomy model" (2022). The bill states that two of the eleven seats on the Mauna Kea Stewardship and Oversight Authority will be reserved for (1) "an individual who is a lineal descendent of a practitioner of Native Hawaiian traditional and customary practices associated with Mauna Kea" and (2) "an individual who is a recognized practitioner of Native Hawaiian traditional and customary practices" (31st Legislature, State of Hawaii 2022). Of course, Kānaka Maoli are not restricted to these two seats; nearly half the members of the first appointed board identify as Hawaiian.

It is too soon to tell how new management of the mauna will affect the kiaʻi's efforts to protect their sacred land. For now, Mauna a Wākea still stands tall on Hawaiʻi Island and in the hearts of those who seek to honor and protect the ʻāina. Mauna a Wākea waits in the wings to emerge once again on stages and in community gathering places. The movement has turned quiet, but it is not silent.

SUSAN JACOB is a Ph.D. candidate in ethnomusicology at the University of Hawaiʻi at Mānoa. Prior to graduate school she worked as a music educator overseas in Tanzania and Malaysia and in her home state of Arizona. She is currently conducting research on Hawaiian protest music and Hawaiʻi hip-hop.

References

Akena, Francis Adyanga. 2012. "Critical Analysis of the Production of Western Knowledge and Its Implications for Indigenous Knowledge and Decolonization." *Journal of Black Studies* 43, no. 6: 599–619.

Archibald, Jo-ann, and Qʼum Qʼum Xiiem. 2018. "Indigenous Storytelling." In *Memory*, edited by Mark Turin Philippe Tortell, and Margot Young, 233–41. Vancouver, BC: Peter Wall Institute for Advanced Studies.

Barrère, Dorothy B., Mary Kawena Pukui, and Marion Kelly. 1980. *Hula, Historical Perspectives.* Pacific Anthropological Records no. 30. Honolulu: Department of Anthropology, Bernice Pauahi Bishop Museum.

Basham, Leilani. 2008. "Mele Lāhui: The Importance Of Pono In Hawaiian Poetry." *Te Kaharoa* 1: 152–64.

Bronner, Simon J. 1998. "The Problem of Tradition." In *Following Tradition: Folklore in the Discourse of American Culture*, 9–72. Logan: Utah State University Press.

Brown, Marie Alohalani. 2016. "Mauna Kea: Hoʻomana Hawaiʻi and Protecting the Sacred." *Journal for the Study of Religion, Nature, and Culture* 10, no. 2: 150–69.

Case, Emalani. 2021. *Everything Ancient Was Once New: Indigenous Persistence from Hawaiʻi to Kahiki.* Honolulu: University of Hawaiʻi Press.

Casumbal-Salazar, Iokepa. 2017. "A Fictive Kinship, Making 'Modernity,' 'Ancient Hawaiians,' and the Telescopes on Mauna Kea." *Native American and Indigenous Studies* 4, no. 2: 1–30.

———. 2019. "'Where Are Your Sacred Temples?' Notes on the Struggle for Mauna a Wākea." In *Detours: A Decolonial Guide to* Hawaiʻi, edited by Hokulani K. Aikau and Vernadette Vicuna Gonzalez, 200–210. Durham, NC: Duke University Press.

Charlot, John. 1985. *The Hawaiian Poetry of Religion and Politics: Some Religio-Political Concepts in Postcontact Literature*. Laʻie, Hawaiʻi: Institute for Polynesian Studies.

Clements, Ann. 2014. "Spirit and Song of the Maori of Aotearoa {New Zealand}." *The Choral Journal* 55, no. 2: 16–22.

Clift, Stephen. 2002. "The Perceived Benefits of Singing: Findings from Preliminary Surveys of a University College Choral Society." *The Journal of the Royal Society for the Promotion of Health* 121, no. 4: 248–56.

Cooper, Danelle, Treena Delormier, and Maile Taualii. 2019. "'It's Always a Part of You': The Connection Between Sacred Spaces and Indigenous/Aboriginal Health." *Indigenous Journal of Human Rights Education* 3, no. 1: 1–29.

Damodaran, Sumangala. 2016. "Protest and Music." In *Oxford Research Encyclopedia: Politics*. Oxford: Oxford University Press.

Degmečić, Dunja, Ivan Požgain, and Pavo Filaković. 2005. "Music as Therapy / Glaba kao terapija." *International Review of the Aesthetics and Sociology of Music* 36, no. 2: 287–300.

Deloria, Barbara, Kristen Foehner, and Sam Scinta, ed. 1999. *Spirit and Reason: The Vine Deloria Jr. Reader*. Golden, CO: Fulcrum.

Denisoff, R. Serge. 1966. "Songs of Persuasion: A Sociological Analysis of Urban Propaganda Songs." *The Journal of American Folklore* 79, no. 314: 581–89.

———. 1968. "Protest Movements: Class Consciousness and the Propaganda Song." *The Sociological Quarterly* 9, no. 2: 228–47.

———. 1970. "Protest Songs: Those on the Top Forty and Those of the Streets." *American Quarterly* 22, no. 4: 807–23.

Eckstein, Lars, and Anja Schwarz. 2019. "The Making of Tupaia's Map: A Story of the Extent and Mastery of Polynesian Navigation, Competing Systems of Wayfinding on James Cook's Endeavour, and the Invention of an Ingenious Cartographic System." *The Journal of Pacific History* 54, no. 1: 1–95.

Edet, Enda M. 1976. "One Hundred Years of Black Protest Music." *The Black Scholar* 7, no. 10: 38–48.

Elbow, Peter, and Reanae McNeal. 2017. "Decolonizing the Classroom: An Essay in Two Parts." *Writing on the Edge* 28, no. 1: 19–32.

Emerson, Nathaniel B., Pele, and Hiiaka. 1915. *A Myth from Hawaii*. Honolulu: Honolulu Star-Bulletin Limited.

Evans, Matthew. 2003. "The Sacred: Differentiating, Clarifying and Extending Concepts." *Review of Religious Research* 45, no. 1 (2003): 32–47.

Feder, Toni. 2019. "Q&A: Kealoha Pisciotta, on Mauna Kea and Conflicts of Astronomy." Physics Today. https://physicstoday.scitation.org/do/10.1063/PT.6.4.20191023a/full/.

Fellezs, Kevin. 2019a. "Nahenahe: The Sound of Kanaka Maoli Refusal." In *Antiracism Inc.: Why the Way We Talk about Racial Justice Matters*, edited by Paula Ioanide Felice Blake, Alison Reed, 231–54. Earth, Milky Way: Punctum Books.

———. 2019b. "Sounding out the Second Hawaiian Renaissance." In *Listen but Don't Ask Question*, 145–82. Durham, N.C.: Duke University Press.

Garcia, Nestor, and Web Staff. 2015. "Hundreds Form Chain at UH Manoa to Protest Thirty Meter Telescope." KHON2. https://web.archive.org/web/20150629004650/http://khon2.com/2015/04/10/hundreds-form-chain-at-uh-manoa-to-protest-thirty-meter-telescope-3/.

Garratt, James. 2019. *Music and Politics: A Critical Introduction.* Cambridge: Cambridge University Press.

Goodyear-Kaʻōpua, Noelani, Craig Howes, Jonathan Kay Kamakawiwoʻole Osorio, and Aiko Yamashiro, eds. *The Value of Hawaiʻi 3: Hulihia, the Turning.* Honolulu: University of Hawaiʻi Press, 2020.

Herman, Doug. 2015. "The Heart of the Hawaiian Peoples' Arguments Against the Telescope on Mauna Kea." *Smithsonian Magazine.* https://www.smithsonianmag.com/smithsonian-institution/heart-hawaiian-people-arguments-arguments-against-telescope-mauna-kea-180955057/

HNN Staff. 2019. "Thousands Take Part in Aloha Unity March through Waikiki." Hawaii News Now. https://www.hawaiinewsnow.com/2019/10/01/aloha-aina-unity-march-set-this-weekend-waikiki/.

Holmes, Barbara Ann. 2004. *Joy Unspeakable: Contemplative Practices of the Black Church.* Minneapolis: Fortress Press.

hoʻomanawanui, kuʻualoha. 2005. "He Lai Hoʻoheno no nā Kau a Kau: Language, Performance, and Form in Hawaiian Poetry." *The Contemporary Pacific* 17, no. 1: 29–81.

Hopkins, J. Uluwehi. 2019. "Moʻolelo as Resistance: The Kaona of "Kahalaopuna" in a Colonized Environment." *Narrative Culture* 6, no. 2: 229–50.

Imada, Adria L. 2012. *Aloha America: Hula Circuits Through the U.S. Empire.* Durham, NC: Duke University Press.

IMUA TMT. 2019. https://www.imuatmt.org/people/.

Ingold, Tim. 2007. *Lines: A Brief History.* New York: Routledge.

Jace Saplan (professor of music) in discussion with author January 2020.

Kaeppler, Adrienne L. 2010. "The Beholder's Share: Viewing Music and Dance in a Globalized World." *Ethnomusicology* 54, no. 2: 185–201.

Kahanu, Noelle M.K.Y. 2020. "I Kū Mau Mau: Restoring Hawaiian Intent, Presence, and Authority." In *Refocusing Ethnographic Museums through Oceanic Lenses,* edited by Noelle M.K.Y. Kahanu Philipp Schorch, Sean Mallon, Cristián Moreno Pakarati, Mara Mulrooney, Nina Tonga, and Ty P. Kāwika Tengan, 21–42. Honolulu: University of Hawaiʻi Press.

Kamae, Eddie, and the Sons of Hawaiʻi. 2008. "E Kuʻu Morning Dew." *Yesterday and Today.* Hawaii Sons. Originally composed in 1973.

Kamahele, Momiala. 2008. "'Ilioʻulaokalani: Defending Native Hawaiian Culture." In *Asian Settler Colonialism: From Local Governance to the Habits of Everyday Life in Hawaiʻi,* edited by Candace Fujikane and Jonathan Y. Okamura, 76–98. Honolulu: University of Hawaiʻi Press.

Kamakawiwoʻole, Israel. 1993. "Hawaiʻi 78." *Facing Future.* Mountain Apple Company HAWAII/Big Boy Records.

Kapuaʻala, D. 1998. "The Backlash Against PASH: Legislative Attempts To Restrict Native Hawaiian Rights." *University of Hawaiʻi Law Review* 20: 321–73.

Kashay, Jennifer Fish. 2008. "From Kapus to Christianity: The Disestablishment of the Hawaiian Religion and Chiefly Appropriation of Calvinist Christianity." *Western Historical Quarterly* 39, no. 1: 17–39.

Keao NeSmith (linguist, educator, and translator) in discussion with author, October 2020.

Kelleher, Jennifer Sinco. 2014. "Protesters Halt Mauna Kea Telescope Groundbreaking." *Honolulu Star-Advertiser*. https://www.staradvertiser.com/2014/10/07/breaking-news/protesters-halt-mauna-kea-telescope-groundbreaking/.

Keller, Mary L. 2014. "Indigenous Studies and 'the Sacred'." *American Indian Quarterly* 38, no. 1: 82–109.

Kim, David, David McCalman, and Dan Fisher. 2012. "The Sacred/Secular Divide and the Christian Worldview." *Journal of Business Ethics* 109, no. 2 (2012): 203–8.

Knopf, Kerstin. 2015. "The Turn Toward the Indigenous: Knowledge Systems and Practices in the Academy." *Amerikastudien/American Studies* 60, no. 2/3 (2015): 179–200.

Kuʻulei Kanahele (professor of Hawaiian studies) in discussion with author, January 2021.

Lewis, D. 1974. "Voyaging Stars: Aspects of Polynesian and Micronesian Astronomy." *Philosophical Transactions of the Royal Society of London* 276, no. 1257: 133–48.

Lewis, George H. 1985. "The Role of Music in Popular Social Movements: A Theory and Case Study of the Island State of Hawaii, USA." *International Review of the Aesthetics and Sociology of Music* 16, no. 2: 153–62.

———. 1987. "Style in Revolt Music, Social Protest, and the Hawaiian Cultural Renaissance." *International Social Science Review* 62, no. 4: 168–77.

Lewis, Hilton. "Director's Message: Maunakea's Future." W. M. Keck Observatory. Last Modified July 7, 2022. https://www.keckobservatory.org/hb2024/.

Liljeblad, Jonathan, and Bas Verschuuren, eds. 2019. *Indigenous Perspectives on Sacred Natural Sites*. New York: Routledge.

Love, Nancy. 2018. "From Settler Colonialism to Standing Rock." *College Music Symposium* 58, no. 3: 1–16.

Luomala, Katharine. 1984. *Hula Kiʻi*. Honolulu: The Institute for Polynesian Studies, 1984.

Makemson, Maud W. 1938. "Hawaiian Astronomical Concepts." *American Anthropologist* 40, no. 3: 370–83.

———. 1939. "Hawaiian Astronomical Concepts II." *American Anthropologist* 41, no. 4: 589–96.

Mākua, Sunnie Kaikala, Manulani Aluli Meyer, and Lynette Lokelani Wakinekona. 2019. "Moʻolelo: Continuity, Stories, and Research in Hawaiʻi." In *Applying Indigenous Research Methods: Stories with Peoples and Communities,* edited by Sweeney Windchief and Timothy San Pedro, 138–49. New York: Routledge.

Mana Maoli. 2020. "Worldwide #Jam4MaunaKea- "Kū Haʻaheo" & "Hawaiʻi Loa"." YouTube. https://www.youtube.com/watch?v=k1Ul5xp4PTg&t=11s.

McDougall, Brandy Nālani. 2016. "Wondering and Laughing with Our Ancestors: Mana Wahine and the Moʻolelo of Hiʻiakaikapoliopele." *Marvels and Tales* 30, no. 1: 24–44.

McLaren, Robert. 2020. "Modern Astronomy on Maunakea: A 60-Year Story (1960–2020)." Virtual.

Miyazaki, Satoshi. "Subaru Telescope Position Statement: Mauna Kea Stewardship and Oversight Authority." Subaru Telescope. Last Modified July 1, 2023. https://subarutelescope.org/en/news/announcements/2022/07/07/3067.html.

Montgomery-Anderson, Brad. 2013. "Macro-Scale Features of School-Based Language Revitalization Programs." *Journal of American Indian Education* 52, no. 3: 41–64.

Moulin, Jane Freeman. 2014. "Trailing Images and Cultural Branding in Post-Renaissance Hawaiʻi." In *The Oxford Handbook of Music Revival,* edited by Caroline Bithell and Juniper Hill, 528–48. Oxford: Oxford University Press.

"Nā Puke Wehewehe ʻŌleleo Hawaiʻi." Ulukau, n.d. https://wehewehe.org.

Nordyke, Eleanor C., and Martha H. Noyes. 1993. "Kaulana Nā Pua: A Voice for Sovereignty." *Hawaiian Journal of History* 27: 27–42.

Osorio, Jamaica. 2021. "Mele Kiaʻi Mauna: Where Creativity and Community Commitment Collide." The Asian/Pacific/American Institute at NYU. Virtual. https://www.youtube.com/watch?v=9mfNn-XeqPE&t=6s.

Papakilo Database (Hawaiian Newspapers Collection). https://www.papakilodatabase.com/pdnupepa/cgi-bin/pdnupepa?a=p&p=home.

Peralto, Leon Noʻeau. 2014. "Portrait. Mauna a Wākea: Hānau ka Mauna, the Piko of Our Ea." In *A Nation Rising: Hawaiian Movements for Life, Land, and Sovereignty,* edited by Ikaika Hussey Noelani Goodyear-Kaʻōpua, and Erin Kahunawaikaʻala Wright, 232–43. Durham, N.C.: Duke University Press.

Pratt, Ray. 2013. "Resistance, Music and." In Grove Music Online. Oxford: Oxford University Press. https://doi-org.eres.library.manoa.hawaii.edu/10.1093/gmo/9781561592630.article.A2252296

Puʻuhonua o Puʻuhuluhulu. 2019a. "Kapu Aloha: A Guiding, Transformational, and Liberating Force." YouTube. https://www.youtube.com/watch?v=AX7kTOHNjYU.

———. 2019b. "Protocol." https://www.puuhuluhulu.com/learn/protocol.

Pukui, Mary Kapena. 1983. *ʻŌlelo Noʻeau: Hawaiian Proverbs and Poetic Sayings.* Honolulu: Bishop Museum Press.

Rabinovich, Silvana. 2018. "Resistance and the Sacred: An Approach to the Various Meanings of the 'Right to the Sacred' in Mexico Today." *Open Theology,* no. 4: 228–35.

Relating to Mauna Kea, H.B. 2024, 31st Legislature, State of Hawaii (2022).

Rodnitzky, Jerry. 2013. "Protest Song." In Grove Music Online. Oxford: Oxford University Press. https://doi-org.eres.library.manoa.hawaii.edu/10.1093/gmo/9781561592630.article.A2252188.

Sarmiento, Fausto, and Sarah Hitchner, ed. 2017. *Indigeneity and the Sacred: Indigenous Revival and the Conservation of Sacred Natural Sites in the Americas.* New York: Berghahn Books.

Saura, Bruno, Maryann Capestro, and Henri Bova. 2002. "Continuity of Bodies: The Infant's Placenta and the Island's Navel in Eastern Polynesia." *The Journal of the Polynesian Society* 111, no. 2: 127–45.

Sheffield, Carrie Louise. 2011. "Native American Hip-Hop and Historical Trauma: Surviving and Healing Trauma on the 'Rez'." *Studies in American Indian Literatures* 23, no. 3: 94–110.

Silva, Noenoe K. 2004. *Aloha Betrayed: Native Hawaiian Resistance to American Colonialism.* Durham, N.C.: Duke University Press.

———. 2004. "I Kū Mau Mau: How Kānaka Maoli Tried to Sustain National Identity Within the United States Political System." *American Studies* 45, no. 3: 9–31.

Stillman, Amy Kuʻuleialoha. 1989. "History Reinterpreted in Song: The Case of the Hawaiian Counterrevolution." *The Hawaiian Journal of History* 23: 1–30.

———. 1993. "Prelude to a Comparative Investigation of Protestant Hymnody in Polynesia." *Yearbook for Traditional Music* 25: 89–99.

———. 1999. "'Aloha Aina': New Perspectives on 'Kaulana Nā Pua'." *Hawaiian Journal of History* 33, no. 1: 113–30.

———. 2021. "Beyond the Coloniality of Authenticity." *American Quarterly* 73, no. 1: 161–67.

Street, John. 2003. "'Fight the Power': The Politics of Music and the Music of Politics." *Government and Opposition* 38, no. 1: 113–30.

Sunday Manoa. 1969. *Guava Jam*. Hula Records.

Swijghuisen Reigersberg, Muriel E. 2017. "Collaborative Music, Health, and Wellbeing Research Globally: Some Perspectives on Challenges Faced and How to Engage with Them." *Journal of Folklore Research* 54, no. 1–2: 133–59.

Tatar, Elizabeth. 1981. "Toward a Description of Precontact Music in Hawaiʻi." *Ethnomusicology* 25, no. 3: 481–92.

Taupōuri Tangarō (professor of Hawaiian studies) in discussion with author, March 2023.

Teves, Stephanie N. 2018. *Defiant Indigeneity: The Politics of Hawaiian Performance.* Chapel Hill: University of North Carolina Press.

thedrakeequator. "What are your thoughts on the Native Hawaiian protests of the Thirty Meter Telescope?" Reddit. Accessed January, 26, 2023. https://www.reddit.com/r/space/comments/zqil9l/what_are_your_thoughts_on_the_native_hawaiian/.

Trask, Haunani-Kay. 1991. "Native and Anthropologists: The Colonial Struggle." *The Contemporary Pacific* 3, no. 1: 159–67.

Tuhiwai Smith, Linda. 2021. *Decolonizing Methodologies: Research and Indigenous Peoples.* London: Bloomsbury.

Twiss, Richard. 2015. *Rescuing the Gospel from the Cowboys: A Native American Expression of the Jesus Way.* Downers Grove, IL: InterVarsity Press.

Urrutia, Doris Elin. 2020. "At Thirty Meter Telescope Protest, Native Hawaiian Elders Leave Mountain over Coronavirus Threat." Space.com. https://www.space.com/coronavirus-shrinks-thirty-meter-telescope-protest-in-hawaii.html.

Way, Lyndon. 2016. "Protest Music, Populism, Politics and Authenticity: The Limits and Potential of Popular Music's Articulation of Subversive Politics." *Journal of Language and Politics* 15, no. 4: 422–45.

Wold, Thor, and Liko Martin. 1975. "Waimanalo Blues," "Country Comfort," "We Are the Children." Ventura, CA: Hana Ola Records.

Zuttermeister, Noenoelani. 2020. "East West Center Spotlight on Hula." Virtual.

Notes

1. Following contemporary usage in Hawai'i, I interchangeably use Kānaka Maoli, Native Hawaiian, and Hawaiian throughout this article to indicate ideas, artifacts, practices, places, and people that are native to the Hawaiian Islands.

2. I use the various iterations on the name Mauna a Wākea (also Maunakea and Mauna Kea) depending on how the name is used within a particular context. For example, I use Mauna a Wākea for the name of the mountain to emphasize the tie with the Hawaiian deity, Wākea. Maunakea is seen as a shortened version of this name, and therefore I use it when referring to the kia'i/ protectors. I use the name Mauna Kea when referring to legal names, such as the access road. This is also the version most often used in news publications.

3. 'Ike has a number of meanings such as to see, know, or recognize, to name a few. This interpretation of the term 'ike can connect to the proverb "ma ka hana ka 'ike" translated as "in working one learns" (Pukui 1983).

4. Hulihia is translated here as "overturn" but can be understood as an overturning through resistance. It is also applied to the rolling or turning of lava: simultaneously causing devastation and generation (Goodyear-Ka'ōpua, Howes, Osorio, and Yamashiro 2020, 5). In resistance circles, the use of this term highlights and frames kia'i efforts as a connection to 'āina (land).

5. I use the name Protect Maunakea to emphasize the main goal for this movement, which is not just to protect the mauna from the construction of a telescope, but from future development overall. Other publications may also refer to this movement as Anti-TMT, No TMT, 'A'ole TMT (No TMT), or Kū Kia'i Mauna (Stand guard over the mountain).

6. See http://www.wehewehe.org.

7. The telling of stories/histories (mo'olelo) is also a widely used form of cultural transmission of knowledge in Hawaiian culture (Hopkins 2019; Mākua, Meyer, and Wakinekona 2019).

8. The Apsálooke reservation in southern Montana (near Billings) is approximately a three-hour drive from their ancestral homeland where Heart Mountain sits in northwest Wyoming.

9. "Gods" is not a direct translation of akua, but much like the term "sacred," it is the closest word to this idea in the English language.

10. In 2013, an estimate was that "Almost 15,000 Hawaiians now use or understand Hawaiian" (Montgomery-Anderson 2013: 53). With increasing education the number is anticipated to be higher.

11. The meanings behind kaona may not be universally understood. For example, pua translates literally as "flower," but when kaona is applied can mean

"child," "genitalia," or "lover." The intention of the composer's kaona is sometimes only meant for a specific audience, therefore its meaning may be hidden even further from others. Kaona, performed beyond simple verbal meanings, is found in dance movements, musical sounds, and performative actions.

12. The renaissance that I refer to here is sometimes called the Second Hawaiian Renaissance with the understanding that the First Hawaiian Renaissance occurred during King David Kalākaua's reign in the nineteenth century (Fellezs 2019b, 147).

13. This renaissance was initiated by the release of the album *Guava Jam* (1969) by the Sunday Manoa (Moulin 2014, 532), a band that included musicians Peter Moon and brothers Robert and Roland Cazimero.

14. Lyrics in ʻōlelo Hawaiʻi appear on http://www.puuhuluhulu.com. The translation is by Nathaniel B. Emerson who published an English translation of the Pele and Hiʻiaka epic in 1915 (p. 226). Emerson's translation is not literal and includes poetic license to aid the flow in English.

15. I cite Taupōuri Tangarō here as the composer of this chant (as is also stated on http://www.puuhuluhulu.com) to give agency to his choice to sample from and modify the original text. He uses repetition of the overall verse and the phrase "Wela i luna . . . ," which is a common mele compositional practice (hoʻomanawanui 2005).

16. "In speech, kē can be a word uttered in disgust, sarcasm, or in arrogant dismissal" (Keao NeSmith, pers. comm.); it can also be described as an onomatopoeic sound of protest, similar to "tsk" or "ugh" in English. Many mele have a vocal tag at the end of each line, usually eā, ē, lā, etc. Kē could serve this function in this chant (Keao NeSmith, pers. comm.).

17. Many scholars have studied the actual and perceived benefits of group musicking, citing improvement in physical and mental health as well as building community and forming social identity (Clift 2002; Degmečić, Požgain, and Filaković 2005; Swijghuisen Reigersberg 2017).

18. Besides meaning the noun "god," the term akua can also be used as a verb meaning to perform extraordinary feats or to become divine or godlike (Taupōuri Tangarō, pers. comm.).

19. Pele is the volcano goddess in Hawaiian lore. McDougall provides an understanding of this important akua in Hawaiian culture in her work *Wondering and Laughing with Our Ancestors: Mana Wahine and the Moʻolelo of Hiʻiakaikapoliopele* (2016).

20. Dr. Saplan is currently an associate professor of music at Arizona State University.

21. In the Native Hawaiian approach to composition, the person who writes the lyrics is considered the haku mele (composer). As stated earlier, Ellen Kekoaohiwaikalani Wright Prendergast is the haku mele of "Kaulana Nā Pua" (1893), but it was later set to music by J. S. Libornio who published a notated version in San Francisco in 1895 (Stillman 1999).

22. In her explanation of precontact styles of vocal performance in Hawaiʻi, Elizabeth Tatar explains the socio-hierarchical system that delineates which mele genres garner the most mana and who can perform them. More divine

genres are generally reserved for the aliʻi and kahuna classes and are only performed by the makaʻāinana (commoners) if under a different name and/or with textual and musical modification (1981, 483–84).

23. Organizers anticipated that roughly ten thousand people would take part in the march on the island of Oʻahu, a number easily exceeded (HNN Staff 2019).

DANA E. POWELL

Life Beyond Ruin: Diné Presence in the Anthropocene

Abstract

This essay is concerned with the overdetermination of frameworks of "ruin" and "loss" in studies of the Anthropocene and the epistemic-political effects of such framings for Indigenous Peoples. While planetary harm is well established, the unique effects of crisis-oriented research on Indigenous Peoples demands critical reflection. I argue that such persistent frameworks of ruin/loss in fact open a space for "settler sustainabilities" to get smuggled in: designs that entrench the status quo of capitalism and colonialism, while at the same time claiming to perform "alternatives." With little comprehension of Indigenous history, politics, and place, settler sustainabilities effectively further Indigenous dispossession and profit from the loss/ruin ontology. Drawing upon collaborative and ethnographic research with Diné (Navajo) colleagues, and thinking with the growing scholarship in Indigenous political ecology, I show through empirical examples how Diné-led projects of territorial care in fact complicate narratives of loss/ruin as foundational framings for Native lives and landscapes. I suggest that attending to the empirics of innovations on the ground show an historical and decolonial sensibility, offering an ethic of land-based practice in times of crisis that does not accept ruin as the defining condition of possibility and futurity for Diné life.

> *Grace put her black hairnet on her dresser before she left.*
> *No one wears black hairnets anymore.*
> *The old women who used to wear them*
> *Seem to have all left Shiprock.*
> *But the black hairnets return every winter,*
> *Stretched out, twirling in the sky,*
> *Forming cylinders, diving, bouncing onto brown farmlands,*
> *And just as suddenly*
> *Bouncing back into cold blue skies,*
> *Diving and playing*
> *Perhaps remembering the old women who wore them*
> *When the women were young and joyful*
> *Laughing and dancing even in the coldest winters in Shiprock.*
>   —"GRACE'S HAIRNET" BY GLORIA EMERSON (DINÉ)[1]

EMERSON'S POEM CALLS US into a landscape that is the biophysical foundation for collective memory and self-determination. This suggests losses have a way of returning, in other forms, as sources of power. Gloria Emerson, a poet, essayist, and artist now in her mid-eighties, tends her family's ranch in rural Waterflow, New Mexico, just off the highway between Shiprock and Farmington, on the northeastern edge of the Navajo Reservation. I have visited with Gloria here over many years.[2] During our last meeting, in June 2023, she took me outside to study the crevassed shadows of the "Hogback": a high desert mountain range reminiscent of a pig's arched torso, its rocky ridgeline an earthen spine against cerulean skies. She sees it as an artist—it has an expressive face, she shows me; but others, white East Coast contemporaries of her Diné grandparents, saw this formation as geological promise of extraction-based wealth.

The oil beneath the Hogback seduced settler prospectors as early as the 1910s, the genesis of what would become a century of a carbon-based economy for the region. During one of our walks along the riverbanks of the San Juan River, just below her home, she was transported into memories of a landscape of riparian wonder: snake stories, old Fords in the wash, her parents picnicking on the fluvial islands. But she also relayed thoughts about more recent times, especially the 2015 incident in which heavy metals spilled into the river from the Gold King Mine upstream and released dangerous chemical pollutants into Diné lands and waters (Chief et al., 2016; Clausen 2021).[3] In an essay on the alarming flow of yellow water that Emerson witnessed following the spill and later painted in a piece she calls "Gold King," anthropologist Teresa Montoya asks, "What does it mean when a baseline starts from a point of existing contamination?" (Montoya 2017, 94).

The question of how to approach ruin, within conditions of settler coloniality, is the central concern of this essay. Emerson's literary and visual work on the changing environment offers one possible response to the politics of impact assessments: although the terms of standardized, quantifiable harm have been established by science, through threshold and "baseline" studies that ignore underlying and ongoing processes of colonialism, there are also lives like Emerson's and so many others that offer alternative orientations for rethinking "ruin" as a primary condition of possibility for Diné life in the Anthropocene. I am concerned about the tendency of popular and academic discourse that engages in tropes of ruin and loss, and what that means for critical Indigenous studies and, more importantly, for Diné and other Indigenous Peoples, like Emerson, Montoya, and so many others, wrestling in various ways with extractivism and its long-term effects. My concern emerges from nearly two decades of collaborative research as a U.S. citizen, white anthropologist in which I worked among diverse Diné communities in the U.S. Southwest, specifically, in the Chinle and Northern Agencies of the Navajo Nation.

The central problem and argument take inspiration from my extended conversations, formal and informal interviews, observations, focus groups, and collaboration with activists, scholars, policymakers, knowledge keepers, and artists over many years and in various forms.[4] We understand that "no intellectual work is authored alone" (Liboiron 2021, viii)—and certainly not this one. This work draws upon immersive coresearch engagements with Diné environmental defenders across two decades, anchored in ethnographic, archival, and landscape-based anthropological research. The particular argument in this essay builds from on-the-ground research conducted in 2018—2019 and follow-up interviews in 2020—2021. The overarching methodology involves engagement across "data sources"—textual, visual-artistic, empirical, humanistic, and experiential—and a commitment to move away from empiricist descriptions and representations of knowledge, and *toward* tracking and sharing practices and concepts for collaborative and decolonial possibilities.[5] Part of the method-as-ethic (Liboiron 2021) employed here is to engage in critical storytelling, with the permission of my collaborators, to offer a counternarrative to contemporary, seductive Anthropocenic accounts of destruction that leave certain lines of political difference, lived experience, and history underexamined.[6]

As such, this essay is an assemblage of stories, arguments, and reflections, woven together around the intellectual politics of what it might mean to see/think/live *life beyond ruin,* in a manner that certainly does not deny damage and loss but refuses to traffic in these alluring tropes and their overdetermining hermeneutics. Ruin as allegory, analogue, moral or literal interpretation has dominated salvage research agendas: What might yet happen, if we decenter this tendency, and more generatively reimagine the "baseline"?

My main observation from two decades of engagement is that, by and large, Diné people do not see their homelands as irreparably destroyed, despite dominant tropes and material legacies of damage. In the broadest sense, even under Anthropocenic conditions in the U.S. settler state, troubled lands, mountains, and waters still constitute Diné sovereignty; though experienced in diverse and even contradictory ways, given the historical collision of extractivism and climate change, this territory is defended as irreplaceable homeland. At stake and present in my overall method are the ways in which Diné and other Indigenous lives are lived on the ground, within and against specific historical conditions, rather than the manner in which such lives are represented in literature that takes ruination or termination as the central ontology. For nearly two decades, I have been humbled and transformed by my Diné friends' stories and projects of tenacity, invention, and restorative labor, as well as frustration and despair, in the face of seemingly intractable impacts of energy extraction, climate change, and other manifestations of environmental vulnerability under late industrial capitalism. I came to notice a gap: a fissure between experience and representation but also between ways of being in Dinétah and ways in which the Diné homeland was discursively cast in wider imaginaries. This is nothing more, perhaps, than the expected fissure between ethnographic detail or the textures of life as lived and the analytic upscaling or sense-making of those details as to become "generalizable" and, as such, translatable to wider publics. This haunting disconnect anchors my concern over the ways in which Anthropocenic narratives of loss and ruination operate to analytically overdetermine Diné experience and futurity.

The essay opens with a seemingly unlikely activist named Ed Singer, to show how situated environmental analytics involve an apprehension of restorative and environmental justice that articulates with Diné sensibilities of natural resource governance on the one hand and self-determination on the other. I tell Ed's story, with his permission, to illuminate the lived experience of a "sustainability" predicament that unveils some of the problems of a colonial politics of scaling and mapping Indigenous territories into larger scales of nation-states and their internal zones of "sacrifice."[7] Next, I examine the conceptual seduction of framings of decay and demise in our times, linking this appeal to traffic in stories of decay, following a central charge to question "damage-centered research" on Indigenous Peoples. I then briefly explore some of the theoretical work on ruin before introducing the idea of settler sustainabilities, linking well-established critiques of sustainability with anticolonial perspectives to see how these designs proliferate in the Navajo Nation. In the final section, I address the dangers of loss and ruination framings, suggesting the epistemic and political limits of a progressive teleology of developmentalist thinking in postcarbon future-making, and the necessity of sovereignty-centered environmental theory.

Chasing the Wind: Sacrifice, Sustainability, and Scale

A decade ago, Diné artist, rancher, elected official, and green energy activist Ed Singer wanted to mount a wind farm on the stark monocline near his home to generate power for rural Diné households, 30 percent of which have no running water or electricity. The commercial-scale wind farm he envisioned for the Cameron Chapter of the Navajo Nation would also export power, perhaps replacing urban dependence on electricity from Diné coal. Ed's experience offers an analytic for the otherwise mundane. Grounded encounters with a colonial politics of scale in which "damaged" lands—in this case, those impacted by Cold War uranium extraction and mid- twentieth-century coal extraction—are all too often perceived as part of a "national whole" of settler governments. These lands (and their peoples, by extension) are framed as unavoidable collateral damage and zones of sacrifice to enable settler futurities (i.e., nuclear weapons to stockpile against the USSR; electrons to move water and power to Phoenix). These become the places acceptable to pollute, develop, militarize, extract, and (eventually) study. Such settler stories of land as irreparably damaged further brackets Diné place-based projects of restoring relations (with the winds, or otherwise) in a manner to advance autonomy within a territory that is intrinsically meaningful unto itself, nonsubstitutable, and whose value is not in relation to a scaled-up national whole but to its own historically and politically particular basis of life. Ed's story illuminates this predicament and the twinned nature of sacrifice and sustainability against a colonial politics of scale.

Ed's story, which I have followed at his invitation and written about in earlier moments of his projects (Powell 2018), vividly frames the problematic of this essay: Diné landscapes and related lives impacted by extraction of various kinds (mineral, financial, intellectual, human, animal, botanical) *still constitute immanent, irreplaceable, nonfungible homelands as the basis of Diné sovereignty.* Ed's story also provokes my own affective mode of ethnography that considers the "charged atmosphere of everyday life" (Stewart 2010) to be portals into broader cultural critique, theory, and most importantly, engagement with material conditions. Transformed by Indigenous research methods (L.T. Smith 1999), ethnography—alongside cothinkers/cocreators like Ed and others we will meet here—exceeds its own representational anchors to become more generatively descriptive, refusive, and relational (A. Simpson 2014). Stay with me, as Ed leads us into the thick of it.

As a land manager who worked closely with livestock and the terrain, Ed knew well the contamination left behind by a settler economy driven by energy mineral extraction and development agendas. Much of Ed's artwork—shown from Gallup to Paris—references this history of colonial capitalist violence, its effects on Diné peoples and lands. In a 2018 painting entitled *Fragile*, Ed depicts the body of a person wrapped in a Pendleton-style blanket, asleep beneath a park bench, their companion animal staring directly at the viewer, as if to ask, "What is your relation and obligation, here?" Painted on the vivid green bench is a blue sign that read, Goldman Sachs. A yellow grassy landscape stretches in all directions until we find, faintly at the horizon, grayish smoke fumes emitting from power plants. In June 2023, Ed took me to his studio in Cortez, where scores of finished art as well as works in progress, across fifty years of painting, stood on easels and were stacked against the walls. There, Ed showed me other visual histories of violence: one painting of a building's interior offered dark commentary on his own experience of boarding school, he explained. Another painting, *T'oh Lits'oh (Yellow Water)*, illustrated the same Gold King Mine Spill that inspired Gloria Emerson's work, an event now emblematic of the recent regional "disasters of late industrialism" (Fortun 2012; see https://edsinger.weebly.com/).

Ed's material-semiotic work has been on canvas but also in the landscape itself, through anemometers, land-use policies, and other infrastructures of localizing electrical production. He admits that his years spent wrestling the winds was unpredictable work. The wind farm proposal was complicated, he admitted, as it involved complex financial and political alliances with a Houston-based wind power developer and a range of federal, international, and private investors. Ed didn't want to go through the Navajo Nation's central government because of what he saw as the slow pace of site development approvals on the reservation, scarcity of capital, and the tribal government being, in Ed's words, "so in love with coal."[8] Indeed, coal extraction has been the major source of revenue for the Navajo Nation since the 1960s. Ed also wanted to test the possibility of local governance, having his Cameron Chapter become a leader in cutting-edge renewable energy, hoping to inspire some of the other 109 chapters across the Nation also rich in wind and solar potential.

This was not simply a struggle against centralized environmental governance. Diné peoples' impressions about wind were impacted, Ed explained, by the high-profile resistance to turbines on Cape Cod due to disruptions of the vista: these rarefied, New England aesthetics inhibited potentially

FIGURE 1. Ed Singer, *Fragile* (2018), oil on canvas painting.

innovative projects in rural Arizona. At the same time, Dutch and Finnish companies contacted Ed, offering their expertise in developing infrastructure in "rugged, rural, out of the way places," while the National Aeronautics and Space Administration (NASA) and other federal agencies interested in the science of air turbulence and high windspeed propeller blades offered to underwrite Ed and his community's vision. Closer to the Southwest, however, new wind and solar farm developments along the Eldorado Transmission Line (owned by Southern California Edison, stretching from Nevada to California) thwarted the Cameron Wind Project; they jumped the line on those waiting to plug in to Eldorado, including the Cameron Project, because it hadn't yet broken ground. "Once we were out of the queue," Ed recounted, "the project lost all value. The biggest part of the feasibility study was that there were transmission lines right there—because it's more expensive to build lines than a wind farm."[9]

Complex "colonial entanglements" (Dennison 2012) led to the project's collapse: the joint venture unraveled due to the logics of extraction *and* of sustainability, processes that go hand in hand in the Navajo Nation, as well as the unexpected intervention of the winds themselves. Grey Mountain's turbine-perfect winds also sculpted the desert landscape in a time of intensifying drought, as gales brought by the changing climate remade sand dunes and dangerously elevated temperatures in the Southwest. Combined with escalating temperatures and lack of rain and snowfall, winds not only give life but also threaten it: transforming livestock watering holes into craters, threatening to bury family homes in sandbanks, and produce blinding sandstorms without comparison in living memory. By the time of my visit to the community of Dilkon (Arizona) in June 2018, not far from Ed's home in Cameron, local herders reported two-hundred dead livestock per week.[10] Such reports were repeated in June 2023, in my conversations with scholars, Elders, and land managers at the Diné Studies Conference at Navajo Preparatory School in Farmington, New Mexico.

The fragile promise of Ed's wind farm gave way, however, to a groundswell of activism in the Nation's Western Agency district in the years following the wind initiative. With policy changes under President Obama, increasing hesitation by financiers due to carbon liabilities, and the economic crisis of 2008, the once-secure future of coal became increasingly precarious in Diné country. The decision to decommission the 1970s behemoth Navajo Generating Station in December 2019 was read by many as a death sentence to the industry. Yet as the Navajo Nation made controversial bids in 2019 to purchase the dinosaur power plant from the utilities letting it go, a crescendo of Diné voices called for a "just transition" (Horseherder 2021) from fossil fuels to wind and solar installations (Montoya 2022). When the wind farm project is considered in this wider political-ecological landscape, it persists not as a failure but as part of dispersed, collective desire for new forms of relocalized environmental governance and infrastructures for the Navajo Nation. In this sense, the legacies of a place long understood in the literature, and among many activists, as a "sacrifice zone" nested within the national scale of settler-state (Kuletz 1998) or the planetary scale of ecological mutation (Latour 2017) may reemerge as its own immanent element and site of meaningful struggle: not divorced from the transit of capital, regulatory agencies and policies, or jurisdictional dilemmas, but endowed with an inalienable set of relations that subsequent violent relationalities do not fully subsume.

Beyond Damage

Projects like the Cameron wind farm challenge popular narratives that cast Indigenous Peoples as tragic victims, Luddites, *or* romantic stewards—in any of these guises, as fully out of step with modernity (P.C. Smith 2009). And perhaps even if those colonial tropes have, at long last, been overturned, more recent liberal tropes of Native bodies, communities, and lands as defined by loss and ruin further perform dangerous theoretical-political work that both pathologizes Indigenous life while also undermining sovereignty by elevating narratives of contamination. These deathly tropes operate as "terminal narratives" (Michael Wilcox quoted in Estes 2020, 1), occluding strategies of presence that offer an alternative epistemology and methodology for the contemporary moment of crisis. Narratives of loss and ruin are deployed strategically in some instances to illuminate the collective crisis all earthlings face in a warming climate and, importantly, used to call for redress where that work remains to be done. These same narratives, however, in academic discourse attendant to crisis, also tend toward an overdetermining weight. At present, they seem to threaten to become a political aesthetic that operates as a Foucauldian "regime of truth" (Foucault 1975) in the environmental humanities, profoundly shaping the ways certain peoples and places are perceived, known, and potentially acted upon, by states, NGOs, investors, and oftentimes activists themselves.

I draw specifically from Eve Tuck's critique of the "damage-centered research" widely characterizing Indigenous Peoples and Nations (Tuck 2009). This kind of damage-centered research, in Tuck's analysis, "looks to historical exploitation, domination, and colonization to explain contemporary brokenness, such as poverty, poor health, and low literacy. Common sense tells us this is a good thing, but the danger in damage-centered research is that it is a pathologizing approach in which the oppression singularly defines a community (Tuck 2009, 413). This approach is not limited to Native communities, but largely shapes research across North America on low-income white communities in Appalachia, African American communities in the Deep South, and emergent research in critical disability studies.[11] It indeed may be a liberal Americanist proclivity to imagine the possibility of redress as an extension of a sympathetic form of recognition, rooted in feeling. As in, "I see/feel you now," to enable an identification that will permit involvement.[12] But the stakes of this "benevolent operation," as Tuck puts it, makes seeing creativity and resistance contingent upon damage, as a foundational ontology. The result of more than a century of this approach has resulted, Tuck confirms, in "feelings of being over-researched yet, ironically, made invisible" (Tuck 2009, 411–12). Such erasure resembles the long-standing "ethnographic silencing" of Indigenous women's knowledge and deeper histories of grounded practices of presence, in the research setting (Bruchac 2014). These analyses show the gendered and racialized nature of scavenging, amassing, and recording in the name of "research," every aspect of what many believed to be a rapidly vanishing "race" (see also Blackhawk 1997; Starn 2004, 2011).

Recent work in Indigenous discard studies mobilizes Tuck's critique of damage-centered research, sharpening it for critical examinations of environmental toxics and toxicity.[13] This work is especially relevant for my discussion, given the widespread, accepted narrative of Diné lands (and the greater Southwest) as an ecological and social "sacrifice zone" for U.S. empire broadly (Cold War era) and urban development specifically (the "Sunbelt" cities). In a trenchant essay that redefines damage for anthropology and the chemical-environmental humanities, Michelle Murphy emplaces Tuck's insight within the dangers of progressivist, liberal moves to document harm as an epistemic strategy for remediation. Murphy writes:

> Focused on collecting the data of damage, much hegemonic North American environmental biomedical research surveils and pathologizes already dispossessed communities. It is hard to perceive the infrastructures of chemical violence in the world at the same time that research attends to molecular manifestations in bodies and communities already living in hostile conditions. *Despite often antiracist intentions, this damage-based research has pernicious effects, placing the focus on chemical violence by virtue of rendering lives and landscapes as pathological.* Such work tends to resuscitate racist, misogynist, and homophobic portraits of poor, Black, Indigenous, female, and queer *lives and communities as damaged and doomed, as inhabiting irreparable states that are not just unwanted but less than fully human.* (Murphy 2017, emphasis added)

The inadvertent "resuscitation" conjures deeply engrained early twentieth-century colonial tropes of disappearing Natives, biologically and politically doomed by settler modernity. Repurposed a century later, these are stories of ruination that go beyond the descriptive (e.g., of climate crisis, species loss, underlying health disparities) to serve an epistemic and ontological function of representation: they become analogs of the lives/lands they ostensibly describe.

Indigenous discard studies offers a critical precautionary principle to assuming damage as the raison d'être for critical research; moreover, it challenges the field of environmental justice studies to engage directly with colonialism as a very specific form of "contemporary and evolving land relations" in which violence (more than "harm") is infra/structural, historical, and in excess of what scientific "thresholds" can measure (Liboiron 2021, 6). When considering the capitalist enslavement of land in particular (as property, as development), Liboiron's radical reframing of pollution, morbidity, and contamination can cast new light on places like the U.S. Southwest, where the foundational violence underpinning land (and water) relations has formed "alterlife relations," wherein biophysical realms (bodies, lands) have been reproduced and transformed so profoundly and yet—are not fully measurable by their "destruction" alone (Liboiron 2021, 108). Drawing as well on Murphy's redefinition of "reproductive justice" as the struggle to reproduce flourishing relations of life, Liboiron confronts the tendency of environmentalists to focus, almost pornographically, on the loss of life: "This is why using photos of albatross to denote destruction rather than the presence of sustained and persisting life is so rude. This is why eating contaminated fish *is life* (as is not eating contaminated fish, from another point of view)" (Liboiron 2021, 108; emphasis added).

Liboiron's contributions to methodology, through the actions of the Collaborative Laboratory in Environmental Action Research they direct, as well as in text, further inform how we might reconfigure an anticolonial environmental humanities for the Anthropocene that resists the appeal of ready-to-wear tropes of loss and ruin as stable, reliable universals. Advancing place-based protocols *that often do not travel well* and a resistance to generalizability invite the ethnographic and historical back into the room, with land relations at the center (Liboiron 2021, 151). This invites not only a fresh kind of experimentation, but of listening well, paying attention, remembering and enacting obligations. This essay, in effect, is part of my own long-standing obligation to Diné Elders, like Ed, Gloria, and Alice mentioned here, but so many others unnamed in this particular text whose pedagogy (with me) has almost always focused on instruction in "the presence of sustained and persisting life" (Liboiron 2021, 108) in the face of untold violence.

This approach, broadly speaking, does not discount the research that has been done (and that which critically remains to be done, and is underway, in many places) that documents and serves as redress for historical wrongs, such as poisoning low-income communities, dispossessing certain populations of land and life, and exploiting certain (gendered and racialized) forms of labor; this is, in essence, the crux of environmental (in)justice scholarship. But discard studies pushes this analysis farther: as Murphy elaborates, "This refusal [of damage-centered research] constitutes a challenge to environmental justice habits" of narrating injury (Murphy 2017). Moreover, the intention is not to devalue the careful work of documenting harm or dismiss the pivotal interventions this work continues to make, instigating (and in some cases, emerging from within) social movements and various forms of action. Tuck's argument that "there was a time and place for damage-centered research" (Tuck 2009, 415) might appear to suggest that the time has now come to move on and reorient toward the future.

Yet a more nuanced reading of this body of work that refuses damage as the object of study moves us beyond an interpretation that is mired in settler logics of "crisis," as these play out through ideas of resistance and temporality. Just as a federal agency intended to manage "native affairs" might be seen as an irrevocable institution of coloniality, as Valerie Lambert shows, Indigenous influence, desire, creativity, and indeed "new paradigms" are forged in spaces that defy ruination as definitive of Native life (Lambert 2022). Colonial institutions are being remade. Similarly, rethinking time as relationships among species resists temporal linearity and thus the "ticking clock" of climate disaster and rather reads for changes in ecological relationships (Whyte 2021). So part of our shift away from damage-centered research includes a more expansive thinking of the institutional, agentive, temporal, and affective registers of "life in crisis" presenting a temporal rupture that demands action (Redfield 2005). This recalls Joe Masco's warning of the "crisis in crisis," wherein public and media debates tend to stabilize existing conditions and the status quo, by turning "crisis" into a "counterrevolutionary idiom" rather than a call for the end of systemic violence and empire (Masco 2017, 2010). As Masco notes, "existential danger" becomes the "affective idiom" and collective basis for "a new kind of governance, one based not on eliminating fears through the protective actions of the security apparatus but rather on the amplification of public dangers through inaction" (Masco 2010, 66). The affective, aesthetic, and political idioms that shape our imaginations of what is and might yet be come into play, when ruination achieves hegemonic grip on environmental analytics.

Such modes of "inaction" on the part of governance undergirds a terrible void in research on a vast range of forms of environmental violence, especially in Indigenous communities. How can we possibly go beyond damage, when damage has yet to be fully documented or understood? To be sure, in Dinétah, there remains an urgent "need to account for how violence calibrates other forms of power in Diné life" (Yazzie 2014, 88). Melanie Yazzie and Jennifer Denetdale assert that systemic forms of violence and racism against Diné peoples occur in the deep "anti-Indianism" and predatory nature of border towns (Denetdale 2016, 2022) but also within the Nation's borders itself, in gendered and heteronormative manipulations of ideas of "Diné tradition" when used for disciplinary and biopolitical ends (Denetdale 2006). Through a critical analysis of colonial tropes of "Indigenous deviance," Denetdale's work reveals how persistent narratives (e.g., of alcoholism, unemployment, contamination, dilapidated infrastructure) operate to stabilize dominant discourses of Indigenous Peoples as intrinsically morally (and otherwise) damaged. Similarly, Melanie Yazzie shows how federal policy strategies have further naturalized these narratives, operating as a "death plan": Yazzie exposes the historical-social construction of damage as part of a design to integrate Diné people into capitalist development in a manner that has transformed Diné lands, bodies, and communities into subsidies for U.S. empire (Yazzie 2018).

And yet, the way out of this morass of apparent loss, as Denetdale writes, is not a re-inscription or aesthetic elevation of damage-centered research that traffics in the terrain of ruin: "Such treatment spells not the end for Indigenous peoples, including the Diné, for we have mapped our way out of multiple life-threatening crises . . . [we see a] Diné refusal to die in a tradition of refusal and resistance that values Iiná or life" (2022, 293). Indeed, assessing violence, harm, and ruin often contains a dialogic position within it, elsewhere described as a "double force of vulnerability" (Gutierrez et al., 2021). Dina Gilio-Whitaker inverts damage narratives in this manner: "Native identities are formed against a backdrop of historical tragedy and ongoing injustice, which often involves the continued struggle to defend what remains of ancestral lands, territories, resources, and cultures (Gilio-Whitaker 2019, 49). The struggle to defend is evident in Gloria Emerson's political ecology and riparian worlding[14] of blackbirds, memory, and refusal to relocate despite known and unknown contamination; it is evident in Ed Singer's bid for a commercial-scale wind farm that engages capitalism and self-determination.

The Radiation Exposure Compensation Act (RECA) of 1990 established a federal system for Diné miners to make claims related to atmospheric nuclear testing and uranium industry employment. Even with its limitations (only partially corrected in later amendments), as a federal compensation measure RECA is celebrated by many Diné activists as significant redress. Loss of health and mortality had to be established, with the U.S. nuclear program as the cause of that ruin. There is a vast body of literature, film, white papers, and other documents detailing the slow material damage done to the Navajo Nation by U.S. nuclearism and industrial coal extraction. And one can read this empirically, in an archaeology of the present, in the hazard signs marking abandoned yet unmitigated tailings piles, drag lines, coal ash pits, oil well pads, and the transmission lines that carry power off the reservation and outward to urban centers, as well as in the more subtle but acutely sensed cancers, asthmas, and birth defects that are both widely reported and underreported.

Locating "ruin" in the movement itself attunes us to a lexicon that acknowledges damage but moves beyond it and the "terminal narratives" noted above (Wilcox cited in Estes 2020) that might otherwise occlude Diné presence in the Anthropocene. Earl Tulley, along with the other cofounders of Diné Citizens against Ruining our Environment (CARE), in the very naming of their organization, identified ruination as something to be resisted (Sherry 2002). Tulley, now a cancer survivor of Cold War toxicity, chuckles when he recalls how the transnational nongovernmental humanitarian aid organization, CARE, attempted to block the fledgling grassroots tribal group from "using their name."[15] What stands out here is not only the "ruination" being resisted—the refusal to succumb to the more obvious forms of ecological degradation due to extractivism and climate change—but the political self-determination that is enacted in "our environment." The name, importantly, is not *the* environment—an abstracted planetary space that we all might share—but rather, the possessive: *our* environment. As such, this name indexes the homelandscape of Dinétah and the collective that dwells within and claims it as an ongoing challenge to the structures and processes of colonialism. The lexical shift appears subtle, but tuning into "our" environment affirms a desire to exist beyond damage and an identification that is not defined by "ruining" but by that which is collectively, irreplaceably "ours": tribal self-determination, belonging, and futurity.[16]

Decentering ruin in this manner shows that at stake is not "merely" naming contamination and enacting environmental cleanup (though this indeed is part of the demand) but a recognition of land relations, territorial integrity, dignity, and the presence and persistence of Diné people in a landscape that has been put to use by colonial capitalism through carbon as a subsidy for modernization. However, as Andrew Curley shows, carbon has also bolstered the sovereignty of the Navajo Nation at the same time it has posed risks of harm (Curley 2023). Beyond Diné land, Nation-building through capitalizing on fossil fuel extraction and energy mineral rights, from the Osage Nation (Dennison 2014; Fixico 2012) to the MHA Nation (Parker 2014) and beyond, shows how resource extraction often enables new forms of citizenship, in a material and intimate manner (Curley 2023, 12). Coal, along with its reviving *and* decomposing infrastructures, as Curley details, is indeed part of Diné land relations. It is not any more synonymous with "ruin" than it is with "wealth": it becomes a meaningful signifier in the labor, legalities, temporal-spatial scales, and place-based practices of colonial capitalism shaping the Navajo Nation (Curley 2023). The colonial politics of scale that approaches Indigenous lands as nested subunits (ruined or not) of the settler whole misses the point that Curley makes, regarding the complex transactions of capitalism:

> In the western half of North America, Indigenous territories are either on top of coveted resources or in the way of transmission lines, pipelines, and waterways that put these resources into capitalistic circulation. These realities of geography create the conditions through which tribal governments seek remedy for decades of colonialism and marginalization through their own participation in resource extraction and the energy industry. (Curley 2023, 185).

Ruination in this instance, if anything at all, is a ruination of relationships wrought by the pipelines and policies of colonial capitalism, remedied through participation in those extractive projects.

Analytics of Ruination

Over the past decade, pivotal works in environmental posthumanism have advanced theories of planetary ruination and demise (Latour 2017; Stengers 2015; Tsing et al. 2017; van Dooren 2014, among others). As a recent genre, they offer critical evidence of what Isabelle Stengers confirms as "the coming barbarism"[17]: an entwined crisis of planetary proportions, both ecological and political, as Gaia takes revenge on our species and our "spokespeople" (politicians) no longer know what to do (Stengers 2015). The diagnostic fits but also carries a blind spot. Dystopia figures not only in the recent present or speculative future, but as Indigenous writers suggest (Whyte 2017, 2021; Dillon 2012) has already occurred and is still unfolding. In this sense, "barbarism" is not forthcoming but entails the conditions of coloniality that persist in the here-and-already. Invocations of planetary crisis, extinction, salvage species operations, and "coming barbarisms" have established a powerful narrative of loss and ruin—indeed, of *terminality*—while saying little of the foundational or ongoing processes of colonialism that structure the workings of capital and the dispossession of Indigenous lands necessary for its operation.

Theories of ruination and the state, such as Laura Ann Stoler's notion of "imperial debris" (Stoler 2013) show the durability of empires in the landscape and have been crucial in disclosing the materiality and temporality of political violence. As Catherine Fennell elaborates in her review of Stoler, empire's formations "linger in the uneven distributions that outlast an empire, in the built environments that continue eroding after capital flees, and in the particles seeping from mines, wells and their many products. And while impermanence is a human condition, so are the attachments, sentiments and residues that tether people to ever-shifting relations, orders and spaces. These attachments, sentiments and residues grant impermanent things a hold on bodies, imaginations and places. And those holds have a way of pressing into the present and futures of those who must navigate them." (Fennell 2018, 520). In the Navajo Nation, such "aftermaths of empire" can be read empirically in the nearly three hundred unmitigated abandoned uranium mines, as shown in Figure 2. These are among the wider legacies of U.S. weapons production during the Cold War—as well as in other "holds" related to extractivism, such as a tribal economy built from the 1920s onward, around energy resources (oil in the 1920s, coal in the 1960s, fracked gas in the twenty-first century). Fennell continues: "Imperial formations proliferate in the present, Stoler argues, because the legal and territorial ambiguities and the distributions of rights and resources characteristic of colonial projects will endure *long after an*

FIGURE 2. Earl Tulley (Diné) points to an abandoned uranium mine in his home village of Blue Gap (Arizona). Photo by author, June 2023.

empire dissolves" (Fennell 2018, 520; emphasis added). Scholars in *NAIS* might question, however, the premise that empire has "dissolved" and thus we face another dogged question for comparative colonialisms (beyond the scope of this paper) in the differences between postsettler versus settler forms of colonialism.

This insight offers a critical theory of and for the present by reading the landscape for empire's durable and material forms of violence. Such analytics offer fresh critiques of capitalism, empire, and productivity, as in Lori Khatchadourian's generative notion of *life extempore,* pushing critical analysis of the production of value under and potentially beyond the conditions of ruin, unsettling standard theories of precarity, degradation, or coping (Khatchadourian 2022). The durability of ruined landscapes wrought by empire and colonialism has also been taken up by U.S. Southwestern studies scholars, especially those examining the legacies of uranium mining for Navajo and other Native Nations (Brugge and Goble 2002; Dawson 1992; Johnston et al. 2010; Kamper et al. 2008; Voyles 2015). In Dinétah, such troubles have been infrastructural long before they were climatic, revealing an environmental history wherein electricity and other energy systems shaped Diné sovereignty in relation to energy minerals and land (Needham 2014; Powell 2015, 2018), to livestock (Weisiger 2009), and increasingly, to water and environmental governance (Curley 2021, 2023).

Indigenous self-determination thus would seem to be the defining difference creating distance and dissonance, empirically and conceptually, from broader theories of ruination. American Indian assertions of self-determination and presence cited throughout this paper build upon a collective historical consciousness and sense of political difference, grounded in territories (Escobar 2008). This reorientation of difference as political-ecological exceeds the current call to "stay with the trouble," to invoke Donna Haraway's provocation for a method of living in the Anthropocene (Haraway 2016). The sovereign difference reminds that crisis is not necessarily recent (e.g., planetary degradation) and that territories impacted by the ruins of capital are also *homelandscapes,* and as such, are often the basis of citizenship and self-determination, even when contested (Dennison 2014; Kuan 2021). Though "trouble" of many kinds indeed shapes Diné experience, for most people, there is little option but to "stay with it." And the "staying with" is embedded in the nonfungibility of specific land relations. Repurposing Haraway further, all beings are indeed entangled in "tentacular practices" of "making kin" and "making with," rather than going alone. But the difference here is twofold: first, Diné self-determination is rooted in a concept of kinship, as *k'e,* that long predates the academic multispecies turn and is formative for environmental governance (Powell and Curley 2009); and second, not all communities are "making with" from the same origin point or for the same purpose.

When damage-centered research has defined what is thought to be possible in places like the Navajo Nation, there is an urgent need for place-based approaches that attend to practices of worldmaking and desire within homelands whose value is not contingent upon being a part-of-a-whole (a broader settler "commons" as it were) or national territory but rather as meaningful, historied places where relations are being (re)established in spite of political-ecological disruptions to botanical, chemical, and animal kin (Carroll 2015; Murphy 2017; Todd 2017). This purview is not to deny the ambit of transnational capital or political economy; it is not a Boasian return to see the damaged individual in need of salvage as representative of the larger scale of loss (Starn 2004); nor a circumscribed cultural ecology (Rappaport 1968). Indeed, as Andrew Curley makes crystal clear, there is perhaps no place on earth more "global" than the rural Navajo Nation in its designs for "carbon sovereignty" (Curley 2023). Rather, this is an analytic—like Ed's wind farm and the food truck and gardens described below—in which Diné lands need not always be narrated as a damaged part of a larger scale but taken seriously within a geopolitical imaginary in which the reference point is not always already weighted to the settler state as the locus of meaning (A. Simpson 2014).

Desire is, as Tuck reminds us, "an epistemological shift . . . and a thirding of the dichotomized categories of reproduction and resistance. Desire fleshes out that which has been hidden or what happens behind our backs" (Tuck 2009, 419–20). Indigenous Peoples, discursively shaped by salvage-oriented, damage-centered research, today face some of the most extreme forms of climate disruption *and* contested environmental governance; for instance, in coastal livelihoods where water often overwhelms (Emanuel and Wilkins 2020; McDermott 2015; Marino 2015; Maldonado 2019) as well as in arid ecologies where water is increasingly scarce (Crate 2008; Redsteer 2011), socioecological vulnerability is a material condition for urgent reckoning. However, research aimed at *only* exposing these layered, cumulative harms must consider the political possibilities for uplifting "desire" that may become unintentionally foreclosed by pathologizing harm. I am concerned with how scholarly analytics may impact communities by naturalizing, fetishizing, and aestheticizing certain conceptual framings that occlude certain kinds of projects, or preemptively frame them as "responses to harm." I am arguing for more than an analytical shift. Rather, I am arguing that our ongoing ethnographic commitments to local contexts and quotidian life offer up fissures in the otherwise seemingly stable meta-narratives of damage and ruination. And since narratives matter, we might yet unsettle dominant stories of loss and ruin by attending to the experimental, playful, desiring, and creative practices that do not exist "in spite of" (but exist in intimate relation with, but perhaps not always in response to) very real experiences of vulnerability. Such a shift, in our necessarily urgent attention to crisis, might illuminate the assertion of other forms of sovereignty and well-being (Hatfield

2020). Our approach for these difficult times then might become, following feminist scholar Eve Sedgwick, moving beyond paranoia (read as "ruin") as an epistemological practice (of what Sedgwick calls "strong negative affect theory"), and instead, toward "reparative readings" of lives complexly lived, in order "to do justice to a wealth of characteristic, cultural central practices, many of which can well be called reparative" (Sedgwick 2003, 147).[18]

As humanities and social science literatures of the nuclear Southwest demonstrates, multiple ontologies of place overlap: it is possible to experience a "geography of the sacred" and a "geography of sacrifice," as Valerie Kuletz shows (1998), as well as to discern competing "technologies of security" among Pueblo Nations, Nuevomexicanx communities, and Los Alamos laboratories, as Joseph Masco's ethnography of U.S. Cold War nuclearism shows (2006). Traci Voyles builds explicitly on Kuletz's work, moving Kuletz's "wasteland discourse" into a focus on the materialization of harm, in what she terms, "wastelanding (2015). Voyles argues that "wastelanding" is an "unexplored component of environmental racism" (2015, 9). However, the prolific writing, digital media, organized actions, and published articulations by Diné activists and scholars that precisely explore the material processes of rendering land pollutable (Begaye 2005; Yazzie and White 2020) seem to indeed address environmental racism and its ruinous effects. Given that the Navajo Nation government itself in 1994 declared uranium mining a "genocide" against the Diné people, and there have been numerous books detailing the damages wrought on Indigenous bodies and landscapes by the midcentury arms race, continuing to emphasize homelands as wastelands may transmit unexamined risks. Despite living in the midst of these conditions, the majority of Diné people express a deep attachment to *Dinétah*, their homeland, and see it as a storied and spiritual landscape, guaranteed to the people by the deities. Certainly, the "imperial debris" of colonialism in the Navajo Nation is impossible to overlook or forget, as violence is etched into the landscape, the built environment, and into bodies. But given that territory is the basis of many Native Nations' sovereignty and political authority, and yet Indigenous lands and waters are increasingly challenged by federal enclosures, rights of way, and easements, we might ask: What is at stake in repurposing such tropes and how does Indigenous self-determination in homelandscapes complicate these analytics of ruination?

Settler Sustainabilities

The collapse of the Cameron wind farm project was complicated, broadly revealing clashes among differing logics of sustainability. For the tribal government, that logic was rooted in extraction; for the outside developer, in a specific technology; for NASA and federal investors, in energy science; for European turbine companies, in rural development; and for Ed, in local governance and self-determination. In the end, wind power is not inherently liberatory or populist but can harness the traumas of colonial dispossession by various agents. In this section, I consider how the loss and ruin analytic sets the stage for *settler sustainabilities* to proliferate: projects, often well-intentioned, yet with little understanding of the tribal-federal relationship, or the complex histories of resource governance in Indigenous lands. Often cast as "green technologies," *settler sustainabilities leave the ongoing processes and structures of colonialism unexamined.*[19] In a word, settler sustainabilities advance what other scholars have elaborated as "settler futurities" (Tuck and Yang 2012). The temporality of green design as a modality of ensuring settler claims on land and economies operates seductively. The idea of sustainability at work in colonial designs within Indigenous territories is indeed an emerging field of critical inquiry: in a careful examination of Southern Sámi representations of wind energy, Susanne Normann shows how turbines invoke colonial enclosures and erasures of Sámi Peoples by Norwegian state and society, and what Aili Keskitalo, the Sámi parliament's president, termed "green colonialism" (Normann 2021). Ethnographic analyses of wind power in Oaxaca, Mexico, show similar findings: "sustainable" technologies in Indigenous territories often operate as avatars of historical, colonial trauma (Howe 2019; Boyer 2019).[20] This is to say, the concept of settler sustainabilities builds upon existing critiques of green colonialism and the failure of many sustainability agendas to adequately address equity—and the situated, unevenly experienced effects of colonialism, in particular.

In the Navajo Nation, geologist and climate scholar Margaret Redsteer challenges this dominant logic, arguing instead that "it is important to understand the distinctive historical, legal and economic contexts of the risk and adaptive capacities of Southwestern Native American communities" (Redsteer et al. 2013, 385). Similarly, Klara Kelley and Harris Francis's research on climate change and Diné clans shows the intrinsic relationality within and between kinship networks—the "*k'e* system," which also orders humans and livestock in the landscape—and the places/environments where these (matrilineally organized) relations find meaning (Kelley and Francis 2019). These authors' holistic, historical, and relational approaches affirm the empirical evidence of climate-induced ruin—for instance, sand dune movement, desertification, and drought—yet they do not overdetermine ruin as the foundational ontology of the landscape and population, itself. This distinction is key.

Sustainability has of course in recent years become more self-reflexive and critical, introducing commitments to "participatory," "endogenous," and other forms of practice. Glen Coulthard diagnoses this turn, as "the significant transformation in the discourse of sustainable development over the last fifteen years" (Coulthard 2014, 77). And yet, without a recognition of the implicit structuring force of loss and ruin as an organizing framework, and without a keen understanding of the legal-political difference that Native sovereignty poses, a mode of settler sustainability often emerges that undermines Indigenous presence and territorial control. Sustainability is thus often figured as an infrastructural and technological response to landscapes of loss and ruin, which have been damaged by rampant capitalist extraction; and colonial relationships are often extended rather than disrupted through state-of-the-art technologies, all in the name of "sustainability" (see Mookerjea 2019; Yazzie 2018).

By settler sustainabilities I mean conceptual designs and material projects that, in foregrounding sustaining Nature (conservation, environmentalism, renewables), may also inadvertently sustain a certain status quo of dispossession. Settler sustainabilities, in fact, further what Escobar calls the persistent "structures of *un*sustainability," which include the political and sociocultural systems that enable occupation and inhibit relationality and habitability (Escobar 2019). As long as concepts such as "alternative sustainabilities"[21] are about sustaining economic forms (e.g., "green jobs"); management regimes that see nature as a "resource"; equity without an analysis of indigeneity as political difference, they fail to interrogate the colonial underpinnings of dispossession and violence. Moreover, they risk sustaining the ongoing structures of colonialism. Rather, how do we shift our sensibilities to read for locally informed projects that do not carry the banner of "sustainability," often exist under the radar or, as Tuck says, "in what happens behind our backs" (2009, 419–20), and as such, may be perceived as not yet scalable to become viable solutions.

Settler sustainabilities travel widely, and efforts within Native Nations are not impermeable to their designs, though they frequently provoke resistance.[22] We can locate them at sites where tropes of loss and ruin are being examined on the ground, and complicated, by Indigenous land defenders. For instance, Andrew Curley shows how green jobs movements in the Navajo Nation have tended to follow neoliberal logics, even in movements attempting to transform the tribal economy away from extractive industries (Curley 2018). In the events Curley describes, and those in which he participated, the fundamental structures of power related to dispossession and developmentalist logics remained intact, despite activists' best intentions. The impasse, he asserts, was that the concept of an alternative economy did not more fundamentally challenge colonialism, capitalism, and federal primacy over Indigenous territory. In another example, in 2007, Diné philosophers, social and natural scientists, and traditional knowledge keepers gathered for three days at Diné College to examine the English-language concept of "sustainability" and consider its relevance for tribal environmental policy. The group concluded that no equivalent concept exists in the Diné language. The very idea of sustainability is an Anglo formation, they found, with minimal relevance for meaningfully addressing the most pressing issues facing the Navajo Nation and Diné people, including climate change.[23] Notably, the outcomes of the meeting upturned settler colonial, romanticist tropes of Indigenous Peoples as the quintessential sustainability experts, while also offering a different epistemic basis for overturning loss and ruin discourses: the research group asserted that the core principles of the Diné ethical framework of Diné Foundational Law provided ample guidance for designing projects oriented toward the promotion of *iina,* or "life," meaning "human bloodline" or "(matri)lineage" as well as life force in all beings. Reoriented around this law, projects would not be evaluated based upon a set of scripted sustainability measures per se, but rather, on their ability to enhance *k'e,* or relationality, among humans and our many relatives.[24]

The concern here is not only with moving beyond shortsighted techno-fixes but with dismantling the legal infrastructure established in U.S. federal Indian law in the 1830s, of "domestic dependent nations."[25] The "structures of unsustainability" (Escobar 2019) are thus designed into the landscape but also built into the political order. One cannot address contemporary food deserts in the Navajo Nation by simply growing more squash. Food deserts have been designs of dispossession for over 150 years, beginning with the 1864 scorched earth campaigns to destroy the fruit orchards in Canyon de Chelly on which thousands of Diné families depended, to the subsequent four-year incarceration of Diné people in a military concentration camp, from 1864 to 1868; then there was the 1930s federal decimation of Diné livestock and the midcentury cultivation of dependency on commodity foods like white flour and canned meat; and finally, the federal assimilation policies that targeted Indigenous knowledge came into place.

Methodologies of "Desire"

Indigenous Peoples and territories have long been framed by outsiders as places of despair and injury. So, as Tuck asks, "What are the long-term costs of thinking of [Native peoples] as damaged?" (2009, 415). At a minimum, when scholars emphasize stories of ruin and loss, other ways of being and "desiring" may be foreclosed. Environmental humanities has taken a decisive turn toward the multispecies, nonhuman world in a commendable effort to write against human exceptionalism (Kirksey and Helmreich 2010). While decentering the human importantly opens up conceptual space for more than humans to come to the fore, some approaches smuggle in the troubling assumption that living with persistent loss and ruin in "landscapes of loss" aptly characterizes the existential predicament of contemporary experience (van Dooren 2014). This durable framework of loss is troubling and has, as Tuck suggests, "long-term costs," as it can operate incidentally to erase the persistence of survival and presence, occluding what Gerald Vizenor has termed "survivance"—that is, projects of resilience, endurance, and desire (Vizenor 1999, 2009). Vizenor argues that survivance projects are "renunciations of dominance, tragedy, and victimry" (1999, 3).

Such projects may include wind farms, food trucks, gardens, and other place-based practices important for sustaining land relations in the Navajo Nation and also include the work of Shiprock artist James B. Joe, whose visual work achieves what affect theory writes about. In this painting, *Past, Present, Future* (Figure 3), we see the unmistakable monolith of Shiprock, with a Diné family and their sheep in the foreground, backed by the colorful high rises of a modern city, recognizable as Albuquerque, with its signature hot-air balloon. At first glance, the painting could be read too simply, as a binary of traditional/modern, rural/urban, Indigenous/settler, agrarian/industrial. It could even be read as a story of loss and ruin: the lifeways left behind, destroyed by colonial capitalism. I read this work, following conversations with Joe about this piece from 2019 to 2023, as a visual method of "desire": a reenvisioning of the San Juan River Watershed and all its entangled and transformed relations. These are coexistent, impure, and interconnected—and at the same time, the material basis for Diné self-determination that does not end at the arbitrary reservation border but extends into wider diasporic spaces. "People just drive by them, just see big rocks, but I give them bright color in my paintings to show their immortality, their presence," remarked Joe, as we surveyed a dozen bright images of Shiprock and other angular landmarks he has painted on canvases in his studio, a purple-walled hogan with a 360-degree view of the formations themselves.[26] The changing image of Shiprock, in particular, has been reproduced for years in sepia-toned photographs for tourist brochures and trinkets—but is simultaneously an affective material icon of Diné sovereignty. In his many renditions of it, Joe centers vibrancy and longevity rather than ruin, as a point of departure for understanding Diné landscapes.

Southeast of Shiprock and the San Juan River, the late Alice Gilmore kept a robust vegetable garden and fruit tree orchard at her home, as well as four dozen sheep on her grazing land. She was among the group of elders, mostly women, who established a roadblock in midwinter of 2006 to prevent construction equipment and tribal police cars from accessing the proposed site for a new coal-fired power plant on her family's customary land. The elders'

FIGURE 3. James B. Joe, *Past, Present, Future* (2020), oil on canvas painting.

roadside vigil went viral through the work of her grandson (by clan), a savvy Dartmouth College graduate who seized Facebook's then two-year-old internet presence, broadcasting the story of this winter occupation, led by grandmothers, around the world. One afternoon, Ms. Gilmore took me out to see the remains of her great-grandparents' stone house, the first structure they inhabited following their return to their Diné homeland following their incarceration at Fort Sumner. They were survivors of the military camp, also called Bosque Redondo, or *Hweeldí,* where 12,000 Diné arrived in 1864 but only 9,000 lived to make the "Long Walk" home, four years later. The ruins of this ancestral home, however, were not ruination for Ms. Gilmore, but the evidence of her family's survival, ongoing presence, and desire to rebuild their life in this place. People reclaimed their homeland from 1868 onward, building hogans, corrals, and stone homes; they renewed their families and their flocks so successfully that by the early twentieth century the Diné were once again a robust presence on the Colorado Plateau.[27] This stone house, the wild edibles, and the lambs that arrived every Spring were her points of reference for a meaningful life. These were the things she defended, she explained, when faced with the prospect of a new coal plant and expanded coal mine. Even in this milieu, loss and ruin are inapt frameworks for capturing the Gilmore family's sensibility, though they are acutely aware of historical trauma and contemporary contamination.

Diné territory remains a precious homeland for the Gilmores and approximately 300,000 others (170,000 Diné live on the reservation, with another 120,000 living in the wider, global Diné diaspora). These are irreplaceable places, infused with life by animals, plants, humans, and the stories of those who came before and remain present. To offer an ontological framing of this homeland as wasted, lost, or ruined risks not only devaluing the cultural and political significance of what such places mean but also risks further undermining already contested land claims. All around Navajo Nation, lands are encroached upon by extractive interests. Moreover, defining land and bodies as ruined dangerously extends the possibility of removal, relocation, and termination: three foundational policies of federal Indian law that defined the nineteenth and twentieth centuries and continue to shape the twenty-first (Cheyfitz et al 2011; Cheyfitz 2023).

Then there is the matter of temporality: if loss as people experience it is not only the recent effect of fossil fuel–based late capitalism but rather has been part of the achievement of settler colonial dispossession, and at the same time, if loss is not definitive of Indigenous experience today, attending to grounded practices of presence offers a methodology for the Anthropocene that does not prefigure its analytic framework. Even in zones of longstanding, large-scale energy extraction and growing climate disruption, like the Colorado Plateau, many Diné critical reflections on environmental and social challenges have been nonapocalyptic. Creative, resourceful, and oriented toward recuperating certain knowledge-practices (often related to food, fuel, and family), activists are working to sustain people and wider ecologies despite an uncertain future. This is not a disavowal of the past but a reattunement to work going on in the present. In several recent conversations about local sensibilities of climate change, my Diné friends immediately turn to reflections on the intergenerational trauma of midcentury boarding schools: "loss," in these terms, is measured through federal Indian policies of assimilation and cultural erasure, such that resistance to loss involves both landscape restoration (i.e., river care projects, uranium tailings piles remediation) as well as maintaining commitments to the centrality of the Diné language in collective political life. For instance, in a 2016 referendum, Diné citizens voted to retain the standing legal requirement that their Nation's president be a fluent speaker of Diné language. There is a recognition that at stake are not only natural resources and toxic wastes but also the sociopolitical impacts of other kinds of systematic losses related to colonial violence: knowledge, language, story, and relationality.

Yet when we consider situated engagements with the empirics of risk *and* survivance, stories emerge that complicate the overdetermining conceptual weight of ruination framings. For instance, in 2018, Diné land defenders Kim Smith and Makai Lewis retrofitted a food truck into a mobile restaurant and research office, shown here in Figure 4. They set out to document local understandings of physical and mental health as these have been impacted by emissions from intensive energy infrastructure in the Navajo Nation's northern New Mexico region. They began their research in Shiprock, along the San Juan River, not far northwest from the Gilmore's land. Shiprock is also within a half-hour drive of San Juan Generating Station coal-fired power plant, just off the reservation, near the border town of Farmington; and a few miles southeast of Shiprock, within reservation boundaries, lies the Four Corners Power Plant, owned by Arizona Public Service Company. For half a century, these plants have created jobs and fostered a certain "moral economy" of labor among male coal workers, as Andrew Curley (2018) argues, but the plants have also created environmental and health risks, and entrenched the tribal economy in a late-industrial model of development (Curley 2023). Thousands of natural gas wells mark the land in between. These are undeniably impacted landscapes and ecologies. Smith and Lewis want to know how this feels for people living in the shadow of these plants, even as they are being de-commissioned, and also what kinds of foods, river restoration work, and new infrastructure and forms of sociality might move their communities toward different kinds of futures.

The food truck pursues the urgent need to cultivate food sovereignty in the Navajo Nation, articulated as early as 2014 in a widely circulating white paper by the Diné Policy Institute, as a movement that is simultaneously nutritive, epistemological, and political (DPI 2014). Smith shared with me some of their motivations:

FIGURE 4. Smith and Lewis with food truck, 2019. Photo courtesy of Kim Smith and Makai Lewis.

There was recently a health advisory that went out about harvesting traditional herbs and medicines. They found that the plants are contaminated and advised herbalists not to collect the herbs and medicines. They've found toxins in cattle and sheep. Farmers can't plant due to the contamination in the [San Juan] River. It is unknown what is in the water besides the [Gold King] mine spill toxins. Coal ash is a huge toxin here, but there are no studies on its toxicity or how long the coal ash has been leaching. We are experimenting on putting in plants that detoxify the soil and water. We have also been reintroducing "permaculture" practices like swells and gabions and building hogans, sweat lodges and bread ovens . . . We need a health impact assessment here because there has been no study done so far in the fifty years of the existence of the power plants.[28]

While toxicity from energy development is the impetus for their work, these activists, and others doing similar work in the region, are engaged in practices of care that derive from a long-term commitment to Diné people and Diné territory. So even as they compile data on peoples' understandings of their health, their research is not exclusively "damage-centered," in

Tuck's sense: their food truck collects data to understand health impacts but retains and promotes dignity, with a menu and convivial method that elicits desire and a sense of possibility (to eat well, to live well, to envision and enact alternatives). And even as they speak of their home as compromised by industrial contamination, they speak of its vitality and potential and work to build infrastructure that promises different kinds of sociality (swells and gabions, sweat lodges and bread ovens). This politics of care recognizes the complexities of caretaking and advocacy when the odds are not favorable. Smith and Lewis are well aware of the staggering rates among Diné youth of type 1 and type 2 diabetes and the related obesity, malnutrition, severe depression, and unhealthy behaviors (Dabelea et al. 2009). This compounds the existing structural violence that underpins health disparities and the more recent entanglements with climate change and the COVID-19 pandemic, intensifying exposure (Emerson and Montoya 2021).

Caring, of course, is complicated: as others have argued, Indigenous forms of care often respond to violent forms of care enacted by the state (Stevenson 2014). While the state offers limited redress in forms such as RECA—a bureaucratic measure responding to state-sanctioned irradiation of Diné people, noted above—the food truck offers redress that recognizes the failures of many statist forms of care (including Indian Health Service and a lack of longitudinal data).[29] Physicians working in the Indian Health Service hospitals on the reservation report their own deep frustrations and anxieties, caring for patients with chronic illnesses, whose everyday lives and immediate environments pose so many risks.[30] Food, for Smith and Lewis, and the conversations that the meals allow, are quotidian modes of care that confront the very complex conditions shaping vulnerable lives and landscapes.

Anticolonial Transitions?

Smith and Lewis understand loss and ruin in historically particular terms: they are the effects of colonization on the individual and collective body. They are also the political effects of anthropogenic transformations of "nature" that have been visible for Diné people at least since New Mexico's first commercial oil well went up in the Navajo reservation, near Shiprock, in 1922. Indeed, the notion of ruin is nothing new: early twentieth-century settler-prospectors perceived New Mexico as "desolate country—sand, mesquite, bear grass and jack rabbits" (Wells 2017). This perception of the Southwest as barren and uninhabited by humans—or humans whose bodies matter—extended to wartime nuclear designs at Los Alamos Laboratories, and aboveground bomb testing in nearby Nevada. Yet this perception of a land already in a state of loss that could be sacrificed for the national interest, through large-scale mining and nuclear explosions, of course contained its own contradiction: the subterranean wealth of energy minerals made this landscape attractive and necessary for the growth of industrial capitalism and the Cold War arsenal.

Twenty-first-century calls for "energy transitions" have had varying reception and slippery meanings in the Navajo Nation, given the collision of a hundred-year economic dependency upon oil, coal, and gas extraction with twenty-first-century calls for climate mitigation (Chamberlain 2000; Curley 2023; Powell and Becker 2022; Powell 2017). Transition movements outside of Indian Country trouble Smith, Lewis, and others, who see in these global movements a dangerous lack of awareness about trust land issues and other territorial and historical constraints facing tribes. At the U.S. Social Forum in Atlanta in 2007, Smith was part of an Indigenous caucus that occupied the Civic Center's stage when large environmental groups pushed for a transition agenda, without any mention of colonialism, intergenerational trauma, or Native treaty rights. I witnessed that challenge, and marveled at how, in a city steeped in civil rights history, mainstream environmental movements still failed to see how Indigenous histories and territories might reorient the terms of their own sustainability platforms. "We want to decolonize transition," Smith explained to me; she laughed, humbled by this aspiration, "with our food truck." This remark signals wider efforts across Native North America to restore Indigenous food systems, including salmon restoration in the Pacific Northwest, buffalo and wild rice in the Upper Midwest, and medicinal foods in the Cherokee Nation (Gilio-Whitaker 2019; 80–82; LaDuke 1999; Carroll 2015). This desire—to "decolonize transition"—responds to forms of settler sustainabilities evident at the U.S. Social Forum but also in the green jobs movement and Ed's wind-farm project, in the Navajo Nation. For Smith, transition has been colonized by certain epistemes that seek technological fixes, pursue trajectories of linear time, and seek resolutions grounded in capitalism.

Their Diné health impact assessment is at least a modest measure toward decolonizing research. After a protracted negotiation with the Navajo Nation's Institutional Review Board and Historic Preservation Office, Smith and Lewis were able to obtain a tribal research permit. They successfully argued that their citizen science as nonexperts (neither researcher holds a master's or doctorate) was legitimate, and their ability to reach study participants was in fact enhanced because they are *not* nonlocal, university-based researchers. Keenly aware of the challenges they face, the duo is emboldened by the participation of area residents in their outreach and by their success in edging tribal research policy toward an appreciation of citizen science. Official tribal approval thus at least implicitly recognizes the need for health data such as these, as there has never been a longitudinal study of the health impacts of the extraction-based tribal economy on its rural residents.[31] The duo's grassroots approach to research methodology is not overdetermined by a damage-centered framework: rather, it desires to fill gaps in the data, enliven food knowledge, reconnect people across rural terrain, and track practices already underway to elevate "the hope, the visions, the wisdom of lived lives and communities" (Tuck 2009, 417).

Energy infrastructure risks for human and nonhuman health have intensified in recent years, with climatic shifts impacting high desert communities like the Navajo Nation. The United States Department of Interior's Office of Indian Affairs set a series of "climate change sustainability goals" in response to Barack Obama's Executive Order in 2013, tasking federal agencies to "prepare the United States for the Impacts of Climate Change" (EO 13653). For the Navajo Region, two official reports have been produced: the first is a "Climate Change Vulnerability Assessment for Priority Wildlife Species" by the Navajo Nation Department of Fish and Wildlife, focusing on adaptation planning for threatened plant and animal species (NNDFW 2013). A second report, "Considerations for Climate Change and Variability Adaptation on the Navajo Nation," authored by University of Colorado scholars, is a more legally driven sector and resource-oriented impacts analysis (Nania et al. 2014). Both reports emphasize nonhumans and the risks to habitat connectivity as aridity and drought become the new norm in the American Southwest. Mule deer and other large mammals (black bear, bighorn sheep, and mountain lions) follow rivers as their movement corridors; as invasive plants overtake riparian environments and river levels drop through evaporation, animals experience a "gap" in their corridor (or traveling pathway). Physical and figurative gaps in this riparian corridor are not only of concern for mule deer but also for the humans whose lives depend on contaminated and politically contested waters and the plants and animals that consume those waters—rapidly diminishing in a period of climate change.

Moreover, the capacity to be responsive depends on *self-determination in relation to* these bodies of water, in a wider geography of contested Indigenous water rights settlements, securities, and regulatory politics, related to the Colorado River (Curley 2021; Wilson et al. 2021; Wilson et al. 2022).[32] Indeed, on June 22, 2023, on the day that many of us met in Farmington, New Mexico, for the opening of the Diné Studies Association Conference, the U.S. Supreme Court issued a 5–4 decision rejecting the Navajo Nation's claim that the Treaty of 1868 ensures water rights to the Nation: the Court ruled that the U.S. holds no "affirmative duty" to provide water (21–1484).[33] This was the latest in many blows to the ongoing struggles over competing claims to the Colorado River and its tributaries. This event elevates the visibility of environmental governance in ecologies highly politicized by ongoing land and water claims. The labor underway to assure Diné stewardship and access to water—even as the Colorado is impacted by energy extraction, agricultural overuse, and climate change—is further evidence of resources/relations worth defending and reclaiming.

Conclusion: Life Beyond Ruin

Projects like Emerson's poetry; Joe's paintings; Smith and Lewis's data activism; Singer's proposed wind farm and artwork; and the Gilmore family's flock and garden, among many wider examples, including intergenerational movements for energy transitions (Horseherder 2021; Kutz 2021), enact projects that resist settler designs of deficit. In doing so, these projects question the overdetermining, damage-centered frameworks that entrench narratives of "blasted landscapes" (Tsing 2015, 2017). As shown in the Navajo Nation, despite their irradiated or extractive biographies, *these territories constitute the material foundation of Diné-centered thought and sovereignty and, as such, are nontransferable*. Territorial value thus does *not* lie in the flourishing of new life amid extractivist or climate change–induced ruination but in long-standing existence as a central base of Indigenous political difference and of past, present, and future land relations. Evidenced by artwork, gardens, localized energy projects, citizen science, and challenges to U.S. federal law and regional utilities, revitalization efforts are diverse, open-ended, and contested, but all point back to a commitment to what Kyle Whyte has called "collective continuance" (Whyte 2018). By extension, these projects resist the durable erasure narrative of the inevitable disappearance and dissolution of Native communities, in need of ethnographic salvage. To the contrary, Diné collaborative research reorients us away from salvage, challenging dominant frameworks for historical analysis: on the one hand, reconceptualizing categories of presence and legibility in the landscape across space and time (Thompson 2023; Campbell 2023), and on the other hand, scaling-up analytics of the conjuncture of structural racism and colonialism in health disparities (Emerson and Montoya 2021). Artists, scholars, and activists are responding to the materiality of political dispossession and environmental harm, but do not regard Diné territory—ancestral homelands—as places anchored in or defined by intrinsic loss. Quite the opposite: their nonsecular, material vitality provides an ethical foundation for land-based sovereignty. As one colleague expressed: "The air may be contaminated, the water may be contaminated . . . and still we sprinkle water on the ground in the morning, making offerings to the rainmaker."[34] And their very material *political* presence, which indeed threatens the settler state—always positioned to retaliate—and inclusive of the everyday and affective practices of sovereignty (Cattelino 2023; Thomas and Masco 2023).

Ed Singer desires yet another design for rethinking ruin: he aspires to turn the uranium-contaminated brownfields around Cameron into solar farms under local control. The 2019 closure of the Navajo Generating Station made a 500-megawatt (MW) transmission line available to his home chapter, running from Page to Phoenix. The Navajo Nation Council has requested proposals for 300 MW (the tribe can only use 200 MW at this time) and he wants to use the land authority of local governance and Diné sovereignty to claim the infrastructure of the existing energy corridor around Cameron, to build something new, where electricity is generated locally and consumed locally, sending only excess power down the line. Solar farms could support a local hub for internet server technology, Singer surmises, transforming Cameron into a provider and agentive center of expertise, for Silicon Valley, and beyond. But the central difference this time is that "the control of it would stay in the community. It would be owned by the people."[35] This desire for sovereignty-based environmental restoration and localization is a response to paternalistic forms of care that throughout the last two centuries have dispossessed Diné people of land, life, and knowledge. It is also a response to settler and capitalist logics that have dominated development in the Navajo Nation, imposing sustainabilities that deploy green technologies to mask colonial designs of dispossession. Whether or not state-of-the-art cloud technology in Cameron will work remains to be seen. Singer, meanwhile, continues to make paintings that critically examine stories of ruin and invite imagination and possibility.

It may be difficult for academics to resist our proclivities to fetishize loss, given the urgencies of climate change and environmental injustice. The sixth mass extinction, habitat destruction, and the violent displacement of millions of humans from rapidly changing environments constitute planetary vulnerability in an almost unthinkable manner. But is this the only—or the most intellectually and politically salient—way to think of and with the world in these times? Are these not, in many ways, settler anxieties and projected futurities about the "end of the world" as we know it? The historical tendency for the scholarship "of" or "about" (but perhaps not "with") Indigenous Peoples, as Vine Deloria Jr. made clear decades ago, has tended to treat Indigenous lifeworlds as salvage projects to bolster settler claims of inheriting the past and the future (Deloria 1969). This "pure research" approach of the time, as Deloria aptly observed, always already approached the "Native" as in the process of biophysical disappearance or assimilation, while at the same time ignoring the urgent exigencies of ongoing colonialism—such as the political disappearance under termination (1969, 81).

Overdeterminations of ruin tend toward a pathologizing of Native life, serving the ongoing processes of empire and rendering homelands as wastelands instead of vibrant landscapes of political possibility. If we shift both our analytics and our concrete capacities for building and tracking collective, collaborative existence, we might better attune our senses to the registers of life where "the trouble" is not an elective positionality but constitutive of historically produced conditions and ongoing processes of settler-colonial relations. If we acknowledge the vital pressure points where important research for redress remains to be done to fully demonstrate cumulative impacts, *and yet* the desire-oriented projects of place-based movements shape quotidian experiences of resistance, we might reposition scholarship toward ongoing projects of self-determination and vitality. How, then, might our conceptual endeavors and methodologies engage in reconnecting and in "rebuilding the context" (L. Simpson 2014), toward restorative and transformative potentials, rather than definitional injury?

DANA E. POWELL (U.S. citizen/white) is an environmental anthropologist working in North America and Taiwan on questions of energy extraction, Indigenous sovereignty, and environmental governance. Powell's first book, *Landscapes of Power: Politics of Energy in the Navajo Nation* (Duke Press, 2018), traces a controversial coal plant slated for Diné lands and the resulting re-articulations of environmentalism and justice. Her current transnational project partners with colleagues in Navajo Nation, eastern North Carolina, and Taiwan to critically examine the lived effects of sustainability and transition projects on Indigenous self-determination, recognition, and wellbeing, within statist projects of social inclusion. Powell has taught at Appalachian State University's Department of Anthropology; Cornell University's Society for the Humanities; National DongHwa University's College of Indigenous Studies; and at Taipei Medical University, where she is currently Associate Professor in the Graduate Institute of Humanities in Medicine. Powell can be contacted at powellde@tmu.edu.tw and danapowell608@gmail.com.

References

Begaye, Enei. 2005. "The Black Mesa Controversy." *Cultural Survival.* 29, no. 5.
Belin, Esther G., Jeff Berglund, Connie A. Jacobs, and Anthony K. Webster. 2021. *The Diné Reader: An Anthology of Navajo Literature.* Tucson: University of Arizona Press.
Ben-zvi, Yael. 2018. *Native Land Talk: Indigenous and Arrivant Rights Theories.* Hanover, N.H.: Dartmouth College Press.

Blackhawk, Ned. 1997. "Julian Steward and the Politics of Representation: A Critique of Anthropologist Julian Steward's Ethnographic Portrayals of the American Indians of the Great Basin." *American Indian Culture and Research Journal* 21, no. 2: 61–81.

Boyer, Dominic. 2019. *Energopolitics*. Durham, N.C.: Duke University Press.

Bruchac, Margaret. 2014. "My Sisters Will Not Speak: Boas, Hunt, and the Ethnographic Silencing of First Nations Women." *Curator: The Museum Journal* 57, no. 2: 153. 171.

Brugge, Doug, and Rob Goble. 2002. "The History of Uranium Mining and the Navajo People." *American Journal of Public Health* 92, no. 9: 1410–19.

Campbell, Wade. 2023. "Reconsidering the 'Pueblito' Phenomenon: Developing a Diné Analysis." Paper presented at the 23rd Diné Studies Association Conference, Farmington, New Mexico, June 24.

Carroll, Clint. 2015. *Roots of Our Renewal: Ethnobotany and Cherokee Environmental Governance*. Minneapolis: University of Minnesota Press.

Cattelino, Jessica. 2023. "Sovereign Interdependencies." In *Sovereignty Unhinged*, edited by Deborah A. Thomas and Joseph Masco, 139–61. Durham, N.C.: Duke University Press.

Cavanagh, Connor Joseph, and Tor Arve Benjaminsen. 2017. "Political Ecology, Variegated Green Economies, and the Foreclosure of Alternative Sustainabilities." *Journal of Political Ecology* 24, no. 1: 200–16. https://doi.org/10.2458/v24i1.20800

Chamberlain, Kathleen P. 2000. *Under Sacred Ground: A History of Navajo Oil, 1922–1982*. Albuquerque: University of New Mexico Press.

Cheyfitz, Eric, N. Bruce Duthu, and Shari M. Huhndorf, eds. 2010. "Sovereignty, Indigeneity, and the Law." *South Atlantic Quarterly* 110, no. 2.

Cheyfitz, Eric. 2023. *The Colonial Construction of Indian Country: Native American Literatures and Federal Indian Law*. Minneapolis: University of Minnesota Press.

Chief, Karletta, Janick F. Artiola, Sarah T. Wilkinson, Paloma Beamer, and Raina M. Meier. 2016. *Understanding the Gold King Mine Spill*. Tucson: University of Arizona Superfund Research Program.

Clausen, Becky, Teresa Montoya, Karletta Chief, Steven Chischilly, Janene Yazzie, Jack Turner, Lisa Marie Jacobs, and Ashley Merchant. 2021. "The Social Impacts of the Gold King Mine Spill to Watershed Communities." In *Gold Metal Waters: The Animas River and the Gold King Mine Spill of 2015*, edited by Peter McCormick and Brad Walters, 190–217. Boulder: University Press of Colorado.

Coulthard, Glen. 2014. *Red Skin, White Masks: Rejecting the Colonial Politics of Recognition*. Minneapolis: University of Minnesota Press.

Crate, Susan A. 2008. "Gone the Bull of Winter? Grappling with the Cultural Implications of and Anthropology's Role(s) in Global Climate Change." *Current Anthropology* 49, no. 4: 569–95.

Curley, Andrew. 2018. "A Failed Green Future: Navajo Green Jobs and Energy 'Transition' in the Navajo Nation." *Geoforum* 88: 57–65.

———. 2019. "*T'áá hwó ají t'éego* and the Moral Economy of Navajo Coal Workers." *Annals of the American Association of Geographers* 109, no. 1: 71–86.

———. 2021. "Unsettling Indian Water Settlements: The Little Colorado River, the San Juan River, and Colonial Enclosures". *Antipode* 53, no. 3: 705–23.

———. 2023. *Carbon Sovereignty: Coal, Development, and Energy Transition in the Navajo Nation.* Tucson: University of Arizona Press.

Dabelea, Dana, Joquetta DeGroat, Carmelita Sorrelman, Martia Glass, Christopher A. Percy, Charlene Avery, Diana Hu, Ralph B. D'Agostino Jr., Jennifer Beyer, Giuseppina Imperatore, Lisa Testaverde, Georgeanna Klingensmith, and Richard F. Hamman. 2009. "Diabetes in Navajo Youth." *Diabetes Care* 32, no. 2: S141–S47.

Dawson, Susan E. 1992. "Navajo Uranium Workers and the Effects of Occupational Illnesses: A Case Study." *Human Organization* 51, no. 4: 389–97.

Deloria, Vine Jr. 1969. *Custer Died for Your Sins: An Indian Manifesto.* Norman: University of Oklahoma Press.

Denetdale, Jennifer. 2006. "Chairmen, Presidents, and Princesses: The Navajo Nation, Gender, and the Politics of Tradition." Wicazo Sa Review 21: 9–28.

———. 2016. "'No Explanation, No Resolution, and No Answers': Border Town Violence and Navajo Resistance to Settler Colonialism." *Wicazo Sa Review.* 31, no. 1: 111–31.

———. 2022. "'Building the Perfect Human to Invade': Dikos Ntsaaígíí-19 (COVID-19) from Border Towns to the Navajo Nation." In *Indian Cities: Histories of Indigenous Urbanization*, edited by Kent Blansett, Cathleen D. Cahill, and Andrew Needham, 290–309. Norman: University of Oklahoma Press.

Dennison, Jean. 2012. *Colonial Entanglement: Constituting a Twenty-First Century Osage Nation.* Chapel Hill: University of North Carolina Press.

———. 2014. "The Logic of Recognition: Debating Osage Nation Citizenship in the 21st Century." *American Indian Quarterly* 38, no. 1: 1–35.

Dillon, Grace, ed. 2012. *Walking the Clouds: An Anthology of Indigenous Science Fiction.* Tucson: University of Arizona Press.

Diné Policy Institute (DPI). 2014. *Diné Food Sovereignty: A Report on the Navajo Nation Food System and the Case to Rebuild a Self-Sufficient Food System for the Diné People.* Tsaile, AZ: Diné Policy Institute. https://www.dinecollege.edu/wp-content/uploads/2018/04/dpi-food-sovereignty-report.pdf.

Emanuel, Ryan E., and David E. Wilkins. 2020. "Breaching Barriers: The Fight for Indigenous Participation in Water Governance." *Water* 12, no. 8: 2113.

Emerson, Marc A., and Teresa Montoya. 2021. "Confronting Legacies of Structural Racism and Settler Colonialism to Understand COVID-19 Impacts on the Navajo Nation." *American Journal of Public Health* 111, no. 8: 1465–69.

Escobar, Arturo. 2008. *Territories of Difference: Place, Movement, Life, Redes.* Durham, N.C.: Duke University Press.

———. 2019. "Habitability and Design: Radical Interdependence and the Reearthing of Cities." *Geoforum* 101: 132–40.

Estes, Nick. 2020. "The Empire of All Maladies: Colonial Contagion and Indigenous Resistance." *The Baffler* 52. https://thebaffler.com/salvos/the-empire-of-all-maladies-estes.

Fennell, Catherine. 2018. "Beyond the Trace." *Postcolonial Studies* 21, no. 4: 520–24.

Fixico, Donald Lee. 2012. *The Invasion of Indian Country in the Twentieth Century: American Capitalism and Tribal Natural Resources, Second Edition.* Boulder: University Press of Colorado.

Ford, Lisa. 2010. *Settler Sovereignty: Jurisdiction and Indigenous People in America and Australia 1788–1836.* Cambridge, MA: Harvard University Press.

Fortun, Kim. 2012. "Ethnography in Late Industrialism." *Cultural Anthropology* 27, no. 3: 446–64.

Foucault, Michel. 1975. *Discipline and Punish.* Pantheon: New York.

Gilio-Whitaker, Dina. 2019. *As Long as Grass Grows: The Indigenous Fight for Environmental Justice, from Colonization to Standing Rock.* New York: Penguin/Random House.

Gutierrez, Grant, Dana E. Powell, and T. L. Pendergrast. 2021. "The Double-Force of Vulnerability: Ethnography and Environmental Justice." *Environment & Society: Advances in Research* 12, no. 1: 66–86.

Hall, Laurie, Sonja Horoshko, Renee Podunovich, and Michael Thompson, eds. 2021. *WET: An Anthology of Water Poems and Prose from the High Desert and Mountains of the Four Corners Region.* Cortez, CO: Sharehouse Press.

Haraway, Donna. 2016. *Staying with the Trouble.* Durham, N.C.: Duke University Press.

Hatfield, D. J. W. 2020. "Good Dances Make Good Guests: Dance, Animation, and Sovereign Assertion in 'Amis Country, Taiwan." *Anthropologica* 62, no. 2: 337–52.

Horseherder, Nicole. 2021. "The Intersection of Climate Change, the Environment, and Race: An Intergenerational Dialogue." *My Life, My Stories.* Online webinar. April 21. https://www.youtube.com/watch?v=3d-MCRyYUwE.

Howe, Cymene. 2019. *Ecologics.* Durham, N.C.: Duke University Press.

Johnston, Barbara Rose, Susan Dawson, and Gary Madsen. 2010. "Uranium Mining and Milling: Navajo Experiences in the American Southwest." In *Indians & Energy: Exploitation and Opportunity.* Edited by Sherry Smith and Brian Frehner. Sante Fe: SAR Press.

Kamper, David, Doug Brugge, Timothy Benally, and Esther Yazzie-Lewis. 2008. The Navajo People and Uranium Mining. *The Western Historical Quarterly* 39: 376.

Kelley, Klara, and Harris Francis. 2019. "Diné Clans and Climate Change: A Historical Lesson for Land Use Today." *American Indian Culture and Research Journal* 43, no. 1: 59–82.

Khatchadourian, Lori. 2022. "Life Extempore: Trials of Ruination in the Twilight Zone of Soviet Industry." *Cultural Anthropology* 37, no. 2: 317–48.

Kirksey, S. Eben, and Stefan Helmreich. 2010. "The Emergence of a Multispecies Anthropology." *Cultural Anthropology* 25, no. 4: 545–76.

Kuan, Da-Wei. 2021. "Indigenous Traditional Territory and Decolonisation of the Settler State: The Taiwan Experience." In *Taiwan's Contemporary Indigenous Peoples*, edited by Chia-Yuan Huang, Daniel Davies, and Dafydd Fell, 184–205. New York: Routledge.

Kuletz, Valerie L. 1998. *The Tainted Desert: Environmental and Social Ruin in the American West.* New York: Routledge.

Kutz, Jessica. 2021. "The Fight for an Equitable Energy Economy for the Navajo Nation." *High Country News*, February 1. https://www.hcn.org/issues/53.2/south-coal-the-fight-for-an-equitable-energy-economy-for-the-navajo-nation.

LaDuke, Winona. 1999. *All Our Relations: Native Struggles for Land and Life.* Cambridge, MA: South End Press.

Lambert, Valerie. 2022. *Native Agency: Indians in the Bureau of Indian Affairs.* Minneapolis: University of Minnesota Press.

Latour, Bruno. 2017. *Facing Gaia: Eight Lectures on the New Climatic Regime.* Medford, MA: Polity Press.

Liboiron, Max. 2021. *Pollution is Colonialism.* Durham, N.C.: Duke University Press.

Maldonado, Julie K. 2019. *Seeking Justice in an Energy Sacrifice Zone.* London: Routledge.

Masco, Joseph. *The Nuclear Borderlands: The Manhattan Project in Post—Cold War New Mexico.* Princeton, N.J.: Princeton University Press, 2006.

Masco, Joseph. 2010. "Bad Weather: On Planetary Crisis." *Social Studies of Science* 40, no. 1: 7—40. https://doi.org/10.4324/9780203077856-15.

Masco, Joseph. 2017. "The Crisis in Crisis." *Current Anthropology* 58, no. 15: 65—76.

Marino, Elizabeth. 2015. *Fierce Climate, Sacred Ground.* Fairbanks: University of Alaska Press.

McDermott, Brian. 2015. *We Are All Related Here.* Swarthmore, PA: EmpathyWorks Films.

Montoya, Teresa. 2017. "Yellow Water: Rupture and Return One Year after the Gold King Mine Spill." *Anthropology Now* 9, no. 3: 91—115.

Montoya, Teresa. 2022. "Stockpile: From Nuclear Colonialism to "Clean" Energy Futures." Theorizing the Contemporary, *Fieldsights,* January 25. https://culanth.org/fieldsights/stockpile-from-nuclear-colonialism-to-clean-energy-futures

Mookerjea, Sourayen. 2019. "Renewable Energy Transition under Multiple Colonialisms: Passive Revolution, Fascism Redux and Utopian Praxes." *Cultural Studies* 33, no. 3: 570—93. https://doi.org/10.1080/09502386.2019.1585464.

Murphy, Michelle. 2017. "Alterlife and Decolonial Chemical Relations." *Cultural Anthropology* 32, no. 4: 494—503.

Nania, Julia, Karen Cozzetto, Nicole Gillett, Sabre Druen, Anne Mariah Tapp, Michael Eitner, and Beth Baldwin. 2014. *Considerations for Climate Change and Variability Adaptation on the Navajo Nation.* Boulder, CO: Getches-Wilkinson Center for Natural Resources, Energy, and the Environment, University of Colorado Law School.

Navajo Nation Department of Fish & Wildlife (NNDFW). 2013. *Climate Change Vulnerability Assessment for Priority Wildlife Species.* Washington, D.C.: The H. John Heinz III Center for Science, Economics and the Environment.

Needham, Todd Andrew. 2014. *Power Lines: Phoenix and the Making of the Modern Southwest.* Princeton, N.J.: Princeton University Press.

Normann, Susanne. 2021. "Green Colonialism in the Nordic Context: Exploring Southern Saami Representations of Wind Energy Development. *Journal of Community Psychology* 49: 77—94.

Powell, Dana E. 2015. "'*The Rainbow Is Our Sovereignty*': Rethinking the Politics of Energy on the Navajo Nation." *Journal of Political Ecology* 22: 53–78.

———. 2017. "Toward Transition? Challenging Extractivism and the Politics of the Inevitable in the Navajo Nation." In *ExtrACTION: Impacts, Responses, and Alternative Futures*, edited by Kirk Jalbert, Anna Willow, David Casagrande, Stephanie Paladino, and Jeanne Simonelli, 211–26. Walnut Creek, CA: Left Coast Press/Routledge.

———. 2018. *Landscapes of Power: Politics of Energy in the Navajo Nation*. Durham, N.C.: Duke University Press, 2018.

Powell, Dana E., and Bidtah Becker. "Situating Energy Justice: Storytelling Risk and Resilience in the Navajo Nation." In *Energy Democracies for Sustainable Futures*, edited by Martin Pasqualetti and Majia Nadesan, 215–24. London: Elsevier, 2022.

Powell, Dana E., and Andrew Curley. 2009. "*K'e, Hozhó,* and Non-Governmental Politics on the Navajo Nation: Ontologies of Difference Manifest in Environmental Activism." *World Anthropologies Network* 4: 109–38.

Rappaport, Roy. 1968. *Pigs for the Ancestors: Ritual in the Ecology of a New Guinea People.* New Haven, CT: Yale University Press.

Redfield, Peter. 2005. "Doctors, Borders, and Life in Crisis." *Cultural Anthropology* 20, no. 3: 328–61.

Redsteer, Margaret Hiza. 2011. *Monitoring and Analysis of Sand Dune Movement and Growth on the Navajo Nation, Southwestern U.S.* Washington, D.C.: USGS.

Redsteer, Margaret Hiza, Bemis, Kirk, Chief, Karletta, Gautam, Mahesh, Middleton, Beth Rose, and Tsosie, Rebecca. 2013. "Unique Challenges Facing Southwestern Tribes." In *Assessment of Climate Change in the Southwest United States: A Report Prepared for the National Climate Assessment*, edited by G. Garfin, A. Jardine, R. Merideth, M. Black, and S. LeRoy, 385–404. Washington, D.C.: Island Press.

Sedgwick, Eve Kosofsky. 2003. *Touching Feeling: Affect, Pedagogy, Performativity.* Durham, N.C.: Duke University Press.

Sherry, John W. 2002. *Land, Wind, and Hard Words: A Story of Navajo Activism.* Albuquerque: University of New Mexico Press.

Simpson, Leanne Betasamosake. 2014. "Land as Pedagogy: Nishnaabeg Intelligence and Rebellious Transformation." *Decolonization: Indigeneity, Education & Society* 3, no. 3: 1–25.

Simpson, Audra. 2014. *Mohawk Interruptus: Political Life Across the Borders of Settler States.* Durham, N.C.: Duke University Press.

Smith, Linda Tuhiwai. 1999. *Decolonizing Methodologies: Research and Indigenous Peoples.* London: Zed Books.

Smith, Paul Chaat. 2009. *Everything You Know about Indians Is Wrong.* Minneapolis: University of Minnesota Press.

Starn, Orin. 2004. *Ishi's Brain: In Search of America's Last "Wild" Indian.* New York: W.W. Norton.

———. 2011. "Here Come the Anthros (Again): The Strange Marriage of Anthropology and Native America." *Cultural Anthropology* 26, no. 2: 179–204.

Stengers, Isabelle. 2015. *In Catastrophic Times: Resisting the Coming Barbarism.* London: Open Humanities Press.

Stevenson, Lisa. 2014. *Life Beside Itself: Imagining Care in the Canadian Arctic.* Berkeley: University of California Press.

Stewart, Kathleen. 2010. "Atmospheric Attunements." *Rubric* 1: 2–14.

Stoler, Laura Ann, ed. 2013. *Imperial Debris: On Ruins and Ruination.* Durham, N.C.: Duke University Press.

———. 2016. *Duress: Imperial Durabilities in Our Times.* Durham, N.C.: Duke University Press.

Thomas, Deborah A., and Joseph Masco, eds. 2023. *Sovereignty Unhinged.* Durham, N.C.: Duke University Press.

Thompson, Kerry. 2023. "*Hooghan* and Hogan: Archaeological Categories and Non-Diné Misunderstandings of Place." Paper presented at the 23rd Diné Studies Association Conference, Farmington, New Mexico, June 24.

Todd, Zoe. 2017. "Fish, Kin, and Hope: Tending to Water Violations in *amiskwaciwâskahikan* and Treaty Six Territory." *Afterall* 43: 102–7.

Tsing, Anna L. 2015. *The Mushroom at the End of the World.* Princeton, N.J.: Princeton University Press.

Tsing, Anna Lowenhaupt, Nils Bubandt, Elaine Gan, and Heather Anne Swanson, eds. 2017. *Arts of Living on a Damaged Planet: Ghosts and Monsters of the Anthropocene.* Minneapolis: University of Minnesota Press.

Tsosie, Rebecca. 2007. "How the Land Was Taken: The Legacy of the Lewis and Clark Expedition for Native Nations." In *American Indian Nations: Yesterday, Today, and Tomorrow,* edited by George Horse Capture, Duane Champagne, and Chandler C. Jackson, 240–79. Lanham, MD: Altamira Press.

Tuck, Eve. 2009. "Suspending Damage: A Letter to Communities." *Harvard Educational Review* 79, no. 3: 409–27.

Tuck, Eve, and K. Wayne Yang. 2012. "Decolonization is Not a Metaphor." *Decolonization: Indigeneity, Education & Society* 1, no. 1: 1–40.

———. 2013. "R-Words: Refusing Research." In *Humanizing Research: Decolonizing Qualitative Inquiry with Youth and Communities,* edited by Django Paris and Maisha T. Winn, 223–48. Thousand Oaks, CA: SAGE.

Van Dooren, Thom. 2014. *Flight Ways: Life and Loss at the Edge of Extinction.* New York: Columbia University Press.

Vizenor, Gerald. 1999. *Manifest Manners: Narratives on Post-Indian Survivance.* Lincoln: University of Nebraska Press.

Vizenor, Gerald. 2009. *Survivance: Narratives of Native Presence.* Lincoln: University of Nebraska Press.

Voyles, Traci Brynne. 2015. *Wastelanding: Legacies of Uranium Mining in Navajo Country.* Minneapolis: University of Minnesota Press.

Weisiger, Marsha. 2009. *Dreaming of Sheep in Navajo Country.* Seattle: University of Washington Press.

Wells, Bruce. 2017. "Making Hole—New Mexico Oil Discoveries." *Greeley Tribune,* July 2. https://www.greeleytribune.com/news/making-hole-new-mexico-oil-discoveries/.

Whyte, Kyle Powys. 2017. "Indigenous Climate Change Studies: Indigenizing

Futures, Decolonizing the Anthropocene." *English Language Notes.* 55, no. 1–2: 153–62.

———. 2018. "Critical Investigations of Resilience: A Brief Introduction to Indigenous Environmental Studies & Sciences." *Daedalus* 147, no. 2: 136–47.

———. 2021. "Time as Kinship," in *The Cambridge Companion to Environmental Humanities*, edited by Jeffrey Cohen and Stephanie Foote, 39–55. Cambridge: Cambridge University Press.

Wilson, Nicole J., Teresa Montoya, Yanna Lambrinidou, Leila M. Harris, Benjamin J. Pauli, Deborah McGregor, Robert J. Patrick, Silvia Gonzalez, Gregory Pierce, and Amber Wutich. 2022. "From "Trust" to "Trustworthiness": Retheorizing Dynamics of Trust, Distrust, and Water Security in North America." *Environment and Planning E: Nature and Space* 6, no. 1: 1–27.

Wilson, Nicole J., Teresa Montoya, Rachel Arseneault, and Andrew Curley. 2021. "Governing Water Insecurity: Navigating Indigenous Water Rights and Regulatory Politics in Settler Colonial States." *Water International* 46, no. 6: 783–801.

Witter, Rebecca, and Dana E. Powell. 2022. "Phantoms Within and Beyond the Frame: Stirrings of Justice Amidst Specters of Rural Capitalism." *Engagement: A Blog Published by the Anthropology & Environment Society.* January 18. https://aesengagement.wordpress.com/2022/01/18/phantoms-within-and-beyond-the-frame-stirrings-of-justice-amidst-specters-of-rural-capitalism/

Yazzie, Melanie K. 2014. "Narrating Ordinary Power: *Hózhǫ́ǫ́ji,* Violence, and Critical Diné Studies." In *Diné Perspectives: Revitalizing and Reclaiming Navajo Thought*, edited by Lloyd L. Lee, 83–99. Tucson: University of Arizona Press.

———. 2018. "Decolonizing Development in Diné Bikeyah: Resource Extraction, Anti-Capitalism, and Relational Futures." *Environment and Society: Advances in Research* 9, no. 1: 25–39.

Yazzie, Janene, with Kimberly White. 2020. *The Planetary Press.* Podcast. October 28. https://www.theplanetarypress.com/2020/10/janene-yazzie-common-home-conversations-beyond-un75/.

Notes

1. Gloria Emerson's poem is reprinted from *The Diné Reader: An Anthology of Navajo Literature,* ed. Esther G. Belin et al. (Tucson: University of Arizona Press, 2021), 51.

2. I first met Gloria Emerson in 2007, when I began to drop into the coffee shop/bookstore/art gallery Awhee' Gowhee' that she ran in Shiprock. From 2007 to 2023, we have engaged in several visual and literary projects together.

3. Interview with Gloria Emerson, September 18, 2019. These reflections draw upon interviews and discussions over many years but especially during visits and interviews at Emerson's home in September 2019 and June 2023 and in email discussions we had related to her and my own chapters. Some of these discussions formed a dialogue in Hall et al. 2021.

4. All formal interviews are noted and acknowledged in the endnotes of this text; inspirations and insights from colleagues are likewise cited as appropriate. All research in the Navajo Nation was conducted with a Class C permit for ethnographic research issued by the Nation's Historic Preservation Department (with chapter resolutions from Blue Gap/Tachee' Chapter). Interviews with individuals named (and aliased) in this essay range from 2018 to 2023, primarily, and are indicated throughout.

5. I am grateful to Judith Farquhar for our 2021–2022 written exchange, which has helped me better articulate this need for deeper reflection on post-empiricist forms of writing.

6. I am especially grateful to Rebecca Witter, my close colleague and research partner at Appalachian State (and beyond), for our ongoing conversations about environmental harm from 2018 to present, via our partnership in the co-directorship of the Eastern N.C. Environmental Justice Co-Lab, pushing me to sharpen my own practice of Max Liboiron's method-as-ethic orientation. Our discussions, collaboration, and cowriting in recent years on the eastern N.C. environmental justice project feeds my analysis immeasurably (see Witter and Powell 2022; Powell et al. forthcoming).

7. I am grateful to one of the anonymous reviewers of this essay, who generatively pushed me on the idea of "colonial politics of scale" and its visibility in how activists (like Ed, and others) are responding to their lands as sacrificial zones.

8. Ed Singer, interview with the author, January 27, 2020.

9. Ed Singer, interview with the author, January 27, 2020.

10. Percy Deal, public statement at The People's Convention gathering, Dilkon Fairgrounds, June 1, 2018.

11. There is a vast literature in environmental justice work that does important work in detailing the damage done in specific communities that bear the weight of disproportionate and cumulative impacts of the siting of hazardous industrial wastes and other forms of environmental harm, expansively defined. Many of these works are reviewed by Gutierrez et al. 2021.

12. I am indebted to Cassie Fennell for this insight.

13. For more resources in this rich and growing field, see https://discardstudies.com/2017/07/10/bibliography-on-critical-approaches-to-toxics-and-toxicity/.

14. I am grateful to the late Diane Nelson for generatively linking the idea of riparian worldings with political ecology (2019 AAA Panel, Vancouver) both in the context of Indigenous Guatemala and transnationally, for those who trace the projects of environmental defense in riverine territories. Nelson's imprint remains vital.

15. Tulley, personal communication.

16. See Ben-Zvi (2018) on the notion of futurity in settler colonial contexts.

17. The term "barbaric," as deployed by Stengers, is unmoored from its roots in ethnological and colonial knowledge regimes built on Indigenous Peoples worldwide.

18. Sedgwick is writing about queer experience and psychoanalysis in this essay, but their analytic of "paranoid" versus "reparative" readings supports

the turn toward desire that Tuck calls for, as ways of (ethnographically) tracking what I see as the significance of *life beyond ruin*.

19. That there are not only different discourses and projects of "sustainability," but hegemony of some over others, is reminiscent of Lisa Ford's analysis (2010) of "settler sovereignties" and how these came into conflict with Indigenous sovereignties in the Americas and Australia.

20. In a collaborative project in which I am involved with other university-based as well as community-based researchers, in Lumbee and African American lands in rural eastern North Carolina, wood pellet biomass and factory-farmed methane biogas capture, cast as "bioenergy," only entrench existing infrastructures of social and economic inequality, environmental racism, and estrangement from territory (Powell et al., forthcoming).

21. The idea of "alternative sustainabilities" has been offered as a way out of unsustainability by some political ecology scholars (see Cavanagh and Benjaminsen 2017), but the alterity of this idea still fails to reckon with the legal and historical imperatives of Indigenous political difference.

22. "Greening" capitalism is settler sustainability par excellence, and by now, feels easy to detect—even when detection is painful, as Curley notes in his article (Curley 2019).

23. Diné Policy Institute 2007 Conference on Sustainability, Diné College, Tsaile, Arizona.

24. Diné Policy Institute 2007 Conference on Sustainability, Diné College, Tsaile, Arizona.

25. This is a reference to Chief Justice John Marshall's rulings in the Marshall Trilogy cases, which establish Native Nations as "domestic dependents" under federal law (Johnson v. M'Intosh, 21 U.S. 543 [1823]; Cherokee Nation v. Georgia, 30 U.S. 1 [1831]; and Worcester v. Georgia, 31 U.S. 515 [1832]). See also Rebecca Tsosie (2007) for a rethinking of the calculated dispossession of Indigenous lands that was part of this early nineteenth-century period.

26. James B. Joe, interview with the author, June 26, 2023.

27. This early twentieth-century flourishing of animal and human life, however, came to be read by federal agents as a threat to soil conservation and led to the infamous "livestock reduction" period (1933–1946) that decimated herds and a subsistence livelihood, forcing many Diné people into a new wage-earning economy. This remains a poignant and painful loss for Diné people today. See Weisiger, *Dreaming of Sheep,* for a full history of livestock reduction and the cultural significance of sheep for Diné people.

28. Kimberly Smith, interview with the author, June 15, 2019.

29. I am grateful to Tomo Sugimoto for helping me see this dialectic of care more clearly.

30. Interview with Indian Health Service physicians and nurses, by the author, October 2008.

31. Though there has been extensive research in epidemiology and environmental harm assessments done by researchers at the Southwest Research and Information Center in Albuquerque, N.M. See http://www.sric.org.

32. See Andrew Curley, "Unsettling Indian Water Settlements."

33. June 22, 2023, U.S. Supreme Court Ruling 21–1484 Arizona vs. Navajo Nation: https://www.supremecourt.gov/opinions/22pdf/21-1484_aplc.pdf.

34. Earl Tulley, interview with the author, May 28, 2021.

35. Ed Singer, interview with the author, January 27, 2020.

REVIEWS

HŌKŪLANI K. AIKAU

Cooling the Tropics: Ice, Indigeneity, and Hawaiian Refreshment
by Hiʻilei Julia Kawehipuaakahaopulani Hobart
Duke University Press, 2022

IT ISN'T VERY OFTEN that a book has the immediate effect of shifting my perspective on everyday life. Hiʻilei Hobart's *Cooling the Tropics: Ice, Indigeneity, and Hawaiian Refreshment* did just that. Her attention to the thermo-politics of coldness, refrigeration, and ice had me hyperaware of how ubiquitous these sensory experiences, technologies, and consumer products are in my everyday life—from my family's dependence on the refrigerator to the life-sustaining necessity of air conditioning in this time of extreme heat. Hobart describes how cooling and freezing technologies emerged and how they have become so normalized and naturalized in Hawaiʻi that they are almost invisible. She shows the reader how "the normative thermal relationships between bodies and environments have developed as a function of American imperial power, arguing that they continue to operate today as embodied expressions of ongoing settler colonialism" (2). While the project spans from nineteenth to twenty-first-century Hawaiʻi, Hobart's attention to the colonial, racial, and gendered dynamics of "thermal colonialism and settler refreshment" makes this book relevant beyond the context of its central case study. Hobart provides richly nuanced readings of multiple texts and archives that include Hawaiian moʻolelo (stories/histories), business ledgers, shipping logs, advertising, as well as commodities such as ice, ice cream, refrigerators, and shave ice. She writes, "Tracing ice and the cold offers a sensorial through line that connects power to pleasure as it traverses the racial and economic terrains of these multiple configurations" (9).

Hobart opens and closes the book on Mauna a Wākea to stress that her project is not singularly about the politics of ice. Rather, in juxtaposing the ontological differences between Kanaka Moali notions of temperature, especially the cold and snow, and the value of the mountain for Western scientific exploration of space, she masterfully demonstrates how notions of temperature are inextricably linked to race, colonialism, dispossession, and extraction. In chapter 1, Hobart contrasts the sacredness of Mauna a Wākea for Kanaka Maoli with the mountain's value for Western science and astronomy. In opening the book with this long-standing controversy, Hobart amplifies the ways in which temperature, its regulation, manufacturing, ideologies, and discourses are part of a much larger project of sustaining settler colonialism.

The three middle chapters trace the history of ice in Hawai'i from its first introduction and decline in the 1850s (ch. 2), to the revival of ice in the islands as refrigeration technology improved between the 1860s and 1880s (ch. 3), to the role of shave ice in manufacturing touristic imaginaries in the early twentieth century (ch. 4). Written as a chronological narrative, each chapter begins by setting the political and social context before moving on to explain how ice, ice cream, shave ice, and cold temperature offer insights into the social and political milieu of Hawai'i. As Hobart explains, while ice, as a commodity, had a relatively small material footprint, as a signifier it carries much weight. Hobart's piercing attention to the thermal politics of temperature makes visible the colonial ideologies, racial projects, and gendered domestication of refrigeration, ice, and the role they play in the settlement and control of Hawai'i.

The final chapter invites the reader to engage in a thought exercise that could be the foundation of a final creative or research project in an advanced undergraduate course or a graduate seminar. What infrastructure, strategic planning, and governance systems would need to be put in place to break free from thermal dependence? Until reading this book, I had not fully grasped the impacts of thermal dependency on our lives and futures. Hobart describes the precarity of melting ice in the context of having to feed hundreds of kia'i (guardians) at the Pu'uhonua o Pu'uhuluhulu, the base camp for the blockade to protect Mauna a Wākea. After reading this book I now realize that my thinking about Indigenous resurgence and futurity needs to also attend to issues of temperature control, refrigeration, and ice. In my own work, I have asked myself many times: How do we feed and sustain Indigenous Nations under present and future conditions of colonialism, racism, dispossessive environmental policy, legal regimes, extractive practices, and violence (in all of its forms). What I had not considered was how temperature—our ability to control and manipulate it—is a key variable in creating the conditions of Indigenous possibility and futurity. Indeed, while we say "water is life," I hadn't truly reflected on the role of ice in this statement. Thanks to Hobart, I do now.

HŌKŪLANI K. AIKAU is director and professor in the School of Indigenous Governance at the University of Victoria.

BRYDON KRAMER

Settler Memory: The Disavowal of Indigeneity and the Politics of Race in the United States
by Kevin Bruyneel
University of North Carolina Press, 2021

IN *SETTLER MEMORY*, Kevin Bruyneel introduces his titular concept to show how racial discourses in the United States often invoke notions of Indigeneity and settler colonialism yet, simultaneously, undercut their contemporary political relevance. For Bruyneel, this occurs through a dual process of "remembering and disavowing" Indigeneity and settler colonial violence to reproduce white settler domination (xiii). By taking this "complicated absent/presence" seriously (2), *Settler Memory* offers a rich discussion on the power of collective remembrance that nuances concepts like the logic of elimination and colonial amnesia to compel readers to be accountable to the multiple histories of the white settler nation-state. In fact, the text's most compelling contribution shows how any "cure" for settler memory must exceed the (liberal) desire to "just know better" (16).

Working through five substantive chapters, Bruyneel traces both the "persistent shaping force" of settler memory (xiii) as well as the concept's implications for racial politics. In chapters 1 and 2, he attends to popular narratives within "antiracist Left memory" to show how engagement with events like Bacon's Rebellion and Reconstruction tend to eschew Indigeneity and settler colonialism (18). As Bruyneel makes clear, tendencies to "drop" Indigeneity and conflate land and property within such literature not only contribute to ongoing colonial violence and dispossession by positioning Indigenous people as "the living dead" (22), but they also limit political analyses by "quarantining" land from labor (47). This obscures the co-constitutive relationship between settler colonialism and slavery as well as how property and (hetero)patriarchy converge to produce white settler domestic spaces.

What makes *Settler Memory* stand out, however, is how Bruyneel adds to concepts like the logic of elimination and colonial amnesia by telling a multistoried history of colonialism in the United States. Building on the work of Black and Indigenous feminist theorists, the author emphasizes disavowal's "*productive capacity,*" which is often glossed over within dominant antiracist and settler colonial analyses. Bruyneel shows how colonial regimes, rather than simply forgetting or erasing Indigenous people and settler violence, rely on the disavowal work of settler memory to invoke depoliticizing references to Indigenous nations. In doing so, he also reveals how radical thinkers like Baldwin's "fraught" relationship with Indigeneity (in chapter 3) can share "common ground" with liberal defenses of racist mascots (124–31) and white supremacist celebrations of colonial conquest (139)—in that, each invokes notions of Indigeneity and settler colonialism while, simultaneously, deflecting from "the implications and obligations" that come with this knowing (3). Although clearly possessing different intentions that he is careful not to conflate, Bruyneel points to these different articulations of settler memory to show how simply naming the ongoing presence of Indigenous people and settler violence is not enough to disrupt settler colonialism. Rather, efforts to decolonize require alternative stories that offer radical interventions and liberating possibilities for all—but especially for Black and Indigenous people.

Perhaps one area where Bruyneel's text leaves me wanting more is its consideration of the liberating possibilities that are opened by stories that refuse settler memory. Although chapters 4 and 5 briefly explore what resisting settler memory can look like via Indigenous resistance at Standing Rock (144) and the work of the Lipan Apache Indian Defense/Strength group (159), Bruyneel primarily attends to diagnosing articulations of settler memory. This compels him to center the work of disavowal in places where one may have hoped for greater consideration of the possibilities that emerge through the refusal of settler memory. Admittedly one of the tasks that lies before all of us living on stolen lands, this hope for the centering of alternative stories and their liberating possibilities is at least partially satisfied when Bruyneel reads Long Soldier's *Whereas* and Sharpe's *In the Wake* in the conclusion. For him, each of these texts serve as examples that coinhabit a "radical poetics and politics refusing settler memory" (170).

In sum, Bruyneel's *Settler Memory* contributes significantly to discussions on relationships between racial justice and decolonization. A crucial read for anyone working within settler colonial contexts, the text clearly reveals how people of all political stripes can perpetuate the work of settler memory. However, it is Bruyneel's consideration of the titular concept's implications for the antiracist Left that will prove particularly insightful for abolitionist and decolonizing movements within Turtle Island and beyond. While it could have had more discussion on historical and contemporary decolonizing possibilities, *Settler Memory* makes clear that any effort to achieve liberation within our current global context will require the centering of Indigenous Peoples and the return of Indigenous lands.

BRYDON KRAMER is a doctoral student in the Political Science Department at the University of Alberta.

ROSE STREMLAU

Allotment Stories: Indigenous Land Relations Under Settler Siege
edited by Daniel Heath Justice and Jean M. O'Brien
University of Minnesota Press, 2021

DON'T PICK UP *Allotment Stories: Indigenous Land Relations Under Settler Siege* looking for a traditional anthology. While this curated collection focuses on historical and ongoing privatization policies enacted by settler governments, it does so creatively and expansively by transcending genre, period, and nation. The volume's coeditors, literary scholar Daniel Heath Justice (Cherokee Nation) and historian Jean M. O'Brien (White Earth Ojibwe), have collected over two dozen essays, poems, short stories, and reflections shared by artists, community scholars, and, yes, some academics. Together, these diverse pieces illuminate both the wide-ranging experiences and impacts of settler laws and the "storied resistance" (xi) to them.

Heath and O'Brien begin *Allotment Stories* with an outstanding introduction that explains historical models of land privatization, particularly allotment policy in the United States, and puts them into a broader context of assimilationist land and resource policies enacted by settler states across the globe in the past and the present. They organize *Allotment Stories* into four thematic sections: "Family Narrations of Privatization," "Racial and Gender Taxonomies," "Privatization as State Violence," and "Resistance and Resurgence."

In the first section, essays explain how land privatization systems work(ed) to dispossess Native people and how they still have rippling impacts on families, communities, and nations. All authors consider their kin's stories across generations and emphasize common themes of painful loss balanced with critical understanding and effective responses to policies whose implementation they could not prevent but that they could critique and blunt. The contributions in section 2 demonstrate the triangulation of land ownership, whiteness, and citizenship/political status. Section 3 provides comparative explanations of how settler states have used both economic development and government bureaucracies as weapons no less destructive than guns and bombs. The breadth of this section—comparing national-level policies in the United States, New Zealand, and Canada—is instructive. In the fourth section, authors explore the diverse forms taken by Indigenous resistance: political, economic, social, spiritual, and cultural.

The broad geographic and chronological scope of this section—covering the Sámi homeland through that of multiple Indigenous nations located within the United States (including Alaska and Hawai'i) and Mexico and Palestine—provides rich context for comparison.

This collection boasts many strengths; in particular, the authors provide a more nuanced analysis of resistance than in any existing publication on allotment. Reflecting a wide breadth and diversity of Indigenous people, *Allotment Stories* enables understanding of the range of strategies through which communities responded to these policies. Perhaps because narratives of forceful opposition or legal defeat in the colonizers' courts are so compelling, we too often overlook the quotidian forms of opposition that are the true handmaidens of cultural and political survival. When preventing the implementation of allotment and other land privatization policies proved impossible (which it often has), attention to myriad forms of culturally appropriate resistance and the practices of dissent not only enriches scholarship but also—and more importantly—can provide models for today and for the future.

An inspiration and invitation for scholarly reconsideration of how we teach and write about violent, pulverizing privatization policies and their correlated agendas of erasure, *Allotment Stories* should be read widely within and beyond the academy. This powerful, compelling, and creative pastiche is an outstanding resource and a model for how to critically and comprehensively engage a central theme in Indigenous studies. Many of the essays are short and digestible for student readers, and the decision to include maps, photographs, and reprints of primary sources makes this collection readily teachable. The success of *Allotment Stories* is that Heath, O'Brien, and the contributors have gifted us with an accessible guide to make sense of the past and to understand how Indigenous Peoples are responding to these policies in the present. As Kelly S. McDonough (White Earth and Irish descent) put it in her outstanding essay on land titles and dispossession in colonial Mexico, "Lessons from the past . . . may inspire renewed recourse to the documentation of memory and history as a strategy to interrupt, if not disrupt, the continued threats to Indigenous territorial and sociopolitical unity today" (245). May it be so.

ROSE STREMLAU is an associate professor of history at Davidson College.

TRACI L. MORRIS

Tribal Administration Handbook: A Guide for Native Nations in the United States
edited by Rebecca M. Webster and Joseph Bauerkemper
Michigan State University Press, 2022

PUBLISHED IN 2022, the *Tribal Administration Handbook* is a sorely needed book for understanding the practicalities of tribal administration. Indian Country should applaud the editors and authors for using a tribally driven participatory approach. While aimed at various audiences, the book remains cohesive and accessible to most readers, despite being an edited volume.

The volume is divided into three sections: "Tribal Management," "Funding and Delivery of Core Services," and "Sovereign Tribes Engaging Settler Governments." Each section includes authors who are practitioners and academics, many of whom are culturally embedded tribal citizens. As an academic and executive director of an applied policy institute working directly with tribes, I found the practitioner chapters particularly useful and recommended the book to several colleagues at the university while I was completing this review.

While the utility of the authors' insights are applicable in many tribal contexts, it would have been beneficial to see this volume reach beyond authors in the Northwest and Midwest to diversify tribal perspectives and experiences. That said, the book is accessible, practical, usable, and generally jargon-free.

Each section's purpose, method, and objectives are clearly delineated, and the "Practitioner Perspective" section at the end of each chapter is easily applicable to real-world practitioners. The book's first part, "Tribal Management," provides excellent insight, but the third part, "Sovereign Tribes Engaging Settler Governments," could have been an excellent first section with a framework for understanding the importance of sovereignty, the legislative process, the federal budget process, and the intergovernmental and state relationship processes—all of which are useful for delineating the boundaries to which Native nations are subject. With those parameters in mind, the other chapters become practical guides for the structure and growth of tribal governments.

In the first part, "Tribal Management," most chapters were very insightful regarding managing a tribe, including the chapters "Authorizing Environment,"

"Strategic Management," "Project Management," and "Tribal Government Human Resources." In addition, each of these chapters includes roadmaps that a tribal employee or tribal enterprise employee could use for structuring their work.

Problematically, in the first part, a chapter by Laural Ballew states that the "theory of leadership is foundational and place-based in connection to each tribal nation. Tribal beliefs and principles are held up by oral traditions for most tribes, and the leadership skills of tradition and practice are fundamental qualifications for their leadership" (56). The author privileges more culturally intact tribes. What if a leader stepped up but was from an urban location? Should they not be eligible for a leadership role? Given that at least 70 percent of Native Americans live in urban areas, should they be deemed unfit for leadership? This chapter provoked more questions than answers.

Part 2, "Funding and Delivery of Core Services," can serve as an excellent roadmap for tribal leadership. In particular, the chapters "Tribal Finance," "Building Tribal Economies through Economic Development," "Community Wellness," and "Tribal Natural Resources" delineate useful topics, procedures, and definitions; they provide concrete recommendations for practitioners and tribal leaders. The two chapters on finance and economies should be required reading for everyone working in a tribal government context. The chapter on wellness reads as a community practitioner or leader's guide with an excellent overview of tribal health systems and funding. The solutions section is instrumental.

The chapter "Human Services" by Katie Johnston-Goodstar, Carey B. Waubanascum, and Donald Eubanks presents a very academic perspective, as some of the language may be inaccessible to practitioners unfamiliar with academic discourse on decolonization. Additionally, while criticism of human services being too Western-aligned may be accurate, it is essential to remember that these services are often tied to federal and state funding, which is not always flexible and provided by understaffed service departments.

Overall, this book is an excellent resource and should be required reading for practitioners, academics, tribal leaders, elected officials, and graduate students. The book would also be useful in American Indian studies upper-division or graduate courses, as the book is an excellent follow-up to *Rebuilding Tribal Economies (2007)*.

TRACI L. MORRIS (Chickasaw Nation) is the executive director of the American Indian Policy (AIPI) Institute at Arizona State University.

VALERIE LAMBERT

Paternalism to Partnership: The Administration of Indian Affairs, 1786–2021
by David H. DeJong
University of Nebraska Press, 2022

RELATIONSHIPS BETWEEN Native people and the Bureau of Indian Affairs (BIA) are fraught for many reasons, one of which is the agency's long history of trying to exterminate Indigenous Peoples and dispossess us of our land. Another is the often very personal nature of the federal-Indian relationship: as one of many expressions of the solemn, treaty-based trust responsibilities of the United States toward our sovereign Native Nations, most of us are tethered to the BIA from womb to tomb or from cradle to grave.

Although the BIA has had and continues to have a significant impact on Indian Country, the scholarship about the BIA is alarmingly sparse. Authored by the federal director of the Pima-Maricopa Irrigation Project, who is a prolific writer and holds a doctorate in American Indian studies, this valuable reference book helps address this lacuna in the literature. For this reason alone, this work makes a valuable contribution to Indigenous studies. Yet readers will, in addition, find much that is of value and interest in this book, including its central focus on the views of Indian Affairs leaders—in their own words—on numerous topics, including Indian land and land tenure, Indian education, Native youth, and tribal economic development.

An introduction and conclusion bookend sixty-five chapters—one on each individual who has headed Indian Affairs. Tackling a period that spans 235 years, the chapters address eight superintendents of Indian Affairs, one chief clerk, thirty-nine commissioners of Indian Affairs, and fourteen assistant secretaries of Indian Affairs. The chapters are composed primarily of extended, uninterrupted excerpts from these leaders' public writings. DeJong mines these officials' words, relying heavily on the annual reports that these leaders produced until 1965. DeJong's undertaking was massive: during the allotment era, for example, certain commissioners' annual reports totaled fifteen hundred pages. DeJong uses these officials' writings to illuminate the conditions in Indian Country as these top bureaucrats saw them, their own and others' Indian policies, major events that were impacting Indian Country, and these leaders' political philosophies. Every chapter begins with a formulaic but comprehensive and usually insightful biography of each leader, helping contextualize subsequent pages of their public writings or oratory.

The initiatives that particular Indian Affairs leaders championed but failed to bring to fruition are especially interesting. The primary sources that ground each chapter reveal that generations before the passage of the General Allotment Act of 1887, numerous heads of Indian Affairs fiercely advocated that our reservation lands be privatized. Other examples of policies thwarted during the years a leader held office include Charles Rhoads's fight to transfer all Indian irrigation projects to the Bureau of Reclamation in the early 1930s and Eddie Brown's battle to remove Indian education from the BIA in the early 1990s—more than a decade before the Bureau of Indian Education was created as a separate unit within Indian Affairs in 2006.

Extensive passages testify to the strident, unapologetically anti-Indian words and actions of the dozens of non-Natives who led the BIA through the late 1970s. As their own words make clear, non-Native officials consistently disrespected the federal trust responsibility, stereotyped Indians as lazy and inferior, insisted that the Indian land base was too large, and problematically racialized Indian identity as part of their larger efforts to undermine tribal sovereignty and nationhood. Their statements contrast markedly with those of the Natives who headed the BIA. The latter insisted that treaties and the trust responsibility were of paramount importance, prioritized the expansion of an Indian land base they understood as too small, doggedly worked to combat the racialization of Indian identity, and fought for tribal sovereignty.

This otherwise outstanding reference book suffers from only a few minor weaknesses. First, the characterization of "partnership" in the title is misleading. Although assistant secretaries of Indian Affairs often speak about partnering with tribes, "partnership" is something that, for BIA leaders, remains mostly aspirational. Assistant secretaries of Indian Affairs are working hard to transform the federal-tribal relationship into a partnership, but to date this goal has fallen short of the reality. In several instances, DeJong alarmingly uses the word "emancipation" as a gloss for termination; and finally, this book's index is insufficient, which compromises the utility of this much-needed work of scholarship about the BIA.

VALERIE LAMBERT (enrolled citizen, Choctaw Nation) is professor of anthropology at the University of North Carolina at Chapel Hill.

SAMUEL R. COOK

Native Agency: Indians in the Bureau of Indian Affairs
by Valerie Lambert
University of Minnesota Press, 2022

FOR AMERICAN INDIANS and those familiar with Indian affairs in the United States, the mere mention of the Bureau of Indian Affairs (BIA) is bound to elicit a preconditioned negative response, even though over 95 percent of its employees are Native. In *Native Agency,* anthropologist Valerie Lambert (Choctaw Nation) challenges contemporary views of the BIA by asking the simple question: "What is the impact of Indians having seized control of this space within the settler state?" (4). The author fuses personal experience as a former BIA employee, historical research, and a theoretical foundation that includes critical perspectives on bureaucracy from Max Weber to Akhil Gupta, to present a realistic assessment of an agency that has been in transition for at least four decades. Lambert's experience as an anthropologist interning at the BIA provides context for her ethnographic research with the actual people working in the agency, delivering a cogent message that for many Indians, working for the BIA is "a way to leverage the power of the settler state to their own ends . . . For many of these employees, working for the BIA [is] a form of resistance to colonial rule" (11).

Chapter 1 provides a brief history of the BIA prior to the advent of Indian hiring in the 1970s. Situating the original Office of Indian Affairs in the War Department, then noting that the transition to the Department of the Interior was based on a settler belief in the "vanishing American" motif, Lambert illuminates one of the central problems with Indian affairs—that non-Indigenous agents are too often credited with definitive policy initiatives, while Native acts of resistance or circumvention go uncredited. While policymakers such as commissioner of Indian Affairs John Collier and President Richard Nixon are credited with some of the most "progressive" initiatives in Indian Affairs, the influence of Indigenous activists in buffering and manipulating the directions of Indian policy are frequently overlooked. Yet the BIA became the de facto "steward" of the trust relationship between Indigenous Nations and the federal government. Thus, chapters 2 and 3 elaborate on how—as "Indian preference" became the norm in federal hiring within agencies dealing with Indigenous issues, Natives in the ranks seized the opportunity to effect a paradigm shift within the Bureau that seeks clarification of the trust relationship as a good faith understanding that Native lands, rights, and sovereignty are sacrosanct.

The remaining chapters rely much more on ethnographic data, as they focus on BIA employees at different levels during and after the mid-1990s (during Lambert's BIA tenure). Chapter 4 focuses on upper-level officials (notably, the assistant secretary for Indian Affairs) and how Native people in that position—particularly Ada Deer and Kevin Gover, for whom Lambert worked in respective terms, held strong convictions about working *for* Indians rather than managing their affairs from afar. Chapters 5 and 6, respectively, deal with rank-and-file employees (housed in the central office), and field employees, demonstrating that many of the constraints of traditional bureaucracies still afflict an Indian-controlled organization, but illustrating that the commitment of most employees to strengthening and upholding the trust relationship has made a difference. While Lambert avoids excessive criticism of some of the more controversial assistant secretaries—notably Ross Swimmer, who served during the first Reagan administration—she provides compelling examples of moments when all BIA employees felt a sense of purpose when confronted with common crises: most notably in the context of the 2009 *Cobell v. Salazar* decision where the Supreme Court determined that the BIA had mismanaged individual trust accounts.

Lambert's book, intentionally or not, serves as a practical guide to how the BIA works, including specifics about operations such as Individual Indian Money accounts and how they are managed at each level of the federal bureaucracy. Lambert is not, however, an apologist. As Native scholars once again endeavor to bring about coherence in Indian law—something that is lacking largely due to centuries of non-Indigenous control—it is critical to acknowledge the Native agents who have been waging that campaign, sometimes at the grassroots level. Lambert provides a compelling glimpse into the convictions of these actors, demonstrating that they are not simply filling positions within a bureaucracy but have a sense of purpose. With the rising popularity of settler colonial studies, scholars too often focus on victimization rather than Indigenous resiliency and agency. Lambert has provided a vital blueprint for dismantling the blind spots that contemporary theoretical perspectives can create when their only object is to explicate oppression.

SAMUEL R. COOK is associate professor in the Department of History and director of American Indian Studies at Virginia Tech.

COLL THRUSH

American Indians and the American Dream: Policies, Place, and Property in Minnesota
by Kasey Keeler
University of Minnesota Press, 2023

WHAT DO a Civil War–era campaign of genocide and a 1992 federal home loan program have to do with each other? A lot, it turns out. Kasey R. Keeler's excellent examination of the politics of land and place in the spaces that became the suburbs of Minneapolis-St. Paul takes a *longue-durée* approach to the question of Indigenous homemaking and the logics and practices of settler colonialism. The result is a book that should be on the shelves and syllabi of scholars interested in the intersection of urban and Indigenous histories—and perhaps on the desks of policymakers as well.

Based on her doctoral research at Minnesota, Keeler's book is a meticulously researched and fine-grained analysis of the ways in which Indigenous people engaged with the so-called American Dream, a potent phrase Keeler tells us was first popularized in the 1930s but emerged from long-standing expectations of Manifest Destiny. Her central argument is this: that Indigenous individuals and families engaged with the politics of home ownership and place-making in complex ways that highlighted their own agency in the face of seemingly overwhelming settler systems of property.

Keeler's introduction begins with the story of her upbringing as a suburban Indian growing up far from her ancestral territories and briefly sets the larger scholarly context of the work within the small but growing field of urban Indigenous histories. Keeler then sets about doing the important work of crafting a deep context for the welter of federal and other programs that are the primary focus of the book. She does this by starting her narrative with the 1862 Dakota War, in which the territories that became the suburbs with which she is primarily concerned were transformed from Indigenous homelands to settler homesteads through profound violence, exclusion, and narrative erasure. From there, Keeler takes us through a complex administrative and bureaucratic history without ever losing sight of the lived experiences of Indigenous people.

One of the great strengths of this book is that it challenges previous scholarly emphasis on formal post-WWII federal relocation programs, recognizing their importance while simultaneously illustrating the many other policies and programs that shaped Indigenous people's relationship with place and property in the suburbs. Here, for example, we learn about the relationship between the Federal Housing Administration, founded in 1934, and the Indian Reorganization Act of the same year, a relationship in which Indian policy and housing policy were, to use Keeler's term, "entangled." When she does turn to postwar federal relocation, Keeler pointedly and usefully reframes it as racialized housing policy. Following this, Keeler provides a close analysis of Little Earth, the first and only Indigenous housing project in the United States, and her final chapter is a detailed discussion of the 1992 Section 184 Indian Home Loan Guarantee Program. Throughout, Keeler deftly keeps policy, the economic realities of Indigenous life in the suburbs, and nuanced questions of identity in play, all the while foregrounding Indigenous voices where they exist in the archives. Despite the array of colonial forces facing Indigenous people in the Twin Cities and their suburbs, this is not a story of mere victimhood or dispossession but rather one of survivance and of Indigenous people's engagement with the shifting and mercurial American Dream.

Ending with a trenchant meditation on present-day Indigenous and racialized houselessness in Minnesota, this book resists the temptation of many urban Indigenous histories to separate the period before settler urbanity from later twentieth-century phenomena. All too often, Indigenous people disappear from urban histories after a war or treaty, then reappear (if at all) in the wake of federal relocation and/or pan-Indian activism. *American Indians and the American Dream* challenges this disjointed and dismembering periodization by articulating the long arc of urban history in which Indigenous people were and are always present.

Keeler has made an extremely significant contribution here, providing an almost unique story of Indigenous suburbanization—and suburban Indigenization—that has heretofore been missed or ignored by those of us working in the spaces where urban and Indigenous histories meet. While many of the details are specific to Minnesota and the United States, scholars beyond those places will also find much here to consider, especially in the way Keeler not only connects the more recent past to deeper histories of colonization but also in her illustration of the ways in which policies and place relations inform each other. Highly recommended.

COLL THRUSH is professor of history and associate faculty in critical Indigenous studies at the University of British Columbia.

MICHAEL D. WISE

People of the Ecotone: Environment and Indigenous Power at the Center of Early America
by Robert Michael Morrissey
University of Washington Press, 2022

OVER THE LAST SEVERAL DECADES the conventional grand narratives of early American historiography have been lurching—if unevenly—toward the acceptance of two profound realities: first, the widespread presence of nontextual archives suggesting the myriad ways Native people shaped political and social transformations both before and after colonial contact; and, second, the legacy of the field of American history itself as an instrument of settler colonialism that, for generations, has probably obscured as much about Native history as it has revealed. Robert Michael Morrissey's *People of the Ecotone* further compels early Americanists to continue this critical Native studies turn by pursuing the field's colonial narratives onto the edge of the tallgrass prairies of the seventeenth and eighteenth centuries, looking to the ecological specificities of these complex patchworks of grass and trees as a source for reframing the region's Native histories and geographies.

Morrissey's geographic focus rests primarily on a vision of seventeenth-century Illinois as a "prairie peninsula" jutting eastward across the Mississippi River (as the ecologist Edgar Transeau put it) and rightfully emphasizes the challenge of imagining this historical landscape in the wake of its modern transformation into homogenized fields of corn and soybeans. For centuries, however, the region represented a dynamic boundary zone between the grasslands to the west and the woodlands to the east, a setting of ecological complexity where Illinois, Meskwaki, and other Native communities thrived on livelihoods that included diverse forms of hunting and agricultural production. Put in the language of another twentieth-century ecologist, Frederic Clements, the Illinois country was an "ecotone," a site where two or more biotic communities shaded into one another. Morrissey uses "a shoreline of grass" as his metaphor for describing this easternmost finger of the tallgrass, which would have been a mosaic of prairies interspersed with forests of oak and hickory (20–23). An extended explication of this historical geography and its changing climate unfolds over several chapters in which Morrissey also traces the eastward migration of bison to the region following the droughts that may have led to the dispersal of Cahokia by the twelfth century. These efforts to reorient the reader's geographical perspective represent a major contribution of the book by insisting that early American historians approach place not simply as a setting on which history "plays out" but as a historical subject requiring its own multidisciplinary analysis.

The latter half of *People of the Ecotone* develops a more conventional historical narrative bookended by the Iroquois raids of 1680 and the conclusion of the Fox Wars in the 1730s. Morrissey convincingly reframes this violence as a contingent outcome of the Illinois's and Meskwaki's circumstances within their ecotonal transition zone, a discussion that adds complexity to the typical textbook explanation of the "Beaver Wars" as a rippling displacement of colonial conflict westward. This analysis will undoubtedly interest many early American specialists, but in the context of the book's larger innovations these final interventions seemed somewhat vestigial.

In that sense, *People of the Ecotone* itself exists in a kind of a transition zone between its broad multidisciplinary approach and its disciplinary textual fetish, which I mean not as admonition but as admiration. The book is at its best when it takes analytical risks. In particular, Morrissey's deep dive into the potential significance of running as a sensory activity vital to Native identities in the tallgrass prairies is brilliant, unexpected, and makes use of a variety of nontextual sources to develop its force and meaning. Morrissey offers us an example of what historians can contribute to interdisciplinary discussions in Native studies when they foreground sensitivities to perception, embodiment, and haptic knowledge as serious subjects of study, and when they eschew the Cartesian assumptions and cartographic rigidities that have long confined the discipline.

For all these reasons *People of the Ecotone* will interest a wide audience of readers across historically oriented fields of Native American studies, as well as critical scholars of Native and Indigenous studies concerned with issues of representation and historical memory. Morrissey's critical approach to the ecotone as unit for geographical analysis will also serve as mode of departure for others who wish to interrogate the spatial logics of colonialism and their possible alternatives.

MICHAEL D. WISE is associate professor in the History Department at the University of North Texas.

JULIANA BARR

The Great Power of Small Nations: Indigenous Diplomacy in the Gulf South
by Elizabeth N. Ellis
University of Pennsylvania Press, 2023

THE GREAT POWER OF SMALL NATIONS had its beginnings in 2006 when Elizabeth Ellis (herself a citizen of the Peoria Tribe of Indians of Oklahoma) worked as part of a research team pursuing archival documentation in support of the Pointe-au-Chien Indian Tribe's petition for federal recognition. Such work investigating the Native presence in Louisiana's southern bayous prior to 1800, while simultaneously grounded in the contemporary concerns of Southern Native polities, provides critical enlightenment about "the disjuncture between the historical evidence and the rigid definitions of community belonging and historical formation that the federal government uses to assess Native nations today" (13). That revelation in turn led Ellis to realize that contemporary questions regarding what constitutes nationhood have blinded us to the diverse political formations of Native nations in early American history. Thus, the book seeks both to redress the misunderstandings that have erased the history of many smaller Native nations from the geopolitical map of the South and to demonstrate the multiple and creative forms of Indigenous community building that bore little resemblance to present-day "Western ideologies of nationhood" but that carried (and continue to carry) the same substantive weight when it comes to sovereign self-governance (13).

Indigenous studies scholars will find great value in Ellis's deep explanation of the workings of nationhood across the lower Mississippi Valley for numerous smaller nations—collectively referred to as *les petites nations* by French colonial officials—as they sought to respond to growing colonial pressures in the seventeenth and eighteenth centuries. Such a collectivity, in French terms, was misleading as these nations encompassed, at minimum, six language groups and had multiple and distinct religious, cultural, and political structures. Simultaneously, however, they shared specific political strategies as they sought to evade not only colonial subordination but also incorporation into larger Native nations. Indeed, they maintained their small sizes with purpose, and smallness was in fact a source of strength. Thus, they chose to migrate, to find and offer refuge, to ally, and to coalesce in multinational settlements where they might defend, protect, and prosper collectively. These strategies explain not only how they survived over three hundred years but also how they held on to portions of their homelands. The expansive tactics of Yazoo, Ofogoula, Avoyelle, Ishak/Atakapa, Tensas, Tunica, Biloxi, Bayagoula, Chitimacha, Tohome, Mobile, and Chakchiuma Nations constantly adapted across an Indigenous borderlands defined here as a space of layered land rights, reciprocal relationships, and plural sovereignty stretching from present-day Alabama to Louisiana. The presence of larger, more powerful Native polities such as Choctaws, Creeks, Chickasaws, Osages, and Natchez proved an equally defining feature of that Indigenous borderlands, and their presence often had more influence on the fortunes of Petites Nations than that of European colonists.

Historical scholars will find compelling Ellis's portrait of the infinitely complex Indigenous political geography within which French colonialism appears more clearly in proportion to actual French demographics. Given the "overwhelming Native power" governing the lower Mississippi Valley in the eighteenth century, each French settlement (outside of New Orleans) operated as just another *petite nation* among many (109). This is nowhere clearer than in fascinating reappraisals of colonial events such as the discussion of Tensa and French responses to the dire crisis of survival during the endless pummeling of English raids that brought devastating levels of disease and depopulation to the region. It was just that the French in Louisiana were as powerless as the Spaniards in Florida, once they became prey to the inexorable slave raids funded and promoted by Englishmen in the Carolinas from the 1670s to the 1710s. French captive-taking and buying bore little resemblance to actions of their colonial peers but looked far more like that of their Tensa neighbors who "forcibly adopted" women and children as everyone, French and Native alike, desperately sought to stabilize ever-diminishing population numbers. Another riveting retelling explains how the Natchez War was in fact the playing out of dramatic Indigenous geopolitics that left Frenchmen even more in thrall to the power of large Native nations. In sum, anything the French could accomplish was possible only with the aid of multinational *petite nation* alliances but, equally, they could accomplish little against the superior forces of Choctaws and Chickasaws. In the end, Ellis leaves no doubt as to archival depth of colonial sources for better understanding even the smallest of Native nations and the value of deep history for demonstrating Native sovereignty undiminished no matter the colonial forces arrayed against it.

JULIANA BARR is associate professor of history at Duke University.

TIFFANY KING

Being Indigenous in Jim Crow Virginia: Powhatan People and the Color Line
by Laura J. Feller
University of Oklahoma Press, 2022

IN *BEING INDIGENOUS IN JIM CROW VIRGINIA: Powhatan People and the Color Line,* Laura Feller chronicles the relentless struggle of tidewater Virginia Indians from 1850 to 1950 to "maintain, assert, reclaim, create, and recreate" their Native identity in the face of Jim Crow statecraft that attempted to erase them (194). Feller homes in on the unique struggles of nonreservation Indians like the Pamunkey, Mattaponi, and Chickahominy. A long history of colonial laws in Virginia (1691, 1866, 1910, and 1924) narrowly defined whiteness through notions of "blood quantum" to protect the white population from intermarriage with Black and Native populations. Feller makes a unique contribution to historiographies of Virginia's path toward the codification of a white-Black binary through a careful study of the 1924 Act to Preserve Racial Integrity.

After the Civil War and prior to the 1924 Act, the migration of "colored" and nonwhite communities from rural to urban areas posed "potential threats to the proper racialized classification of Virginia's citizens" (55). The anxious architects of the 1924 law argued that "Native Virginians, because their appearance cloaked their Black blood, might more easily blend into the white population" and disrupt the white-Black color line (56). Feller focuses on the Act as a modern form of race craft designed to "ensure that no one in Virginia could escape Jim Crow by claiming to be Indian rather than Black (7)." The author mines a range of archival material, including Virginia census data, Canadian census data, Virginia Bureau of Vital Statistics, U.S. Southern Claims Commission, Records of the Virginia Council on Indians, Virginia State Department of Education Indian Schools, University of Pennsylvania Museum Archives, Baptist Church records, tax records, newspapers, and family letters.

Chapter 1 travels with the extended family and descendants of Lucy Pearman Scott and William Scott from Richmond, Virginia, to Canada and back to Virginia as they attempt to maintain their Indianness in the 1850s. The Scotts and their extended family asserted their Indianness by living in proximity to one another through Chickahominy endogamy or "paired-sibling marriage" (36) and the strategic use of alternative forms of racial documentation like the U.S. Southern Claims Commission.

Chapter 2 explores how the 1924 Act to Preserve Racial Integrity consolidated and codified a white-Black binary. Engineers of the law asserted that there were no real Indians (Native people without Black ancestors) in Virginia. To enforce the law that established a white-Black racial order, an army of physicians, midwives, undertakers, local registrars, county clerks, and census enumerators interpreted and enforced the 1924 Act in ways that erased Indigenous presence.

Chapter 3 attends to tidewater Natives' creation of institutions like separate Baptist churches and schools to construct and assert Indigenous identity while distinguishing themselves from African Americans. Tribes also creatively appropriated colonial institutions like universities and museums to gain public recognition.

Chapter 4 explores tidewater Natives use of white anthropologists as resources. Some white anthropologists like Frank Speck became allies who corresponded with white educators, lawyers, and public officials to make the case that tidewater Natives possessed distinct cultural identities.

Feller's fifth chapter is devoted to the kinds of obstacles that the 1930 and 1940 census, World War II draft, and federal laws like school desegregation posed to Virginia nations. In the epilogue, Feller recounts the recent efforts of several Virginia nations to gain recognition, such as the Pamunkey who gained federal recognition in 2016.

Feller's analyses of archival material are deft and layered. The author is at their best when tracing the racial classifications of a person like John Howell across different archival documents. Feller follows the shifting classifications of John Howell from "mulatto" in the 1870 and 1880 census to Pamunkey in the U.S. Southern Claims Commission's files of 1870. The comparative archival reading practices are more compelling than Feller's attempts, in chapter 1, to interpret letters written by Lucy Pearman Scott as possible evidence of Scott's racial motivations, anxieties, and desire to distance herself from Black people. Feller might have made a stronger case about the presence of anti-Black sentiments and practices with a more substantive analysis of the tax records that document Scott's family member's ownership of enslaved people. While the chapter on white anthropologists does a masterful job of discussing the methods and advocacy used by anthropologists, little attention is devoted to the discussions and debates that Native organizations had about their choice to work with ethnographers.

As a storyteller, Feller constructs a fascinating narrative about tidewater Indians' resistance to Jim Crow racialization. By and large, *Being Indigenous in Jim Crow Virginia* treats the struggle for Indigenous sovereignty in the Southeast and Virginia with the assiduousness that it deserves.

TIFFANY KING is Barbara and John Glynn Research Professor in Democracy and Equity and associate professor of women, gender, and sexuality at the University of Virginia.

MICHAEL P. TAYLOR

Assimilation, Resilience, and Survival: A History of the Stewart Indian School, 1890–2020
by Samantha M. Williams
University of Nebraska Press, 2022

WITH U.S. DEPARTMENT OF THE INTERIOR Secretary Deb Haaland's 2021 creation of the Federal Indian Boarding School Initiative, a long-awaited opportunity arrived for increased national attention to and acknowledgment of boarding school histories and their intergenerational legacies. Soon after Secretary Haaland's announcement, K. Tsianina Lomawaima and Brenda Child published pieces in the *Washington Post* challenging readers to recognize that the genocidal project of federal Indian boarding schools continued the long-standing strategy of removing Indigenous Peoples from their home communities and lands. As they have been doing since the 1990s, Lomawaima and Child set the discursive tone for the emerging era of reconciliation in the United States. By documenting the entangled histories of U.S. settler colonialism that came to a head in the creation and decades-long administration of boarding schools, historians and Indigenous studies scholars have the urgent responsibility to assertively engage, and thereby shape, public discourse and policy with Indigenous communities and leaders. It is the duty of scholars to imagine and develop what reconciliation and healing might look like for Indigenous Peoples in the United States.

This long-view approach to boarding school histories is what Samantha M. Williams does so well in her 130-year history of the Stewart Indian School, *Assimilation, Resilience, and Survival.* Williams refuses to tell an oversimplified story of the school or a reductive history of the students, alumni, and survivors. This willingness to represent the complicated, even contradictory, experiences and attitudes toward Stewart emerges out of an ethical obligation to the relationships Williams developed with the families, administrators, and community members that shaped the Stewart Indian School then and now. In so doing, *Assimilation, Resilience, and Survival* joins a growing body of locally specific and collaborative boarding school scholarship that traces the continuation of assimilationist education agendas into the late twentieth century, including such important works as Clifford E. Trafzer, Matthew Sakiestewa Gilbert, and Lorene Siquoc's *The Indian School on Magnolia Avenue* (2012), Kevin Whalen's

Native Students at Work (2016), and Farina King, Michael Taylor, and James Swenson's *Returning Home* (2021).

What makes *Assimilation, Resilience, and Survival* such an important contribution to boarding school histories is the Stewart Indian School's position as being among the first schools created and one of the few remaining in operation. Stewart's unique longevity allows Williams to guide readers from the origination of boarding schools through each era of assimilation, protest, reform, termination, relocation, self-determination, and reclamation. Divided into five chapters organized around important reinforcements of or shifts in Indian policy, Williams moves fluidly between national, tribal, and school-specific contexts. Though the book is primarily about the Stewart Indian School, with ample images, tables of data, and survivor testimonies, readers are introduced to the boarding school system in its entirety, demonstrating that at its core—even in the most progressive eras—the system was designed to forever remove Indigenous children from their homelands, communities, and cultures.

Williams prioritizes direct stories of Stewart students and survivors without pushing a singular narrative or argumentative agenda. When she shares a student or survivor's experiences of harsh discipline and abuse, she validates the stories by referencing national data of student abuse and neglect. At the same time, when she shares positive student experiences, she commends the teller's resilience, never questioning the authenticity of the teller's experience, but she also never allows such testimonies to be apologetic for the larger assimilationist system. In our current era of growing political, communal, and interpersonal division, Williams strikes a vital historiographical balance between agency and accountability, holding space for multiple truths at the same time without losing sight of the underlying boarding school agenda whose posterity continue to work against the self-determination of Indigenous families, communities, and nations.

As comprehensive and well-crafted as Williams's book is, it compels me to think more about the collaborative methodologies and the continuance of community relations developed and sustained through each part of—and well beyond—the research and writing process. As a settler scholar myself, Williams leaves me wondering how I might do more than gather and prioritize Indigenous voices in my own scholarship. This book represents a radical restructuring of academic-community relations, a reimagined reciprocity of resources with multilateral benefit, in which our scholarship is but a representative branch of a much broader relationship that reflects the expressed interests of Indigenous families, communities, and nations at least as much as it serves academic and public institutions.

MICHAEL P. TAYLOR is associate professor of English at Brigham Young University.

LYNN STEPHEN

Scales of Resistance: Indigenous Women's Transborder Activism
by Maylei Blackwell
Duke University Press, 2023

THE DECOLONIZATION of Western knowledge is a tall order, but one that Maylei Blackwell successfully fills in *Scales of Resistance.* Centering conversations on how Indigenous women's activism brings Indigenous cosmovisions, balance, and relationality to the table, Maylei Blackwell pushes us to rethink categories of colonialism, the settler/Indigenous binary, and the ways that gender permeates local, regional, national, and global Indigenous organizing. Blackwell's book is driven by a multigenerational accompaniment of Indigenous women, social movements, Indigenous and other intellectuals, and activists.

Blackwell incorporates scale into the structure of the book. She begins with a focus on Indigenous women in Mexico and in diaspora who are engaged in national movements for Indigenous autonomy and explains how they organize to preserve autonomy in their homes, communities, and through local forms of justice and governance. As the author notes: "Indigenous women moved the struggle for autonomy from a discourse of rights to a practice of autonomy by scaling down to the levels of the community, the home, and the body." (42).

Blackwell then explores how women from the Coordinadora Nacional de Mujeres Indígenas (CONAMI), founded in 1997 in Oaxaca City, also began to participate in hemispheric spaces of women's organizing such as the Enlace Continental de Mujeres Indígenas de Ayba Yala (ECMIA). Blackwell centers the concept of Abiayala but also the tensions that emerge from using it as an organizing concept. "Abiayala forges a trans-Indigenous political frame that names an alternative sense of relations and responsibility to one another and a way in which Indigenous actors at multiple scales root their own nations' and communities' struggles to broader international Indigenous rights frameworks and practices of solidarity" (109). Abiayala became, however, unscalable in Blackwell's scheme of multiple scales as women moved simultaneously between local, national, transnational, international and trans-Indigenous and transborder scales of organization—also producing new identities, kinds of consciousness, and strategies. As global consumption, tourism, and different forms of extraction ramped up in the 1990s and 2000s, weaving, as well as medicinal and agricultural knowledges, for example, went from local discussions to national and global arenas. Simultaneously, Indigenous women engaged in intense confrontations with hegemonic Western feminism centering Indigenous women's knowledges and their own sense of gender justice bound to collective rights and autonomy.

Women also engage in their own forms of gender-based advocacy to shape community decisions from the bottom up. Long-standing practices of comunalidad have been key to women's success in empowering themselves. Through deep analysis of the life histories and testimonies of Indigenous women leaders in Oaxaca and Guerrero, Blackwell documents how communal work, kinship, ritual life, and assemblies have been used by women to empower themselves locally and regionally. These structures are rooted in long-standing Indigenous forms of governance.

Blackwell uses her multidecade relationship with women in the Frente Indígena de Organizaciones Binacionales (FIOB) to illustrate how the Indigenous male and female leadership worked across colonial and national borders to increase women's and youth leadership. Trying to change discrimination against Indigenous women and empower them as communal leaders across a binational organization is a major challenge. The election of the FIOB's first binational female leader, Odilia Romero Hernández, in 2017 marked a shift in the organization; however, she bore the marks of many years of debates, doubts, and incredibly hard work in her body and biography.

Indigenous Los Angeles bears the ongoing structures of multiple colonialities, Tongva territory, a large population of "relocated" and "detribalized" Native Peoples from the U.S. because of U.S. government policies of termination, and a large diaspora of Indigenous Peoples from Latin America and Oceania. How do you theorize diasporic Mesoamerican (and other) Indigenous Peoples in the tribal homelands of others using Indigenous concepts? Seeking to avoid the settler/Indigenous dichotomy, Blackwell uses the Tongva concept of Kuuyam/guest to refer to the three hundred thousand Indigenous Oaxacan and Mayan Indigenous Peoples in diaspora in Los Angeles. Being a guest focuses on relationship and responsibility to the land and the Indigenous Peoples of that land—offering the possibility of the abolition of white supremacist logics. If Indigenous Oaxacan women in Los Angeles who build their lives in transpueblo spaces that connect multicity transborder communities are Tongva guests, then the possibility exists for transregional Pan-Indigenous relations.

Scales of Resistance is a remarkable record of Indigenous women's organizing across the hemisphere and of Blackwell's documentation, accompaniment, and theorization.

LYNN STEPHEN is Philip H. Knight Chair, professor of anthropology, and graduate faculty in Indigenous, race, and ethnic studies at the University of Oregon.

GILLIAN CALDER

Reconciliation and Indigenous Justice: A Search for Ways Forward
by David Milward
Fernwood Publishing, 2022

THIS IS AN IMPORTANT BOOK, not just in the story it tells but also in the way it tells that story. It is an invaluable resource for all those living with or learning about the complicated dimensions of reconciliation, Indigenous justice, prison abolition, intersocietal legal orders, ethics and morality, restorative programming, spirituality, principles of sentencing, and the importance of a search for ways forward. It takes on many of the most difficult issues that we face as a shared society, and it does so with grace, careful research, and a sense of hope.

The book's power rests in the clear connection it draws between the experience of residential schools and the grave problem of overincarceration of Indigenous Peoples in Canada today. It troubles the ways that standard punitive policies of the Canadian state continue to be applied to Indigenous peoples living with the social legacies and enduring harms of residential schools; and then it offers concrete means to repair relationships, to further harmony in the context of conflict, to rethink approaches to punishment, and to reimagine accountability, responsibility and safety.

Part of what enables David Milward to accomplish his aims is the decision he makes to approach the issues and questions of reconciliation as a "Word Warrior." Drawn from the work of Anishinaabe political scientist Dale Turner,[1] Word Warriors are academically trained Indigenous philosophers who act as bridges and advocates for Indigenous people within a democratic state. They are people with the capacity to move between languages, across dichotomies, and within ways of thinking about the world. As Inuvialuit legal scholar Gordon Christie has written, Word Warriors must be able to take up, deconstruct, and continue to resist colonialism—but they are also skilled in their ability to engage the legal and political discourses of the state.[2]

Milward responds to those who see the work of change as only possible through the realm of direct action by offering that it is as a Word Warrior that he is likely to be the most persuasive within corridors of power; to effect change in the realm of criminal justice policy is to align—he argues—Canadian self-interest with Indigenous aspirations.

Embracing words as effective tools of social justice, Milward shows how residential schools, through their legacies of abuse, planted the seeds of intergenerational trauma in Indigenous communities. He then painstakingly follows each sprout through case law where he teases out judicial recognition of residential school factors that have played a role in the accused's conflict with the justice system and ultimately in overincarceration. And while it is painful, he moves through questions of substance use, mental health, racism, cultural losses, deficient parenting, intimate partner violence, sexual abuse, poverty, family policing, and the intersections that coexist. He then offers law as remedy: as a scythe in a garden full of weeds, a sprinkler for parched soil, and fertilizer for ideas that need more nurturing to break the surface.

Cognizant that hope can be fleeting, Milward concludes by drawing a narrative of reconciliation, resurgence, and revitalization into the text. He shows what might grow from investment in community, from critical programming both inside and outside of prison, and from a principled reallocation of resources. He uses his Word Warrior toolkit to bridge colonial laws to Indigenous legal orders: highlighting questions of safety, responsibility, family relations, and care. And ultimately, with a reminder that words are sometimes the most powerful tools available, he leaves his readers with some reasoned optimism and a way forward.

GILLIAN CALDER is professor in the Faculty of Law at the University of Victoria.

Notes

1. Dale Turner, *This Is Not a Peace Pipe: Towards a Critical Indigenous Philosophy* (Toronto: University of Toronto Press, 2006).
2. Gordon Christie, "Response to *This Is Not a Peace Pipe: Towards a Critical Indigenous Philosophy* by Dale Turner," *APA Newsletter* 10, no. 2 (2011).

KRYSTAL S. TSOSIE

Inventing the Thrifty Gene: The Science of Settler Colonialism
by Travis Hay
University of Manitoba Press, 2021

IN *INVENTING THE THRIFTY GENE: The Science of Settler Colonialism,* non-Indigenous historian Travis Hay writes a compelling critique of James Neel's flawed "thrifty gene hypothesis," a concept that still pervades many settler-geneticists' understanding of Type 2 diabetes mellitus in Indigenous people. This hypothesis is an extension of similar "mismatch" narratives; it posits through an evolutionary biology lens that a disease state emerges due to a divergence between Indigenous Peoples' supposedly innate and genetic predisposition to storing higher blood glucose levels attuned over centuries of traditional diet patterns and periodic famine that have become maladaptive to recent or "modern" carbohydrate- and starch-rich industrialized diets. This narrative is repeatedly substantiated in Western settler-scientists' explorations of diabetes, although it has been discredited by many who have rightfully pointed to colonial and structural factors—such as forced removal of culturally based foodways, destabilized food sovereignties, and inequities in preventative healthcare—as more evidence-based contributors to the diabetic state in Indigenous peoples compared to reductionist, simplistic narratives rooted solely in DNA.[1] Hay cites these works, but he also weaves a readable and accessible history of how these concepts and dichotomies (Indigenous versus Western, "premodern"/ancestral versus modern/industrial) can be misused and serve as settler hubris reified as "science" through a singular, narrow lens of genetics.

Much of Hay's book is an extended exploration of how Western academia has foundationally situated race as a biological construct in the fields of human genetics and genomics, anthropology, and even medicine. While contemporary human genetics and genomics research tries to eschew its eugenicist past—which led to dangerous, hierarchical constructions of genetic racism—academic scholars still must check each other to ensure that studies based on exploring genetic variation and differences between populations do not biologically reify "race." For instance, a 2018 open letter signed by sixty-seven scientists and researchers criticized geneticist David Reich's book *Who We Are and How We Got Here* for substantiating differences between groups as being of genetic not social constructions.[2] As long as researchers continue to push for increased inclusion of Indigenous Peoples in genetic studies, the need will remain for a book such as Hay's, which questions the situation of Indigenous bodies as sources for settler-science's extraction and benefit. As Hay writes, just as Indigenous lands and resources were usurped by colonialism, "Indian blood, like diamonds, and oil, thus became supremely valuable to settlers" (90).

As a part of an intensive diagnostic analysis of Neel's genetic interest in Indigenous Peoples, Hay deconstructs Neel's "obsess[ion] with Indian blood" as a preoccupation "with his own biological self," which is an interesting critique of the man often regarded as the father of modern human genetics (87). The emergence of Hay's book comes fortuitously timed with recent and ongoing conversations to include Neel's legacy that has impacts for policy and the reckoning of genetic science.[3] However, in considering the centricity of damage that one settler-scientist can do, we must also take care not to grant too much power in storifying the influence of one man as a proxy of the fields' sins at large. After all, in terms of the study of Indigenous genetics, settler-science already has a lot to atone for as it moves forward.

KRYSTAL S. TSOSIE (Diné/Navajo Nation) is assistant professor in the School of Life Sciences in the Center for Biology and Society at Arizona State University.

Notes

1. Southam et al., "Is the Thrifty Genotype Hypothesis Supported by Evidence Based on Confirmed Type 2 Diabetes- and Obesity-Susceptibility Variants?" *Diabetologia* 2009 52, no. 9: 1846—51.

2. "How Not to Talk about Race and Genetics" Buzzfeed Opinion, March 30, 2018, https://www.buzzfeednews.com/article/bfopinion/race-genetics-david-reich).

3. "Response to Allegations against James V. Neel in Darkness in El Dorado, by Patrick Tierney," American Society of Human Genetics 70, no. 1 (2002): 1—10, https://www.ncbi.nlm.nih.gov/pmc/articles/PMC384880/; and "ASHG Documents and Apologizes for Past Harms of Human Genetics Research, Commits to Building an Equitable Future" (press release) January 24, 2023, https://www.ashg.org/publications-news/press-releases/ashg-documents-and-apologizes-for-past-harms-of-human-genetics-research-commits-to-building-an-equitable-future/.

JAMES H. COX

The Makings and Unmakings of Americans: Indians and Immigrants in American Literature and Culture, 1879–1924
Cristina Stanciu
Yale University Press, 2023

STANCIU OPENS her book with a *New York Times* article from 1923, near the end of the forty-five years under her consideration. In familiar Progressive Era fashion, the article represents Indigenous people and immigrants as "problems" to solve as part of the process of forming a U.S. national identity. Stanciu's study shows Indigenous people and immigrants as agents in this process: What role did they play, she asks, in the conversations about Americanization and what it means to be an American? What impact did they have on definitions of American identity? How, too, did their contributions align in heretofore unacknowledged or understudied ways, especially by rejecting exclusion while also preserving cultural specificity in the decades between the opening of Carlisle Indian Industrial School and the passing by Congress in 1924 of the Immigration (Johnson-Reed) Act and Indian Citizenship Act? Stanciu addresses these questions by drawing on the methods of Indigenous studies, American studies, settler colonial studies, and literary and film studies.

The introduction and first two chapters establish the foundational historical and political contexts in which Indigenous people and immigrants navigated the forces of assimilation and acculturation. Specifically, Stanciu outlines the legal landscape of citizenship and naturalization for both Indigenous people and immigrants and the history of Americanization as a specific movement driven by the federal government and numerous public and private institutions. Each chapter contains memorable insights characteristic of Stanciu's research. In the first chapter, Stanciu notes that the Competency Commission's citizenship ceremonies influenced the creation of naturalization ceremonies for immigrants. In the second, which includes a sharp, compelling analysis of the politics of an unrealized memorial to American Indians in New York, she assesses the turn from the identification of Indigenous people as "vanishing Americans" to "First Americans" as a strategic response by white Americans (specifically, the descendants of earlier groups of European colonizers) to an increase in immigration primarily from central and southern Europe.

The following six chapters alternate focus between Indigenous people and immigrants and the various media in which they participated as authors and creators and in which they were represented. Chapters 3 and 4 take student writing at Carlisle and in the foreign language press, respectively, as their focus; chapters 5 and 6 consider the writing by the leaders of the Society of American Indians and by immigrant authors; and chapters 7 and 8 look at industrial films and silent films of the early Hollywood era. Each chapter examines the tools of coercion used by teachers and school administrators, politicians, corporations, filmmakers, and others to facilitate Americanization and the strategies used by Indigenous people and immigrants to get their voices, experiences, and perspectives heard.

Stanciu finds strategic affiliations (a poet writing in Yiddish draws a correlation between Jewish and Indigenous experiences of oppression; Carlos Montezuma speaking on the shared desire of Indigenous people and immigrants to become citizens) and divergences (increasing anti-immigrant sentiment in the Society of American Indians at the end of the First World War; settler-colonial attitudes and stereotypes of Indigenous people in immigrant writing) between the two groups. She identifies a wide range of views within each group, too, as individuals—novelists and filmmakers, journalists and editors, students and activists—and their allies decided how best to face the political and economic power of the Bureau of Naturalization, Ford Motor Company, Americanism Committee of the Motion Picture Industry, and Hollywood, among other institutions working to enforce a narrowly defined U.S. national identity (Christian, capitalist, English speaking) and to restrict U.S. citizenship by race, nationality, and religion. Dissent in this hostile environment often appears in subtle forms: students at Carlisle attempt to Indigenize the school's publications; James Young Deer/James Young Johnson tells a story of surviving rather than vanishing in *White Fawn's Devotion* (1910); Abraham Cahan illuminates the poignant consequences of his protagonist's effort to assimilate in his novel *The Rise of David Levinsky* (1917).

Stanciu's book reorients the conversation about Americanization by situating Indigenous people and immigrants at the center of it. The study raises important, challenging questions about how scholars interpret the choices made by people under constant duress by state and corporate institutions in a racist, xenophobic, and certainly not unique era. Stanciu provides a model of how to read texts full of vexing nuances and contradictions. *The Makings and Unmakings of Americans* is a meticulously researched and argued cultural history of Americanization, one that sets a robust foundation for more studies of the sites where Indigeneity and immigration meet.

JAMES H. COX is Jane and Roland Blumberg Centennial Professor of English and Distinguished Teaching Professor at the University of Texas at Austin.

KAI PYLE

Making Love with the Land
Joshua Whitehead
University of Minnesota Press, 2022

JOSHUA WHITEHEAD'S *Making Love with the Land* is deeply concerned with the ethics of writing as a queer Indigenous person. From the first essay, which asks, "Who names the rez dog rez?" and demands that the reader reconsider who exactly they think these essays are written for, the book flows through ten essays that are distinct from one another but related through ongoing themes. The second essay, "My Body Is a Hinterland," sets up a number of these major themes connecting land, body, mind, dreams, and writing in one sinuous thread. "Writing As a Rupture" forms the centerpiece of the book, a long essay in which Whitehead grapples with the question of genre, trying on several different terms for his writing and settling on none with satisfaction. The remaining essays deal intensely with topics of the body, illness, grief, healing, and mourning. "Me, the Joshua Tree" is a vivid and beautiful piece written in a series of flashbacks to a moment of transitioning a relationship away from romantic and sexual partnership but toward something no less powerful. With the last essay, "The Pain Eater," we find ourselves in the present as Whitehead describes the entwining of "end" and "beginning" in the era of COVID.

One of the most striking things about the book is the way Whitehead continuously finds ways to interweave land, body, mind, and writing. In one of the more explicit statements of this relationship, he asserts, "I posit my stories as an umbilical space between the body of text and the body of the writer, and furthermore, as woven from the surrounding larger bodies: the basket as a body of land that holds a body of water—which is to say that the stories I produce herein are a body of text umbilically tied to the exquisite ache of my physical body, which is bound within the cuppings of Treaty 7 and Treaty 1." (95) Throughout the book, he makes the case that this connection is as literal and physical as it is ephemeral or creative.

The draw of this book for many people will likely be the fact that the author is a queer Indigenous person and already a prolific author, and it would not be wrong to say that Whitehead has written these essays while thinking intensely about what it means to be queer and Indigenous in the settler colonial nation-state of Canada today. Yet he is also clearly deeply ambivalent about the gaze that this brings to his work; a major theme running through the book asks whether writing and consuming creative nonfiction by a queer Indigenous author under these circumstances can ever be more than a form of a "voyeurism of a genre" (21). Indeed, issues of writing as a practice and form suffuse almost every single essay in this book, and I suspect this aspect of *Making Love with the Land* will receive less attention than the identity categories the author draws upon. Yet in addition to questioning the ethics of writing in relation to non-Native audiences, Whitehead also discusses connections between writing and dreaming ("My Body Is a Hinterland"), taking inspiration from art and video games ("On Ekphrasis and Emphases," "The Year in Video Games"), and writing as a form of mourning ("My Aunties are Wolverines"). In spite of his frequent concerns about whether "narrative is a type of stripshow," (133), he also recognizes the healing power of narrative, whether it is self-healing through the narratives others have written, or healing of a community through the honoring and remembrance of kin.

The prose of *Making Love with the Land* is thickly embedded with imagery, much of it culturally specific in ways that might escape those unfamiliar with the Plains Cree language. In "A Geography of Queer Woundings," Whitehead replaces all pronouns with the equivalent in Cree syllabics, forcing those who do not read Cree to experience a reversal of the alienation he has faced in white queer spaces. While the text is clearly informed by academic debates in Native studies (such as those concerning the complexities of sovereignty for queer Indigenous bodyminds), Whitehead resists conforming to academic textual norms. The result is a book that will be valuable to readers outside the academy, while also offering rich insights for those in Native studies, disability studies, and gender studies. Gorgeously written and profoundly rooted in Indigenous thought, *Making Love with the Land* will undoubtedly offer continued insights long after the first read.

KAI PYLE (Métis/Sault Ste. Marie Ojibwe) is an Assistant Professor in Gender & Women's Studies and American Indian & Indigenous Studies at the University of Wisconsin - Madison.

CHRISTOPHER PEXA

The Dakota Way of Life
by Ella Deloria (Raymond J. DeMallie and Thierry Veyrié, eds.)
University of Nebraska Press, 2022

ELLA DELORIA'S ETHNOGRAPHY, *The Dakota Way of Life,* gathers in 581 magisterial pages material that had previously existed as a finished but unpublished manuscript. The book's long editorial provenance—and the failure of publishers to bring it (and her novel, *Waterlily*) to light while she lived—is certainly part of its significance for contemporary readers: first completed in 1945, the manuscript passed between numerous hands until DeMallie began editorial work on it in the 1980s.

Deloria hailed from Standing Rock and was Iháŋktuŋwaŋ or Yankton Dakota, but her main focus here is the Thíthuŋwaŋ or Teton people, the Lakota-speaking bands of the Ochéti Sakówiŋ Oyáte or People of the Seven Council Fires. As in her other writings, but especially in *Speaking of Indians* (1944), Deloria foregrounds kinship as underpinning Dakota life at all scales: the individual (chapters 11–13); the family or immediate relatives (chapters 8–10); the tʼiyošpaye tʼípi, the "group of relatives living" together or extended family (chapters 1–7), and ultimately the oyáte, or all Ochéti Sakówiŋ people. Throughout, Deloria's savvy accounting of the richness of Dakota life, whether at the level of the everyday or of the philosophical, is astonishing.

Deloria's use of "Dakota," because she writes as a Dakota woman, implies Dakota-, Nakota-, and Lakota-speaking people, or who she names "Santees," "Yanktons," and "Tetons" (2). She explains her focus on Tetons or Lakota as their being "the largest division" who "were able to retain their culture for a longer period than the Yanktons east of the Missouri, or the Santees still farther east" (2). This framing of cultural preservation/loss is typical of Deloria's time and was no doubt influenced by her close relationships with the anthropologists Franz Boas, Ruth Benedict, and Margaret Mead. But despite the influence of salvage anthropology, Deloria's wry humor and ability to track continuities between past and present express the persistence of Dakota values and ways of life that Deloria documents.

While the content of the volume is remarkable, so is its curation. Raymond DeMallie's role in caring for and shaping Ella Deloria's work is documented in the book's introduction as well as in a moving afterword by Deloria's great nephew/grandson, Philip Deloria, who evokes DeMallie's close kinship with the Deloria family over some sixty years. Despite this intimate connection, I found myself wishing for clearer tracking of the choices made by DeMallie and Veyrié. The text is presented without noting specifically how the editors "excised [. . .] repetitions, reduced the excessive length of some of the prose, [. . .] revised some of the wording to improve clarity, mitigated some of the stylistic excesses, and added footnotes and scholarly context" (xxvi). In striving to produce an air of seamlessness, Deloria's hesitations, her repetitions—in short, the effort of decades of intellectual labor, of interviewing community members and relatives, of translating Lakota language into English—are effectively erased. The book's editors account for this choice as a way of avoiding an even longer text, but I found that this fluent presentation domesticates the very real challenges Deloria encountered in her fieldwork.

Likewise, DeMallie's and Veyrié's endnotes are also often couched in binaries—especially those of the sacred/secular and the natural/supernatural—that were alien to pre-reservation Dakota life and ways of knowing. To be fair, these annotations follow Deloria's own usages. But hers are far from unequivocal and reflect instead the difficult translational dynamic Deloria navigated as a Yankton Christian woman and ethnographer. For instance, when Deloria glosses the term "wak'ą" (or wakȟáŋ) as "sacred," the editors note that "wak'ą is the Dakota spiritual concept of the supernatural" (376). But Dakota lifeways were historically not theistic, and Deloria's own explanation of lightning and hail images on a tipi links them to "those unfortunate men and women under temporary bondage to the Thunder Beings," who are not gods but rather powerful beings with whom certain humans (heyók'a) may have relationships.

This complex dynamic appears again in Deloria's discussion of the verb, wač'ékiya, which Deloria describes as meaning "'to address by kinship term' and 'to pray.'" Although she avers it is "only by the context whether it is secular or religious," her subsequent discussion of this word's usages effectively erases this binary. As she shows throughout this book and elsewhere, to address someone as a relative is to remember all our relatives—human and otherwise—without recourse to hierarchy or privilege and, implicitly at least, to wish only the best for them.

I am deeply grateful for this book. It is unquestionably important for scholars and community members involved with Ochéti Sakówiŋ lifeways, knowledge, and history and is also, as Philip Deloria notes, invaluable as a document that both uses and complicates the tropes of twentieth-century anthropology. Its greatest value may yet prove to be for those readers interested in N/L/Dakota-language learning and revitalization since it provides nuances of linguistic and historical meaning from relatives, raconteurs, and "informants" whose knowledge of these endangered languages remains all too precious.

CHRISTOPHER PEXA is associate professor of English at Harvard University.

CELIA HAIG-BROWN

The Boy from Buzwah: A Life in Indian Education
by Cecil King
University of Regina Press, 2022

"**THE PURPOSE OF THIS WRITING** is to finally set to paper the story of my life" (1). This humble beginning leads to a wealth of insights not only into Cecil King's life growing up in his home community of Two Clock but also into developments of "Indian Education" across Canada. Affirmation of frustrations encountered, resistance to clichéd narratives, and most importantly King's indomitable spirit relishing his Indigenous roots and branches all breathe life into the text. Narration and counternarrative complicate reductionist understandings of what it means to be Odawa within the "*Niswi Shkoden Wiikanendowin* (the Three Fires Confederacy)," overlayed but never overshadowed by the colonial state called Canada (2). The book is organized around his early life "on the reserve," residential school, his varied careers in education, the amazing educational "revolution" in Indian education in Canada starting in the 1970s, and finally his reflections on the meaning he now takes from the life he has lived so far.

Born in 1932, King was raised by grandparents trained at residential school to recognize the power of the English language and knowledge system. Combined with the parallel power of the third adult in his household, Kohkwehns, "the teacher that stands out from all the others" and her traditional Ojibwe knowledge and language, King's strong foundations grounded his forays into the larger world (5). His considerations detail: time with Kohkwehns in the bush as somewhat disapproving grandparents go off to work, four qualified First Nations teachers in his elementary school, serving as valedictorian at his Indian residential school graduation, using Ojibwe language for success with rural students, the 1960s' return to the power of drum and dance in his community, his role in Indigenous teacher education programs in several provinces, his archival study of Jean-Baptiste Assiginack, and the list goes on.

King's discussion of his residential school experience exemplifies his ability to consider each facet of his life from a range of perspectives over time. He circles into ever-deepening understandings of the impacts. Having "done well . . . in the high school entrance exams" following his first eight years of schooling in his home community, he left in the big black bus to attend Garnier Residential School (Spanish) (113). His grandparents told him he had more to learn. There the Jesuit priests focused on classic Western education. King points out that he and his friends never felt that Christianity was being pounded into their heads: it was already a part of his life through his grandparents' teachings, and the boys "were as devout as the average little Catholic boys anywhere!" (119). He takes particular exception to academics who refute or dismiss his stories and those of his friend Basil Johnston in his 1988 book *Indian School Days*: King did not experience sexual abuse: he was not a victim of the schools. In fact, he thrived in the educational context. For older students who came to the schools with an express purpose, the scholarly work could prove quite positive even as the priests' racist attitudes had less immediate impact. The boys were told they would never "measure up" to become priests themselves; later in the text, King comes to see a shortcoming of the schools in not preparing students to "live with other Canadians" (156). In his doctoral studies, reading Jesuit history and their documented attitudes, he recalled retreats at his school where students were "upbraided for our barbarism" (246).

The book is about much more than residential schools. The revolution in teacher education based in the landmark document *Indian Control of Indian Education* (NIB 1971) provided direction as King headed the development of ITEP in Saskatchewan. He held a Rockefeller Fellowship with the Newberry Library, worked on Indigenous languages for Manitoba's legal system, made continuing contributions to teacher education across provinces, and connected with so many familiar and famous players: Mary Lou Fox, Clive Linklater, Murray Sinclair, Verna St. Denis, Rita Bouvier, Stan Wilson. Throughout the text, King's gentle approach prevails: never angry, his matter-of-fact tone when referring to the racist practices, policies, and attitudes he encountered shows his strength as a survivor, a warrior, and a teacher—according to the late Mohawk scholar, Patricia Monture Angus. No victim mentality here—not even for a moment. Instead, the reader is presented with the tensions wrought by the encounter between a superbly intellectual mind and the crazy divisiveness of a persistently colonial world. Along with all his accomplishments, King leaves the reader with a final challenge: "There is *so much* to do" (original emphasis, 339).

CELIA HAIG-BROWN is a (white) professor in the Faculty of Education at York University in Toronto, Canada.

DAVID DELGADO SHORTER

Dancing Indigenous Worlds: Choreographies of Relation
by Jacqueline Shea Murphy
University of Minnesota Press, 2022

IN HER LATEST BOOK, Jacqueline Shea Murphy continues the enriching scholarship that she so beautifully embodied in her previous work, *The People Never Stopped Dancing* (2007). Murphy devotes her attention here to how Indigenous choreographers are laboring toward a decolonized future. To explicate the methods and effects of these choreographic "resurge-instances," as she terms them, Murphy accentuates relationality in her research methods, her book structure, and her theoretical formulation (20).

The book contains a lengthy introduction that delineates how Murphy understands the current project as building substantially upon her previous research and other works in Indigenous dance studies. She offers two chapters on relational reciprocity and perspectival relationality, respectively. While the first chapter brings us to Aotearoa, the second focuses on movement workshops led by Rulan Tangen. Both chapters embody the relationality in the author's methods. Murphy resists taking sole authority for her representations by including the voices of Jack Gray, Rulan Tangen, and others. The text engenders a polyvocality and centering of Indigenous intelligence that further illustrates a way of producing scholarship *with* rather than *about*.

Next, Murphy offers an interlude, an ethnographic play-by-play of a 2010 work by Tanya Lakin Linklater at the annual Ode'min Giizis Festival. The images included here are particularly useful and poignant. Readers are shown how dance can bring history into the sensorial realm. Continuing her speaking *with* approach, Murphy makes the effective decision to include Tanya Lukin Linklater's written response to Murphy's written representation of her and her work. This section engenders a form of grace that scholars could model as they think, write, and represent with others. Murphy's own characterizations are held accountable by the artists in the focus of her analysis. I imagine this "interlude/pause/provocation" section to be one of the most useful as a stand-alone assigned reading in a course. Murphy demonstrates how scholarly interpretation can richly include our collaborators in the research rather than simply objectifying them in the scholarly gaze (266).

In the last two chapters, Murphy proposes the lenses of abun-dance and refusings. Murphy maintains a commitment to relational research and writing, as the chapters feature a study of the work of Emily Johnson and Australian choreographic works of refusal; we gain Indigenous perspectives on the research through Murphy's inclusion of others' voices (Mishuana Goeman, Rosy Simas, Tonya Lakin Linklater, and Daystar/Rosalia Jones). Not satisfied with quotes or short phrases from these peers, Murphy clearly knows that we gain more value in reading first-person insights. Murphy's text puts her theory into practice: she makes good kin in an academic mode of knowledge-making.

Murphy conveys an extraordinary amount of insight through her writing, gems not quite showcased in the table of contents or the unfortunately sparse index. With over two hundred pages of complex and highly associated thinking, I initially found myself looking for a subject in the index that did not appear to be listed. Then in the reading, I was elated to see the subject was in the body of the text. And while Murphy does give an (oddly framed) discussion of what "Indigenous" might mean (32–38), she avoids the contentious issue of who is Indigenous, a prominent line of inquiry in contemporary discussions of erasure.

To be clear, Murphy's text cannot be faulted for not doing enough. This book seems to burst at the seams (or "binding" as the case may be). I was particularly impressed by her ability to cover such a wide range of issues in Native studies, such as epistemology, memory, temporality, queerness, narration, and dramaturgy. While some of her scholarly touchstones might not be obvious choices, she clearly knows the field well. Jaqueline Shea Murphy demonstrates with agility her range of influences, from dance studies, performance studies, and Indigenous studies simultaneously if not equally. The writing magnetically keeps the reader not only engaged but constantly aware of the stakes. How important is dance to decolonization? Murphy quotes one of her interlocutors wonderfully to answer that dance provides the methods to move "'through disequilibrium and divining ways through spaces made for infinite possibility' not (only) to negotiate the disequilibrium and precocity of these spaces but to enact beyond them" (257).

DAVID DELGADO SHORTER is professor in the Department of World Arts and Cultures/Dance at the University of California, Los Angeles. He also serves as the editor in chief of the *American Indian Culture and Research Journal*.

CARTER MELAND

Dance of the Returned
Devon A. Mihesuah
University of Arizona Press, 2022

HAVING JUST COMPLETED teaching my Spring 2023 course on Native genre fiction, I was eager to jump into Devon A. Mihesuah's *Dance of the Returned* before I even knew it was a supernatural thriller. I thought it was a detective novel, the third in Mihesuah's series centering on the Chahta (Choctaw) police detective Monique Blue Hawk. I haven't read the other two books. Maybe they are all supernatural thrillers; however, unlike a good detective, I'll lead with my assumptions rather than the facts.

I assumed it was a detective novel because the plot initially concerned the disappearance of East James, a Chahta man in the Norman, Oklahoma area. Monique's investigation into East's disappearance is met with a startling lack of concern on the part of most of his friends and family members, including his wife and their children. Over the course of the next few days, Monique learns that East was involved in a Renewal Dance, a ceremony she's never heard of, under the guidance of her uncle Leroy Bear Red Ears. She meets other Renewal Dancers, who all appear weak and exhausted, sunburned (and windburned), but seemingly rejuvenated. When East returns, as exhausted as the others but seemingly at peace, Monique decides, after questioning her uncle Leroy, to try the Renewal Dance herself. It's at this point the novel ceases to be a detective novel and becomes something more mysterious, more compelling: something I shouldn't say too much about for fear of spoiling it for readers.

I will say it becomes an adventure tale and a kind of time-travel story, as well as a piece of historical fiction, one meditating on the tension between what the novel deems the Nationalist Chahta people, who want to keep the ancestral ways, and the Progressivists, who believe accommodation to white ways is best. Fasting and dancing under the guidance of her uncle, Monique and her companion dancers (who represent a cross-section of Chahta people, ranging from traditionalists to hippies to war vets) find themselves lifted out of their present and into a time and place without twenty-first-century comforts. Along with the dancers, readers may find themselves wondering where they are and how they will survive. Through their adventures we get a crash course in living off the environment (as their ancestors had) as well as reflections on history (their "removal" from the present echoes the Chahta removal from the Southeast to what is currently Oklahoma). As one of the dancers puts it amid their tribulation, "Looks like we got our wish to be decolonized," only it is muttered in resignation not celebration (227). This statement gives Monique the opportunity to point out that living in a precolonial manner is not what decolonizing is about. "Decolonization," she says, "means to retain traditions, to fight for treaty rights, and to ensure cultural sustainability in modern society" (228). It means to use traditions to understand how to live with cars, smartphones, and settler peoples—to live as twenty-first-century Chahta, not as imitation white folk.

The book's decolonizing move, of looking beyond the dichotomy of either living in the manner of ancestors from dozens of generations past or total assimilation, is to acknowledge that modern life is Chahta life, and Chahta modernity needs to be rooted in Chahta cultural ways, not settler ones. Decolonizing means you can have an iPhone and be a Chahta traditionalist because of how you think and live with reference to ancestral teachings. With such an understanding of decolonization, we can also think about another important decolonizing move that Mihesuah's novel makes. Earlier I identified the book as a supernatural thriller, which is a marketing category in the contemporary economy and important to drive sales (and I hope this book achieves such sales), but if your cultural cosmology allows for what to settler eyes looks like slippages between this time and others—and if such slippages are allowed and expected in certain ceremonial conditions—then is it really supernatural? Even if it is a part of how, in this case, the Chahta universe works, does that not mean that Monique's journey to another time is as natural as the sun rising in the east? Perhaps Mihesuah's *Dance of the Returned* is best viewed as a natural thriller. One you should read. Naturally.

CARTER MELAND is associate professor in the Department of American Indian Studies at the University of Minnesota, Duluth.

FREDERICK WHITE

Raven's Echo
by Robert Davis Hoffman
University of Arizona Press, 2022

WHEN WE ENCOUNTER Raven from Tlingit artist and poet Robert Davis Hoffman's perspective, the artist engages in a modern recasting of Raven's power and influence from a traditional Tlingit and settler fusion. He quotes "Raven's rhythm" in the preface, claiming these words "are Raven's echo," and his rhythmic movement is "Raven's heartbeat" (x). He explains the context of writing those lines: at that point in his life, he viewed Raven as "an unpredictable and restless Trickster who intervenes in human affairs, often making life miserable, plagued with fear and uncertainty" (xi). Raven is also the creator, though journeying through the collection, there is not much reverence for him, but that is apropos for most tricksters.

In "Raven tells stories," irreverence for Trickster is immediate as the speaker prays "Raven, gather us to that dark breast, / . . . / keep us distracted from all this blackness" (7). Typically, it is always wise not to trust anything Tricksters say, but we see that greatly emphasized as the poem ends. The speaker describes the lack of hope Raven offers and also references the physical traits of his tongue, saying one cannot trust anything that comes out of Raven's mouth. The imagery instantiates alienation from self, from the tribe, and from the creator, but it is hard to reconcile that such words could be Raven's echo and that the speaker is merely echoing what Raven has uttered. While tricksters are often unaware of their actions or words and their impact on creation and humanity, they are at least cognizant of themselves: it is unlikely such words come from their own mouth about themselves.

In "Saginaw Bay," very basic Indigenous themes emerge, including missionary colonialism, "I've heard of men in black robes who came" teaching the Tlingit about God and how those who heard listened, indicating that the message from the missionaries impacted the Tlingit culture forever (13). The loss of land and the environment emerge as well when he addresses the logging industry's impact on the environment and how the sky was full of trees to the horizon; but now it is only a treeless horizon with the scars of stumps everywhere (16). We see the extent of the destruction of Tlingit culture and environment echoed in "Soul Catcher" where nature is cognizant of mistreatment because trees know "know how easy it is to disappear" (21). The environment's sentience bespeaks its own demise which the Tlingit could not discern until it was too late.

There are very vulnerable moments when Hoffman addresses his family. In "Daddy," we find a sense of wonder as the speaker describes a faded memory: "Our eyes are full of each other" though the memory is fading: he can only partially recall a familiar tune he is whistling, and he almost missed hearing his Tlingit name as they quietly spoke to each other (28). Yet another poem dealing with his father, "Game," reveals a tenderness that anticipates positivity. But what occurs is alienation from both humanity and nature as he listens to his father and his companions discuss hunting stories. The poem ends with the speaker awakening to a rifle shot and can only vocalize the sound of a deer as his dad and others laugh at him.

As in most Indigenous literature, alcoholism is a common theme. In "What the crying woman saw," "Outgrowing ourselves," "He was a dancer," and "Rock of Ages" a surprisingly sympathetic tone arises, that such behavior is not only understandable but acceptable given the circumstances, although you can hear mainstream commentary "dismissing the shameless drunk" (67). Alcoholism is a difficult reality across Indigenous nations and communities, but Hoffman offers hope in returning to traditional knowledge and practices to overcome the trap of alcohol.

This two-part collection starts with a prayer, invoking Raven to gather them to his dark heart, and ends with a confession where the speaker divulges his desire to emulate a beloved uncle who encourages the speaker to stop fighting so hard because only then will the speaker get what he wants (91). The speaker's concluding words exude encouragement and hope. It is also an apropos culmination of the "Reconstruction" section and portends potential growth as the speaker desires to emulate a precious uncle, most likely a brother of his mother, since Tlingits are matrilineal. Hope is eternal and a great foundation for reconstruction.

FREDERICK WHITE is a citizen of the Haida Nation and associate professor of English at Slippery Rock University (PA).

JOSÉ ANTONIO LUCERO

Cinematic Comanches: The Lone Ranger in the Media Borderlands
by Dustin Tahmahkera
University of Nebraska Press, 2022

WITH *CINEMATIC COMANCHES: The Lone Ranger in the Media Borderlands*, Dustin Tahmahkera (Comanche) offers a lively, theoretically engaged, and often humorous exploration of the intersections of Native studies, cinema and media studies, and Comanche history. Tahmahkera's book represents a cinema-centered version of Leanne Howe's (Choctaw) "tribalography," her influential term for the connective work that Native storytelling does in "integrating oral traditions, histories, and experiences into narratives and expanding our identities."[1] Working across several genres, texts, and conversations, Tahmahkera offers an expansive consideration of the "media borderlands" that connect "real and reel Comanches" (xi).

From the very first word of the text, *maruawe* (a greeting in the Comanche language that can be rendered as "tell it"), the book centers Comanche perspectives. Such tribal specificity, however, does not keep the book from offering deep and broad lessons about Native representation relevant far beyond Comanchería: "As a method, maruawe is a call to report on a media-centric borderlands of Comanche history *as* representation and of Comanche representation *as* history" (x). This borderlands account includes plenty of critique and investigations into what is playfully rendered in the Comanche language as *isa kwitapu,* or "bullshit" (xiii). As a history of Hollywood westerns that runs from *The Searchers* to *The Lone Ranger,* there is plenty of isa kwitapu, for sure. At the same time, that history is full of many moments of Comanche agency and kin-making that will make for many lively classroom conversations. Readers are invited into accessible and informed discussions about "representational jurisdiction" or "who represents whom" (chapter 1), a reconsideration of the casting of Johnny Depp in the role of Tonto as an extension of the history of Comanche captivity and kinship (chapter 2), an analysis of "cinematic justice and injustice" in Disney's *The Lone Ranger* (chapter 3), and finally a tribally specific discussion of Comanche viewing and criticism of the Disney film (chapter 4). Spoiler alert: *The Lone Ranger* is a site of meaningful Comanche action and also a story of missed opportunities. Importantly, this book is much more than a consideration of one film; it is also a conversation between the author and his ancestors and relatives like his great-great-great-grandmother Cynthia Ann Parker ("white-captive-turned Comanche"), great-great-grandfather Quanah Parker ("the last 'chief' of the Comanches"), and high-profile aunties like Juanita Pahdopopony and Ladonna Harris. Readers will want to bring some popcorn for the engaging ways that family history become film history, and vice versa.

I appreciated (but some readers might take issue with) the way Tahmahkera avoids some of the debates in Comanche studies that have generated more heat than light. I am thinking specifically of the debates over the work of Finnish historian Pekka Hämäläinen and his use of "empire" as an analytic to understand Comanche and other Native peoples' territorial expansion. Tahmahkera uses "Comanche empire" unabashedly and without qualification. While I am curious what Tahmahkera thinks about the critiques of Hämäläinen lodged by historians like Ned Blackhawk and Nick Estes, I can also see how some of those debates have unintentionally centered the European historian more than the Native histories.

The most controversial part of this Native history involves, of course, the adoption of actor Johnny Depp into the Comanche Nation by Ladonna Harris. While it is risky to bring Depp so centrally into the story, it remains one of Comanche agency and creativity. Harris suggested "with a grin" that "we made [Depp] a Comanche so he'd learn to act like one" (20). The jury is probably still out on how well that bet has paid off, especially since the defamation trials of Depp and his former partner Amanda Heard. At the same time, such complexities are reminders that not all relations are good and that kinship is not conflict-free. That said, while Depp's behavior should not detract from the book's arguments, one can be forgiven for wishing that timing would have allowed Tahmahkera to include less Depp/*Lone Ranger* and more about the 2022 film *Prey,* which Hulu viewers can opt to watch entirely in the Comanche language. Tahmahkera has elsewhere written eloquently about the consulting work that he and his late auntie Juanita Pahdopony did for the film, which in many ways is a continuation of the real/reel histories so compellingly told in *Cinematic Comanches*.[2] Indeed, it is validation for one of the main themes of this book: when it comes to Comanche histories and futures, there is much more to tell.

JOSÉ ANTONIO LUCERO teaches in the Comparative History of Ideas Department and the Henry M. Jackson School of International Studies at the University of Washington.

Notes

1. Leanne Howe, "The Story of America: A Tribalography," in *Clearing a Path: Theorizing the Past in Native American Studies*, ed. Nancy Shoemaker (New York: Routledge), 2002: 29–48.

2. Dustin Tahmahkera, "Prey: Behind the Scenes with Cinematic Comanches," *World Literature Today,* August 31, 2022, https://www.worldliteraturetoday.org/blog/culture/prey-behind-scenes-cinematic-comanches-dustin-tahmahkera.

AMY GORE

"Vaudeville Indians" on Global Circuits, 1880s to 1930s
Christine Bold
Yale University Press, 2022

BOLD TAKES RECOVERY WORK in a new direction by taking up the subject of vaudeville, one of the most popular forms of mass entertainment during the turn of the century. Vaudeville brought to the stage a fast-paced variety of brief performances by a host of singers, actors, dancers, comedians, trained animals, and other spectacles. At an affordable price, an individual or a family could enter a vaudeville theater and be entertained for hours by an ongoing array of these short performances, an experience not unlike modern social media entertainment such as YouTube and TikTok. While many correlate Indigenous performances at the turn of the century with Wild West shows, vaudeville remains a distinct stream of entertainment with its mashup of Native and non-Native acts, stand-alone spectacles not tied to a common theme, and a somewhat greater degree of creative control for Native performers than the Wild West shows. Vaudeville had an immense impact on the entertainment industry, one that receives far too little attention for the ways in which it impacted modern American culture. Bold's research highlights the key role Indian performances and Indigenous Peoples played in vaudeville, and in doing so, Indigenous contributions to modernity and popular culture.

Bold structures *"Vaudeville Indians"* largely around a handful of performers. After an introduction that provides the foundational history of vaudeville and an overview of the more than three hundred Indigenous people who participated, Bold details her approach over the past twenty-five years to such a complex and under-researched topic. She identifies her research exchange with Indigenous actors and communities, and she writes transparently and humbly about her dedication to the principles of Indigenous research methodologies and nonextractive scholarship. After laying the groundwork for vaudeville history and her research methodologies, Bold organizes the rest of her book around selected performers. Chapter 2 follows the career of Go-won-go Mohawk, a transatlantic Seneca playwright and performer. The third chapter largely focuses on Esther Deer/Princess White Deer, one of several multigenerational Mohawk family members who circled the globe as vaudeville entertainers. Then, in an unexpected but appropriate turn, the last two chapters explore vaudeville performers whose Indigenous identities are either unclear or appropriated. The fourth chapter delves into the story of Princess Chinquilla, who self-identified as Southern Cheyenne but faced challenges in her claim to Indigeneity, and the fifth chapter traces the career of German redface trick cyclist Chester Dieck, who played Indian on stage for more than six decades. Bold justifies her inclusion of these non-Native or indeterminate identities by explaining, "Indian vaudeville was built from the entanglement of Indigeneity and Indianness, and a pattern recurs through this history whereby the energetic ingenuity of the first repeatedly saves vaudeville from the tired stereotypes of the second" (270). While she centers these four biographies, she mentions many more Indigenous performers encountered during her research, as their stories intertwine with other performers and Indigenous community members. Bold weaves sensitively and adeptly between Native, non-Native, and indeterminate identities of vaudeville performers, and each chapter is exceptionally dense with information.

Bold intersperses four shorter "Vaudeville Numbers" between each chapter, and in the spirit of vaudeville, I anticipated that each of these would give me a more visual sense of a specific performance. Instead, each one primarily traces a specific performer rather than a single act, which redirected my expectations and made the interludes less distinctive from the chapters. As Bold readily acknowledges, "The ephemeral nature of the form and the huge number of acts made for sparse reviews," and therefore reconstructing the acts is understandably challenging (129). While Bold is sometimes able to find details that allow her to re-create the spectacle and emotions of an act, at other times those details are simply missing. This leaves Bold in the difficult position of "telling" rather than "showing" in her accounts of vaudeville history, sometimes leaving the reader missing an immediate sense of the subject at hand. However, the moments in which Bold re-creates the stage as well as its history shine brightly, such as when she details the riotous slapstick of Chinquilla's act (195). As a result, not only the archival resources but also vaudeville itself feel somehow ephemeral, ubiquitous enough to escape the intensive documentation that comes with notoriety. And yet vaudeville unmistakably set in motion a profound cultural influence, forerunning motion pictures and the staccato entertainment ubiquitous in our modern lives. *"Vaudeville Indians"* stands as a corrective to the perceived absence of Indigeneity's relationship to vaudeville and an impressive resource for any further research into the subject.

AMY GORE is assistant professor of English at North Dakota State University.

MARK MINCH-DE LEON

Visualizing Genocide: Indigenous Interventions in Art, Archives, and Museums
edited by Yve Chavez and Nancy Marie Mithlo
University of Arizona Press, 2022

GENOCIDE CREATES a problem for visuality. The problem is in both the effacement of violence through normalization and the demand to render it visible in a colonial visual field. This issue is amplified by the conditions of invisibility that settler states create for Indigenous Peoples. Recently, this overdetermined invisibilization has begun to dissipate, thanks largely to the work of Indigenous activists but also to changing attitudes toward the recognition of genocide, raising the need to attend to the politics of visibility anew. Yve Chavez and Nancy Marie Mithlo's coedited book, *Visualizing Genocide: Indigenous Interventions in Art, Archives, and Museums*, does just this by engaging the issue of genocide's visibility in the context of Indigenous art. The twelve chapters and ten authors, from an Indigenous viewpoint, engage the question of how genocide registers in the material practices of Indigenous artists, archives and their formations and uses, and museums and exhibitionary narratives with attention to the impact on communities.

A vast literature exists on the problem that genocide creates for visuality, in relation to truth and reconciliation, the destruction of records, the value of testimony of survivors, of thresholds of violence and the means through which violence is made visible or invisible, and of the ethics of reproducing and/or reprising the violence. Much of this work hinges on the question of proof, which has led many scholars to be critical of human rights frameworks for the damage that reliance on the archival dimensions of documentation can have on communities, communal memory, and forms of healing when those processes of recognition and validation are controlled by the same state and epistemological formations that initially produced the violence.

The turn to art and its powers of visualization is an important intervention, moving as it does from the realm of documentary to forms of collective memorialization and the material, aesthetic, and epistemic consequences of violence on the visual field. Unburdened by the logic of the archive, Indigenous artists are able to explore more deeply the impact violence continues to have on communities and their forms of memory and creative and collective energies outside the bounds of state-centered recognition of violence and the aftermath of sociologically defined trauma and harm.

In their introduction, Chavez and Mithlo write, "In an era characterized by fragmented knowing, decontextualized sound bites, and instant access, how do we know with certainty the difference between truth and distortion when contemplating past atrocities? . . . Our analysis contends that it is in the open registers of artistic practice and reinterpretation of archival holdings that facts previously considered 'unknowable' can be clearly documented" (4). I'm intrigued by the irreverent conflation of art and fact, but I wonder about the implications of reading art as the space of truth-making. Is there a risk of replacing the creative imagination with the impetus to document organized around an archival conception of truth? Chavez and Mithlo address this issue by acknowledging the inherent bias of archival sources and the need to attend to cultural specificity, authorial voice, and positionality in assessing historical claims, but does this approach risk being *included* as "active interventions in the [colonial] historic record"?

One of the ways that Chavez and Mithlo address this issue is by focusing on the figure of the witness (5). Indigenous artists are often confronted with a public desire for the performance of authenticity and tradition. An associated impulse is the demand for Indigenous people to perform their trauma. In the context of the politics of truth and reconciliation, for instance, Dian Million locates a state-centered biopolitical force in the demand/desire to testify that raises important questions about the effect of interpreting Indigenous art as a form of witnessing. In other words, we should be cautious about which forms of legitimation we adopt in order to contest the forces of invisibilization and the destruction of agency in the ongoing genocidal structures of settler colonialism.

Chavez and Mithlo, together with the other authors in this collection, have produced an important and thought-provoking book, jump-starting the conversation about Indigenous genocide outside the bounds of the official narrative. So-called expressive culture has long been a site where Indigenous creators and knowledge and culture bearers have addressed the histories and ongoing relations of genocide in settler colonial contexts, as has the discipline of museology, and yet the legal and historiographic fields have largely held a monopoly on these discussions. This book is a welcome intervention and invitation for us to begin to talk about the histories and ongoing effects of genocide through collective and relational Indigenous lenses. It also significantly highlights the inventive work of Indigenous artists and curators in this regard.

MARK MINCH-DE LEON is assistant professor of English at the University of California, Riverside.

NEW FROM UNC PRESS

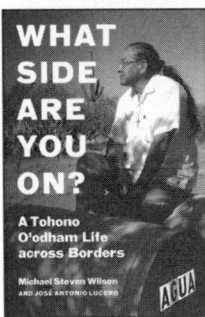

WHAT SIDE ARE YOU ON?
A Tohono O'odham Life across Borders
Michael Steven Wilson and José Antonio Lucero

"An effective, engaging, and valuable book. By tacking between Wilson's first-person life history and Lucero's contextual 'interludes,' this collaborative work provides both an intimate account of lived experience and a historical analysis of the larger structures of power that have a hand in shaping life as an Indigenous person along the US-Mexico border."
—**Shannon Speed**, University of California, Los Angeles
216 pages $24.95 paper

VITAL RELATIONS
How the Osage Nation Moves Indigenous Nationhood into the Future
Jean Dennison

"Dennison's book takes an important place among Indigenous and institutional ethnography, showing the fine details and complex negotiations of tribal governance as they unfold in both ordinary and official settings. Dennison paints a highly contoured and complex picture of the Osage Nation as a site of struggle, contestation, cooperation, and care."
—**Clint Carroll**, University of Colorado
256 pages $29.95 paper

ON THE SWAMP
Fighting for Indigenous Environmental Justice
Ryan E. Emanuel

"Emanuel takes you on a fascinating journey through time on his Lumbee homelands, focusing on contemporary tribal environmental protections efforts. The Lumbee tribe's quest to preserve their natural environment and water is a valuable story of how many tribes try to mitigate the risk of climate change while knowing they'll bear a greater burden of ecological harm for all of society. Emanuel captures in beautiful detail how tribes use traditional values around caretaking the environment while asserting their sovereignty."
—**Karen Diver**, Fond du Lac Band of Lake Superior Chippewa
312 pages $19.95 paper

THE RICH EARTH BETWEEN US
The Intimate Grounds of Race and Sexuality in the Atlantic World, 1770–1840
Shelby Johnson

"This text joins a growing conversation on the solidarities between African diasporic and Indigenous communities of the Atlantic World. The creativity, care, and deep, multifield engagement that Johnson brings to her primary sources is a model for what scholarship on this period can be."
—**Greta LaFleur**, Yale University
230 pages $32.95 paper

WHAT JANE KNEW
Anishinaabe Stories and American Imperialism, 1815–1845
Maureen Konkle

"An incredible achievement and one that will stand as the definitive account of the Johnston family and their literary legacy. Konkle's scholarship here is beyond reproach, demonstrating her exemplary skills as a researcher, critic, and writer."
—**Daniel Heath Justice** (Cherokee Nation), University of British Columbia
448 pages $29.95 paper

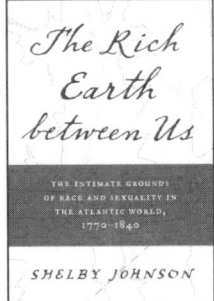

 Most UNC Press books are also available as E-Books.

UNC Press books are now available through Books@JSTOR and Project Muse – and North Carolina Scholarship Online (NCSO) on Oxford Scholarship Online.

THE UNIVERSITY OF NORTH CAROLINA PRESS
at bookstores or 800-848-6224 • uncpress.org • uncpressblog.com

NEW FROM MINNESOTA

Indigenous Archival Activism
Mohican Interventions in Public History and Memory
Rose Miron

"A necessary volume on the intersection of Indigenous knowledge loss, recovery, and production in the context of settler colonialism. Rose Miron challenges an accepted narrative about a vanished people with a deeply researched project that centers their persistence and relevance."
—**Jacki Thompson Rand**, Choctaw Nation of Oklahoma, University of Illinois at Urbana-Champaign

$30.00 paperback | 312 pages

Producing Sovereignty
The Rise of Indigenous Media in Canada
Karrmen Crey

"Crey speaks to the decolonizing force of Indigenous media—not only as expressions of Indigenous cultural sovereignty but as destabilizing forces within contemporary settler societies." —**Marian Bredin**, coeditor of *Canadian Television: Text and Context*

$27.00 paperback | 216 pages | Indigenous Americas

Solar Adobe
Energy, Ecology, and Earthen Architecture
Albert Narath

How a centuries-old Indigenous architectural tradition reemerged as a potential solution to the political and environmental crises of the 1970s

$32.95 paperback | 304 pages

Medicine Wheel for the Planet
A Journey Toward Personal and Ecological Healing
Jennifer Grenz

"Through an exquisite weaving of lived experiences, storytelling, and regional Indigenous wisdom, Dr. Jennifer Grenz guides us . . . into the deeper promise of true relational ecology." —**Lyanda Lynn Haupt**, author of *Rooted*

$25.95 hardcover | 280 pages
Available May 2024

Prairie Edge
Conor Kerr

"Expertly capturing the contemporary Métis spirit, *Prairie Edge* is truly an essential story for our time." —**Waubgeshig Rice**, author of *Moon of the Turning Leaves*

$25.95 hardcover | 272 pages
Available June 2024

University of Minnesota Press | www.upress.umn.edu | 800-621-2736